THE LIFE-CHANGING POWER
OF THE HOLY SPIRIT

THE
LIFE-CHANGING
POWER
OF THE
HOLY SPIRIT

INSIGHTS
FROM CLASSIC
CHRISTIAN LEADERS

LEONA FRANCES
CHOY

WingSpread Publishers
Camp Hill, Pennsylvania

WingSpread Publishers
3825 Hartzdale Drive · Camp Hill, PA 17011
www.wingspreadpublishers.com

A division of Zur Ltd.

The Life-Changing Power of the Holy Spirit
ISBN: 978-1-60066-155-6
LOC Control Number: 2007938445
© 1990, 2003 by Leona Choy

Previously published by Christian Publications, Inc.
First Christian Publications Edition 1990
First WingSpread Publishers Edition 2007

Unless otherwise indicated, Scripture taken
from the Authorized King James Version of the Bible.

The Life-Changing Power of the Holy Spirit
was previously published under the title *Powerlines*.

CONTENTS

Contents

CONTENTS

CONTENTS

Contents

FOREWORD

THIS BOOK IS A GRAND SYMPOSIUM of great Christian leaders from the past, a roster of spiritual saints – some of them giants – all on the first team who would be saints in any denomination, and who, by their lives and spiritual depth still speak today.

The author adopted a fresh interview style, letting each tell his or her own story of how he or she entered the Spirit-filled life. To recast it all like this called for great care, and the author did her homework well.

Their testimonies are vivid, though they vary a lot, which is good. Like horses eager for the race, they all finally come to a similar starting gate where they must "enter in." Somehow they all have to get into that gate! For some it is a real "crisis experience" and they back off more than once. A few really sweat it out. Many are especially shy at the term "baptism" of the Spirit. Others walk right into it without blinking or argument. But they all finally *enter there*, and from then on they run their Christian race for all it is worth!

No matter how you say it, or what terminology you use, getting through that gate is really crucial. That is what this book is all about: How they all viewed that gate, got through it, entered the "deeper life" and ran for the prize of the high calling in Christ Jesus.

1

They all paid a high price to get into that race. This book will tell you all about that.

How they got through that gate is really exciting. Though they disagree on terminology—"baptism of the Spirit," "second blessing," "crisis experience"—they all finally come to agreement on one important thing. It is an experience *subsequent* to conversion—not the same thing—calling for *full surrender*, *active obedience* and *faith* in response to the *Word of God*.

It all makes a colorful story! Never stale. We get to see a lot into the inner world and workings of these tried and tested leaders.

Here, for example, are a few:

> **Andrew Murray:** Always near the top of anybody's list. Saw into it all in his full and vigorous life and ministry—always abounding in the work of the Lord. He knows how to weave great distinctions and distinctives into beautiful harmony—without compromise.

> **Samuel Chadwick:** Great in Christ's life and ministry by any standard—speaks out very dynamically and with great authority. He highlights more distinctions with much discernment, both with the Word of God and in his witness.

> **E.M. Bounds:** Who can compare with him in the mighty field and force of prayer? Rising daily at four a.m. to pray, he knew what he was talking about. He is so impelling and believeable, and he wrote from the solid depths of his being. He relates the working of the Holy Spirit to prayer—fully. And this is needed. I often say we are bound to pray when we read Bounds!

> **R.A. Torrey:** Another giant—has no problem with

the term "baptism" of the Spirit. In fact, D.L. Moody urged him to speak on it at his conferences. That term was used quite freely before the Pentecostals entered the field.

G. Campbell Morgan: Quite adamant in insisting that we should not call this the "baptism" of the Spirit. But if we stay with him in his many writings we find him very strong and equally insistent on the need for the great power and working of the Holy Spirit. In fact, I talked with Dr. Morgan in London in 1938, and he told me the greatest need in the Church today is the Holy Spirit: "they hardly know the Holy Spirit [in churches today]."

Samuel Logan Brengle: Should never be forgotten in one's quest for the Spirit's filling. What a godly man! One who had such effective meetings all the time after the Lord filled him. His story is most helpful in the way he highlights the deep *cleansing* and *holy love of God*—in his own experience and then in his ministry. He was of the "holiness" school and movement, but was free from sectarianism. He was another of those saints, like Fletcher of Madley, who would be a saint in any denomination.

A.B. Simpson: Helpful because he lived through so much. His gospel was a *full* gospel. He relates his deeper experience to sanctification as well as to power for service and ministry. He comes through with much-needed clarity and distinction between the gifts and graces (fruit) of the Spirit. And—what is of particular importance—he relates all to the church. This could be said to be a weakness with many, because Pentecost was experienced by a *whole congregation*. The Holy Spirit filled *all* as well as *each*. It was both corporate and individual. Not too many pay attention to this. Above all, Dr. Simpson became a pathfinder in relating everything to Christ in a new and wonderful way. His Christ became so big that he literally took everything over as his *All in All*. His "deeper" experience should help everyone.

F.B. Meyer: His name is almost a household word among Christians because of his many illustrious writings. In them he gives a lot of secrets and fitting helps. He also had a vivid experience of entering into the Spirit-filled life. I know ministers who were helped "in" through F.B. Meyer.

Charles G. Finney: What an experience he had! And what a modern giant he has become for revivals, especially for churches—*so needed right now!* His experience in what he calls the "baptism" of the Spirit is so penetrating and permeating that we wonder if he could call it anything else. The author gives a lot of space to this, and it is good. Because with it we get to see into the great secret of Finney's power and of his strong revivals. His lifetime track record of revivals has hardly been surpassed. It is very timely today, this story, because there is a lot of prayer and concern for revivals in our churches.

L.S. Chafer: Comes to the gate in his own way and also gives us a lot of teaching. While avoiding the term "baptism" for this experience he covers the ground and also arrives at the truth of the "spiritual man." He is very strong on the Holy

Spirit, and for the need for being Spirit-filled Christians.

This is a very valuable volume—the bibliography alone makes it such. The author has done her home-work well. She asks the right questions and draws out some great answers. It should also prove to be a fine source-book for the Spirit-filled life and for prayer and revivals.

Armin R. Gesswein
Founder-Director
Revival Prayer Fellowship

PUBLISHER'S INTRODUCTION

THE *LIFE-CHANGING POWER OF THE HOLY SPIRIT* will both teach and inspire you. Its unique interview style will effectively focus your mind to help understand what these great men and women of the faith believed about the working of the Holy Spirit. You will be charged as you read how the Holy Spirit became real to these individuals. You may even be led into a deeper understanding of His workings.

However, it is important to remember what this book is: a historical understanding of various evangelical leaders' views of the Holy Spirit. It is not intended to be the doctrinal statement of WingSpread Publishers. Rather, it represents a panorama of individual views, some of which are almost opposite each other.

Our reason for publishing this book is not to confuse but to inform the reader. *The Life-Changing Power of the Holy Spirit* is an easy-to-read, fast-paced book that allows readers to see and understand what great evangelical leaders taught about the Holy Spirit. It is not biased toward a particular doctrinal position nor is it intended to help you come to one.

Although there are individuals in the book whose positions WingSpread Publishers fully agrees with, no attempt was made to make them more prominent. Chapters are simply arranged alphabetically.

When you look at our list, you may wonder why some leaders were not included. That too was not due to our own censorship. Some prominent evangelical leaders of the era did not write books so the author could not "interview" them. Others wrote, but did not say much about the Holy Spirit, so that too kept them out of the book.

As you read *The Life-Changing Power of the Holy Spirit*, our prayer is that its powerful message will cause you to desire more of the Holy Spirit in your own life, just as each of the individuals in this book did.

INTRODUCTION

L ET US UNDERSTAND THESE MEN AND WOMEN in the context of their times. The movement of the Holy Spirit in any age is in line with the broad sweep of God's sovereignty and, at the same time, His purposes for His people.

We do not always know why He moves as He does; and we only partially discern His moving, like the Divine Wind. Our present age has the advantage of hindsight as we try to evaluate the experiences of these giants. We may even be mistaken in our judgment because our present age will in turn be evaluated by the age to come, if the Lord tarries. Posterity may conclude that we also only saw "through a glass darkly" compared to what the Holy Spirit will yet reveal of His work.

Unity in diversity

You will begin to notice certain broad generalizations on the work of the Holy Spirit emerging from these interviews. While details may understandably differ, similarities in the pattern of God's working by His Spirit anywhere are striking. You will be able to pick these out for your own spiritual profit and understanding.

Let us appreciate that each spiritual leader described the *same precious jewel* from a distinctly *personal* aspect. The brilliant flashes have different colors reflecting their setting, yet each facet gives us a fuller revelation of the creative, varied ministry of the Spirit in the world expressed through the ages.

No boxes or walls

As a perceptive reader, you will undoubtedly conclude that the Holy Spirit's moving in our present age is not new after all. The Holy Spirit sometimes moves in surprising ways – perhaps unconventional, in our opinion. We cannot box Him in to any human formula, nor can we second guess Him. He continues to work according to God's perfect, permanent and sovereign blueprint! Man-made fences, walls and divisions, including ecclesiastical and denominational ones, topple before the powerful work of the Holy Spirit. He seeks to accomplish the will of the Father and glorify the Son.

If we had been there

If we were transplanted into the times of some of these giants of the faith, our reactions might have been the same as their contemporaries. Would we have been on the side of the convinced or the doubters?

How would D.L. Moody's "uncouth appearance and country-bumpkin preaching style" have affected us? Would we have looked down upon Evan Roberts's youth and lack of training? After all, his evangelistic band was composed of enthusiastic "kids" in their teens and early 20s. Would we have criticized Hannah Smith as a "woman preacher"?

In fact, how would we have responded to Jesus and His unorthodox teachings and miracles if we had lived in the first century? Each age of church history has its conservative traditionalists who are reluctant to accept anything beyond their comfortable status quo, suspicious that the source of any change must be from man and not God.

Wake up calls

Each age also has its open-hearted, seeking believers who are willing, if the principles are not contrary to the Scriptures, to boldly press on with God in uncharted ways. They recognize that God is always impelling His children forward. He wants to get on with the perfecting of the saints, the nourishing of the Bride, the completion of the Church—which usually means waking her from sleep.

Revivals, renewals, restorations—personal and collective—are among God's vehicles to rouse His church. God is always seeking to fill human channels with Himself, drawing them both to move on with Him and show others the way. The giants you will meet in this book are among that band of pioneers.

Expressing God's fullness

Inevitably, emotions seem to attend such awakenings. Emotions in themselves should not be disparaged and avoided if their source is from God and under His control.

The Father expressed love, the greatest emotion, by sending His only Son to redeem the world. Love in and through us is the priority fruit of the Holy Spirit. Disappointed in the church's loss of first love, the Lord declared in Revelation 3:15 NIV "I know your deeds, that you are neither cold nor hot. I wish that you were either one or the other." Is not our generation a lukewarm one that could stand some heating up?

Praise, tears of repentance, anger and hatred toward sin, shouts of exulting joy, bursts of genuine and prolonged prayer, zeal that thrusts out believers to witness to others in holy boldness—all are emotions accompanying God's work among men throughout recorded history.

Today's sophisticated, intellectualized, polished, padded-pew churchianity may resist or shun emotional expression—but it has always been God's way. It is no surprise to find it echoed in the experiences of these giants of the faith.

Let's not miss the boat!

God has moved. God is moving. God will certainly move by His Holy Spirit in future awakenings all over the world in our lifetime until He returns. We "kick against the pricks" in vain. God will be God. He insists on doing things His way, on His terms, and when He chooses. Let us instead *welcome* the work of His Spirit.

"Even so, come, Lord Jesus!"

Through the time tunnel

Have you ever wanted to meet and ask questions of certain giants of the Christian faith? I have! Let's imagine our way together through the time tunnel of the past century or two.

These great men and women were eager to tell their own generation about the source of spiritual power in their experience, teaching and ministry. Now let's ask them to share their open secrets with *our generation*. That is the theme of this book.

Several giants made us dig hard for their priceless answers from the deep mines of theological seminary archives and second-hand bookstores. Others wrote volumes on the subject and their gold lies closer to the surface. We will discover that some of them knew each other and were laterally influenced. Their answers complement and supplement aspects of the subject because the same Holy Spirit was moving among them.

I have been spiritually enriched through my encounter with these giants–I know you, too, will share that experience.

Format

Our format will be similar to a talk show on radio or television. As the "host," I will introduce our "guest" in each chapter and let you know in what year our interview is taking place. Then I will deliberately ask corresponding questions of each interviewee to provide you with an unbiased and comprehensive perspective.

Who's who?

I selected these individuals from a long list of notable possibilities, picking out people who are generally well known in church history from the 19th and overlapping into the early 20th century.

Why have I used that cut-off point? Those whom I interviewed lived, or at least "answered" me, before the founding of the Pentecostal denominations at the beginning of the 20th century. They were obviously not a part of that movement nor of the charismatic renewal as we know it today–it did not exist at that time.

This fact is significant since my purpose is to deal with the teachings and experience of the Holy Spirit *before* that era. When these men and women speak of "the baptism of the Spirit" they are doing so in the context of their own answers and as they personally interpreted certain biblical passages.

Speaking for themselves

We will let the giants use their own terminology to describe "the abundant life" as Jesus termed it, or "being filled with the Spirit" as the apostle Paul described it. "The victorious life" and "becoming a fulfilled Christian" are some other terms you will encounter. Generally these spiritual leaders will be referring to an on-going fuller Christian life of power and effectiveness. Sometimes they will be referring to a crisis which launched that abundant life, and sometimes to the results of that experience.

Not a debate

Each interview may stand alone. I have tried to follow the particular person's train of thought from his or her writings. I did not argue with his or her answer when it differed from that of another. I refrained from pointing out to any of them something that seemed like an inconsistency or an error when viewed from our generation's perspective or my personal interpretation. This is not a panel discussion or debate.

I asked each the questions that I was sure he or she had already answered in his or her writings. I planted the questions, so to speak. It follows that I did not ask a particular person anything he or she had not addressed in his or her books. Each interview took whatever direction the interviewee determined from his or her writings.

Please trust me!

I have made honest effort to maintain integrity and not put words into the mouths of any of these men and women or take their answers out of context. I researched prime sources, memoirs, autobiographies, biographies and their own expository writings. This has been extensive; usually I found it necessary to study several books on or by each person to gain an accurate perspective. Of course I have had to be selective. They "told" me far more than I had space to share with you, even about our fixed subject.

The lengthy bibliography points out the impossibility of footnotes, which would surely have distracted you. Detailed notes would have turned this book into an academic exercise rather than a free-flowing, informative and hopefully inspiring volume. I can verify the source of their statements and invite the reader to trust my integrity.

"You are there" flavor

My one liberty in presenting the answers of these men and women has been to slightly contemporize some of their sentence structure instead of allowing ponderous word-for-word quotes to stand as written. Their sometimes out-dated syntax, and lengthy, involved, multi-punctuated sentences were much admired in their times. We respect that. Flourished syntax tends to confuse us as modern readers.

On the other hand, I have tried to avoid paraphrasing, keeping as closely as possible to their exact vocabulary, their original flavor, style and phraseology. Usually I retained their answers in the passive voice for the style it represents. Their complex sentences are part of their style as well. When one used "Holy Ghost" and another "Holy Spirit," I let it stand. We don't expect them to speak in 20th-century colloquial terms.

Enjoy the atmosphere of their era as if "you are there"! Smile when they speak of the "rush and hurry of life"–they only traveled by horse and carriage! Some complained about "these evil and Satanic days" a hundred years ago! They used examples of steam-driven engines and trolley cars–all lived before atomic or nuclear power and men walking on the moon. They talked about "the turn of the century" meaning the 20th. We face the 21st. They spoke of the nearness of "the end of the age" and the "soon coming of the Lord." We are nearer than they were. Some looked forward to spiritual awakenings—we interviewed others later who were already experiencing them.

Let's bring on our first guest . . .

Edward McKendree Bounds

[1835–1913]

THE HOLY OIL
OF POWER

ORN IN SHELBY COUNTY, MISSOURI, E.M. Bounds received his common school education at Shelbyville. As a young man, he practiced law for a few years until his call to preach the gospel at the age of 24. His first pastorate was as a circuit preacher in the Monticello area.

While he was serving as pastor of a church in Brunswick, war was declared and young Bounds was made prisoner of war because he would not take the oath of allegiance to the Federal government. Authorities sent him to St. Louis and later transferred him to Memphis, Tennessee.

Eventually securing his release, he traveled on foot nearly a hundred miles to join General Pierce's command in Mississippi. He served as chaplain of the Fifth Missouri Regiment until nearly the end of the war. He was captured at the last minute and held as prisoner at Nashville, Tennessee.

After the war, Bounds pastored churches in Tennessee and Alabama. In 1875 he became pastor of St. Paul Methodist Church in St. Louis and served there for four years. In 1876 he married Emmie Barnette who died 10 years later, leaving him with two young daughters. In 1887 he married Emmie's sister, Hattie, and had five children by his second wife.

After serving several more pastorates in Missouri, he became the editor of the St. Louis *Christian Advocate*. Bounds was a deep thinker and forceful writer whose books have been translated into many different languages. He spent the last 17 years of his life in Georgia with his family, reading, writing and praying most of the time. His habit was to rise at four every morning for prayer and study of the Bible. Considering prayer to be his business, Bounds exemplified the life of prayer about which he taught and wrote.

* * *

APPROXIMATE DATE: 1899

QUESTION: Why is prayer the one theme of all your books?
E.M. BOUNDS: I believe that what the church needs today is not more or better machinery, not new organizations or more and novel methods. She needs men whom the Holy Spirit can use—men of prayer, men mighty in prayer. The Holy Spirit does not flow through methods, but through men. He does not come on ma-

chinery, but on men. He does not anoint plans, but men – men of prayer!

Q: *How does that apply to the leadership of the church?*
BOUNDS: Everything depends on the spiritual character of the preacher. In its life-giving forces, the sermon cannot rise above the man. Dead men preach dead sermons, and dead sermons kill. The gospel of Christ does not move by popular waves. It has no self-propagating power. It moves as the men who have charge of it move. The preaching man must be the praying man. Prayer is the preacher's mightiest weapon. An almighty force in itself, it gives life and force to all. Prayer makes the preacher. Prayer makes the pastor.

Q: *Does the ministry lack spirituality today?*
BOUNDS: The pulpit of this day is weak in praying. The pride of learning is opposite to the dependent humility of prayer. Prayer in the pulpit is all too often only a performance for the routine of the service. Every preacher who does not make prayer a mighty factor in his own life and ministry is powerless to advance God's cause in this world.

One of most serious and popular errors of the modern pulpit is the inclusion of more thought than prayer in its sermons. It is easier to fill the head than to prepare the heart, to make a brain sermon than a heart sermon. Praying gives sense, brings wisdom and broadens and strengthens the mind. The prayer closet is a perfect schoolteacher and schoolhouse for the preacher. Thought is not only brightened and clarified in prayer, but thought is born in prayer.

Q: *Is there a difference between proclaiming God's*

Word and doing so with an anointing of the Holy Spirit?

BOUNDS: There is a great difference. Anointing is that indefinable, indescribable something which pierces the heart because it comes immediately from the Lord. Some call it unction. It makes the Word of God "quick, and powerful, and sharper than any two-edged sword, piercing even to the dividing asunder of soul and spirit, and of the joints and marrow, and . . . a discerner of the thoughts and intents of the heart" (Hebrews 4:12). Anointing gives the words of the preacher point, sharpness and power, and stirs many a dead congregation.

Q: How does the Spirit's anointing change a preacher who has lacked it before?

BOUNDS: The preacher who receives a baptism of anointing has divine inspiration upon him. The letter of the Word is now embellished and fired by this mysterious power, and the throbbings of life begin. The anointing pervades and convicts the conscience and breaks the heart. There is a wide spiritual chasm between the preacher who has it and the one who does not.

Q: What is a simple definition of anointing?

BOUNDS: Anointing is simply allowing God to be in His own Word and on His own preacher. By mighty, great and continual prayerfulness, anointing is the preacher's entire potential. It inspires and clarifies his intellect, gives insight, grasp and projecting power. It gives him heart power, which is greater than head power. Tenderness, purity and force flow from his heart by this anointing. Growth, freedom, fullness of thought, directness and simplicity of utterance are the results of this anointing.

Q: Is earnestness the same as anointing?
BOUNDS: Earnestness is often mistaken for anointing. He who has divine anointing *will be earnest* in the very spiritual nature of things. But there may be a great deal of earnestness *without* the least bit of anointing. Earnestness and anointing look alike from some points of view. Earnestness may be readily and without detection substituted or mistaken for unction. It requires a spiritual eye and a spiritual taste to discern the difference.

Earnestness may be sincere, serious, ardent and persevering. It goes at a thing with good will, pursues it with perseverance and puts force in it. But the results do not rise higher than the mere human. The *man* is in it—the whole man, with all that he has of will and heart, of brains and genius, of planning, working and talking. He has set himself to some purpose which has mastered him, and he pursues to master it.

Q: What is the basic lack of one who is only earnest?
BOUNDS: There may be *none* of God in it. There may be *little* of God in it, because there is *so much of the man* in it. He may present pleas in support of his earnest purpose. The result will be to please, touch, move or overwhelm people with his own conviction of their importance. He may move along earthly ways, propelled only by human forces. But earthly hands made its altar, and earthly flames kindled its fire.

Q: Does Spirit anointing have other look-alikes?
BOUNDS: The anointing may be simulated. Many things look like it. Some results resemble its effects, but they are foreign to its nature. Genius is one, but true anointing is not the gift of genius. Genius is gifted and great but it takes more to win estranged and depraved hearts to God, to repair the breaches, and to restore the

church to purity and power. Pathetic or emotional sermons may look like the movements of divine anointing. But they are not radical—neither sin-searching nor sin-curing.

Q: *Is prayer the only way to receive the anointing?*
BOUNDS: Because it comes directly from the Holy Spirit, it comes to the preacher not in the study, but in the prayer closet. It is heaven's distillation only in answer to prayer. It is the sweetest exhalation of the Holy Spirit. It impregnates, suffuses, softens, percolates, cuts and soothes. It carries the Word like dynamite. It makes the Word a soother, an arraigner, a revealer, a searcher. It makes the hearer a culprit or a saint—makes him weep like a child and live like a giant. It opens his heart and his purse as gently, yet as strongly, as springtime opens the leaves.

Q: *When a man receives the Spirit's anointing, does it last a lifetime?*
BOUNDS: Holy Spirit anointing is not an inalienable gift, but a conditional gift. Its presence is continued and increased by the same process that secured it at first—unceasing prayer to God. We must count all else loss and failure without it. His holy oil only fills praying hearts. Prayer is the sole condition to maintain this anointing. Without perseverance in prayer, the anointing, like leftover manna, breeds worms.

Q: *How important is prayer in behalf of God's servants?*
BOUNDS: Just as it is absolutely necessary for the preacher himself to pray, it is an absolute necessity that people pray for the preacher. These two propositions are wedded into a union which ought never to be di-

vorced. It will take all the praying the preacher can do, and all the praying he can solicit, to meet the fearful responsibilities and gain the largest, truest success in his great work. The preacher, next to the cultivation of his own prayer life in its most intense form, should greatly covet the prayers of God's people.

Q: Why does this not seem important in the average church?

BOUNDS: Somehow the practice of praying for the preacher has fallen into disuse or is depreciated. Some even think it is a criticism of the ministry, a public declaration that the ministry is somehow inefficient. Perhaps praying for the preacher offends his pride of learning and self-sufficiency. If that is the case, it *ought* to offend and rebuke him. The more holy a man is, the more he should estimate prayer.

Q: What basis do we have from Scripture to pray for leadership?

BOUNDS: The apostle Paul continually requested prayer for himself. If Paul was so dependent on the prayers of God's saints to give his ministry success, how much more do we need to center our prayers on the ministry of today!

In Romans 15:30, Paul asked believers to strive with him in prayers to God for himself. In Ephesians 6:18–19, Paul exposed his very heart: "Praying always with all prayer and supplication in the Spirit, and watching thereunto with all perseverance and supplication for all saints; *And for me*, that utterance may be given unto me, that I may open my mouth boldly, to make known the mystery of the gospel." Colossians 4:3–4, First Thessalonians 5:25, Second Corinthians 1:11 and Second Thessalonians 3:1–2 are echoes of Paul asking believers to pray for him. Part of their work was to lend a helping hand in prayer.

Paul did not feel that this urgent plea for prayer lowered his dignity, lessened his influence or depreciated his piety. What if it did? Let dignity go; let influence be destroyed; let his reputation be marred—he must have their prayers. Called, commissioned and the chief of the apostles, all his equipment was imperfect without the prayers of his people.

Q: *Praying is not easy.*
BOUNDS: Spiritual work is always taxing work, and men are loath to do it. True praying involves serious attention and time, which flesh and blood do not relish. Few people have such strong fiber that they will make a costly outlay when inferior work will pass just as well in the market. To be little *with* God is to be little *for* God. It takes much time for the fullness of God to flow into the spirit. Short devotions cut the pipe of God's full flow. We live shabbily because we pray meagerly. This is not a day of prayer. Few men pray. In these days of hurry and bustle, of electricity and steam, men will not take time to pray. Prayer is out-of-date—almost a lost art.

Where are the Christlike leaders who can teach modern saints how to pray and put them at it? Do we know that we are raising up a prayerless set of saints? Only praying leaders can have praying followers. We greatly need somebody who can set the saints to this business of praying!

* * *

Writings by Bounds and *books used in research (not intended to be exhaustive):

The Essentials of Prayer

Heaven: A Place, A City, A Home
The Necessity of Prayer
The Possibilities of Prayer
*Power Through Prayer
*Prayer and Praying Men
*Purpose in Prayer
The Reality of Prayer
Satan: His Personality, Power, and Overthrow
The Weapon of Prayer

Samuel Logan Brengle

[1860–1936]

MAKE ROOM
FOR POWER

S AMUEL'S FATHER DIED IN THE CIVIL WAR, and his mother raised him on an Indiana farm. He counted his conversion from a childhood decision in a small Methodist church. After college, he became a circuit preacher in Indiana. Two years later he left for seminary in Boston full of high ambitions for a prestigious ministerial career.

After personal deeper experiences with the Lord in 1885, Brengle gave up his plans for a secure Methodist pastorate, and sailed for London to join the little-known Salvation Army under General William Booth. He was assigned to small, new, pioneer works on America's East Coast in rough communities. Brengle wrote many articles in the Army's *War Cry* magazine, which were later compiled into a book.

Used mightily by God to 76 years of age in ministries large and small, Colonel Brengle's preaching was scholarly, yet humble, non-ranting, straightforward and based solidly on the Word of God. His was a "Holiness" teaching of the "Second Blessing" in its sincerest form because he was an example of the sanctified living he proclaimed.

* * *

APPROXIMATE DATE: 1899

QUESTION: Why did you switch from a secure and prestigious Methodist pastorate to the little-known and lightly regarded Salvation Army?
SAMUEL LOGAN BRENGLE: I hungered for complete consecration to the Savior and holiness of life. It meant emptying myself before that longed-for filling could come in. My pride and ambition took up much of the space.

Q: Colonel Brengle, please tell us what happened.
BRENGLE: I saw the humility of Jesus in contrast to my pride and temper, the lowliness of Jesus against my ambition and selfishness. I wanted to be a great preacher, and in some ways I sought the Holy Spirit to accomplish that. I rationalized that I could glorify the Lord more if I became a great preacher rather than a mediocre one. After the Lord dealt with me deep in my soul, I prayed in utter desperation: Lord, I wanted to be an eloquent preacher, but if by stammering and stuttering I can bring greater glory to Thee, then let me stammer and stutter!

Q: What Scripture did God use to bring you into that experience?
BRENGLE: I shall never forget my joy, mingled with awe

and wonder, when First John 1:9 suddenly dawned upon my consciousness. For several weeks I had been searching the Word, ransacking my heart, humbling my soul and crying to God almost day and night for a pure heart and the baptism with the Holy Ghost. One glad, sweet day, January 9, 1885, it stood out boldly: "If we confess our sins, he is faithful and just to forgive us our sins and to cleanse us from all unrighteousness." I believed without any doubt that His precious blood cleansed my heart, even mine, from all sin.

Shortly after, I read again the words of Jesus to Martha, "I am the resurrection, and the life: he that believeth in me, though he were dead, yet shall he live; and whoever liveth and believeth in me shall never die" (John 11:25–26). Instantly my heart melted like wax before fire. Jesus Christ revealed Himself to my spiritual consciousness and filled my soul with unutterable love. I walked in a heaven of love.

Q: *Were you aware at the time of what God had done in your life?*
BRENGLE: Not altogether, until one day with amazement I said to a friend, "This is the perfect love about which the apostle John wrote—but it is beyond all I dreamed of! In it is personality—this love thinks, wills, talks with me, corrects me, instructs and teaches me." Then I knew that God the Holy Ghost was in this love, and that this love *was* God, for "God is love."

Q: *Is there some danger in overemphasizing a deeper experience of the Holy Spirit?*
BRENGLE: Great heights are always opposite great depths, and from the heights of this blessed experience many have plunged into the dark depths of fanaticism. But we must not draw back from the experience

through fear. We can avoid all danger by meekness and lowliness of heart, by humble, faithful service, by esteeming others better than ourselves and in honor preferring them before ourselves. We must keep an open, teachable spirit by looking steadily unto Jesus, to whom the Holy Spirit continually points us. He would not have us fix our attention exclusively upon Himself and His work *in* us, but upon the Crucified One and His work *for* us. We must walk in the steps of Him whose blood purchased our pardon and continues to make and keep us clean.

Q: *Many Christians through the ages have had similar deep experiences. But they seem to differ in their use of terms, or the time and order of the baptism or fullness of the Spirit.*
BRENGLE: I believe four classes of teachers have differing views. First, those who emphasize cleansing, who say much about a clean heart, but little, if anything, about the fullness of the Holy Spirit and power from on high. Second, those who emphasize the baptism of the Holy Ghost and His fullness, but say little or nothing of cleansing from inbred sin and the destruction of the carnal mind. Third, those who say much on both, but separate them into two distinct experiences, often widely separated in time. Last, those who teach that the truth lies in the union of the two, that while we may separate them in their order, putting cleansing first, we cannot separate them as to time. It is the baptism that cleanses just as darkness vanishes before the flash of the electric light when we touch the right button.

Q: *What is your view?*
BRENGLE: I believe sanctification – cleansing, being made holy – comes first, then filling, divine union with the Father and the Son through the Holy Spirit. But the

cleansing and the filling or baptism are not separate in time. The cleansing is not *before* the baptism, but *by* the baptism. The act and state of believing, which is man's part, and the act of baptizing with the Holy Ghost, cleansing as by fire, which is God's part, bring about the one experience of entire sanctification. We must not and cannot logically look upon them as two distinct blessings, any more than the act of the husband and the act of the wife are two separate experiences in marriage.

Q: *Do we receive the Holy Spirit initially at this time of the baptism?*
BRENGLE: No, He already dwells in the believer. "If any man have not the Spirit of Christ, he is none of his" (Romans 8:9b). Every child of God, every truly converted person, has the Holy Spirit in some gracious manner and measure, otherwise he would not be a child of God. I am speaking of a further experience for one who is already a believer.

Q: *Many Christians object to the term "second blessing."*
BRENGLE: Advocates of entire sanctification as an experience brought about by the baptism with the Spirit following regeneration do call it "the second blessing." But many good people who object to that term also say that they have received a first, second, third, or fiftieth blessing. No doubt they have. Yet the people who speak of "the second blessing" are correct in the sense in which they use the term – in that sense there are only the two blessings.

Q: *Is conversion the same as the baptism or fullness of the Holy Spirit?*

BRENGLE: Not the same. Great and gracious as is the work of the Holy Spirit in regeneration, it is not the fiery pentecostal baptism with the Spirit which Jesus promised. Conversion is not the fullness of the Holy Ghost to which God's Word exhorts us. Conversion is only the clear dawn of the day and not the rising of the daystar. It is only the initial work of the Spirit. It is perfect in its kind, but it is preparatory to another and fuller work of the Spirit.

Q: Can both happen in one experience?
BRENGLE: Surely this is possible. Since the day of Pentecost, we may receive the Holy Spirit immediately if we have repented of all sin and believed on Jesus and thus have been born again. Some have assured me that they were indeed sanctified wholly and filled with the Spirit within a few hours of their conversion. But often this work is slow, for the Holy Spirit can only work effectually as we work with Him, practicing intelligent and obedient faith.

Q: Please explain further about your use of the term "second blessing" describing this fullness or baptism of the Spirit.
BRENGLE: Let us be sure not to become confused by disputing over terms and wrangling about words. The first blessing in Jesus Christ is salvation with its negative side of remission of sins and forgiveness and its positive side of renewal or regeneration. That is the new birth. It is one experience.

The second blessing is entire sanctification with its negative side of cleansing and its positive side of filling with the Holy Ghost—one whole, rounded, glorious, epochal experience. And while *many refreshings*, girdings, illuminations, secret tokens and assurances of love and favor may follow, there is no third blessing in this large sense, in this present time.

When time is no more, when God has lifted up the everlasting doors and the King of Glory, forever redeemed and crowned, comes in with His Bride, and makes us sit down with Him at His throne—then in eternity we shall have the third blessing—we shall be glorified!

Q: Is the baptism of the Spirit for work and service only?
BRENGLE: It does bring power, the power of God, and it does equip for service, probably the most important service to which God has commissioned any created beings—the proclamation of salvation and the conditions of peace to a lost world. But that is not the only purpose—in fact, not the primary one. The primary work of the baptism is cleansing.

Q: What happens when we give ourselves fully to God and His filling?
BRENGLE: Our hearts and lives overflow. The blessed Holy Ghost comes in and Jesus becomes all and in all to us. The blessing is too big to contain—it just bursts out and overflows through the life, the looks, the conversation, the very tones of the voice. It gladdens and refreshes and purifies wherever it goes.

Jesus calls it rivers of living water (John 7:38). Love and peace and joy overflow. It makes the face shine; it glances from the eye; it bubbles out in thanksgiving and praise. You never can tell when one who has the blessing will shout out, "Glory to God! Praise the Lord! Hallelujah! Amen!" Patience and longsuffering, goodness and generosity overflow. You must not hold the blessing of this fullness selfishly for your own gratification, but let it overflow to the hungry, thirsty, fainting world about you.

Q: How can we maintain or abide in this experience of fullness?

BRENGLE: Remember, however blessed and satisfactory our present experience may be, we must never rest in it. Our Lord has yet many things to say to us, as we are able to receive them. We must stir up the gift of God that is in us and say with Paul, "One thing I do, forgetting those things which are behind, and reaching forward unto those things which are before, I press toward the mark for the prize of the high calling of God in Christ Jesus" (Philippians 3:13–14).

It is at this point that many fail. They seek the Lord, they weep and struggle and pray, and then they believe. But instead of pressing on, they sit down to enjoy the blessing, and lo! it is not. The children of Israel moved when the pillar of cloud and fire moved. And when the Comforter comes, we must follow if we want to abide in Him and be filled with all the fullness of God. Oh, the joy of following Him!

Q: What evidences will confirm that we have the genuine fullness of the Spirit's blessing?

BRENGLE: The blessing is never a harsh, narrow, unprogressive exclusiveness which often calls itself by the sweet, heavenly term of "holiness." It is expressed in the vigorous, courageous, self-sacrificing, tender, Pentecostal experience of perfect love. Our desire is both to save ourselves and enlighten the world. Our converts will be strong; those entering the work will multiply and will be capable, daredevil men and women. Our people will be like the brethren of Gideon, of whom it was said, "Each one resembled the children of a king."

The question is, "Have *ye* received the Holy Ghost since *ye* believed?"

* * *

Writings by and about Brengle and *books used in research (not intended to be exhaustive):

*Samuel Logan Brengle: Portrait of a Prophet
*They Found the Secret
*When the Holy Ghost is Come

Samuel Chadwick

[1860–1932]

SAINTS OF THE FIRE-HEART

ORN OF METHODIST PARENTS in Burnley, Lancashire, Samuel accepted Christ at the age of 10. From the time he was eight he worked 12 hours a day in an English cotton mill. When he was 15 he felt a call to the ministry and began to study until midnight after each long work day to compensate for his lack of basic education. His was an unlikely background for a noted English preacher, educator, Bible expositor and evangelist, but Samuel Chadwick shook his generation awake by the power of God.

As a young man preparing for the ministry, he relied on his own meticulous sermons to move men. His personal spiritual revolution took place during his first village pastorate at age 21. Dramatically changed from that point forward, Chadwick launched a ministry of aggressive evangelism and Bible teaching in Edinburgh, Glasgow, Leeds, London and other cities.

He became principal of Cliff College in Derbyshire, a Methodist school for training young men to become evangelists. Editing its weekly newspaper, in which his own articles regularly appeared, helped to spread his godly influence nationwide. As president of the Methodist Conference, Chadwick conducted conventions each weekend for many years in strategic centers throughout England.

His messages centered on essential evangelical truths of Christianity. His lengthy sermons were studded with rich biblical truth, quickened by the Holy Spirit whom he acknowledged as energizing him. Chadwick called men to their evangelistic task, but never failed to caution them, "Do all in the power of the Holy Spirit."

* * *

APPROXIMATE DATE: 1898

QUESTION: Mr. Chadwick, what do you think about the condition of the church relative to the Holy Spirit today?

SAMUEL CHADWICK: No doctrine of the Christian faith has been so neglected. The blunders and disasters of the church are largely, if not entirely, accounted for by the neglect of the Spirit's ministry and mission. The church is helpless without the presence and power of the Spirit. The lust for talk about work increases as the power for work declines. Conferences multiply when work fails. We see that the church has lost the note of authority, the secret of wisdom and the gift of power through persistent and willful neglect of the Holy Spirit of God. Confusion and impotence are inevitable when the wisdom and resources of the world are substituted for the presence and power of the Spirit.

Q: Is the problem with the church caused by wrong theology?
CHADWICK: The church still has a theology of the Holy Spirit but it has no living consciousness of His presence and power. Theology without experience is like faith without works; it is dead.

Q: Outwardly there seems to be a great deal of church growth and Christian activity.
CHADWICK: Certainly, but the church that is man-managed instead of God-governed is doomed to failure. A ministry that is college-trained but not Spirit-filled works no miracles. The church that multiplies committees and neglects prayer may be fussy, noisy, enterprising, but it labors in vain and spends its strength for nothing. It is possible to excel in mechanics and fail in dynamic. There is a superabundance of machinery; what is lacking is power. To run an organization needs no God. Man can supply the energy, enterprise and enthusiasm for things human. The real work of a church depends upon the power of the Spirit. Certainly the energy of the flesh can run bazaars, organize amusements and raise millions of dollars; but it is the presence of the Holy Spirit that makes a temple of the Living God. Things will get no better until we get back to the realized presence and power of the Holy Spirit.

Q: How did you personally come into a special experience of the Holy Spirit?
CHADWICK: To give you a background, I had a very great struggle to become educated. Since I was from a poor family in England, I worked since I was a child of eight.

I was converted as a boy in a Methodist chapel and from my mid-teens I was conscious of a call to the ministry. At 21 I finally became a lay preacher in a neighboring village church. I had been taught to prepare sermons with meticulous care and believed that if a minister preached interesting sermons, the people would flock to listen.

Q: *Would you say your ministry was spiritually effective at that time?*
CHADWICK: Definitely not. Soon my little stock of excellent sermons was nearly exhausted and nothing much had happened. I became concerned about my lack of power. Then I began to hear testimonies of people who had been quickened by a new experience of the Holy Spirit. I became intrigued. I persuaded my friends to enter into a covenant with me to pray for revival. As I searched my Bible and prayed alone and with my friends, the Holy Spirit gradually led me to the place of renewal.

Q: *Please share more of your story.*
CHADWICK: It was a Saturday night when I was alone in my room praying for blessing on the work of the morrow. Soon the Holy Spirit was searching and convicting me. He threw His searchlight on those wonderful sermons of which I was so proud. The struggle went on into the early hours of Sunday morning. Then I rose from my knees, took my precious stock of sermon manuscripts, put them into the empty grate and set fire to them. It was a crisis of obedience. When it came I could not explain what had happened but I was aware of things unspeakable and full of glory.

Q: *What changes did you experience?*

CHADWICK: Some results were immediate. There came into my soul a deep peace, a thrilling joy and a new sense of power. My mind was quickened. I felt I had received a new faculty of understanding. Every power was vitalized. My bodily powers were quickened. There was a new sense of spring and vitality, a new power of endurance and a strong man's exhilaration for big things.

Q: Was your ministry affected?

CHADWICK: Things began to happen. What we had failed to do by strenuous endeavor came to pass without effort. From the first day of my Pentecost I became a seeker and winner of souls. The very next day's ministry was powerful and I saw seven persons converted—one for each of my barren preaching years! The next week I called my people to a week of prayer. During that week the Spirit of God fell upon the people and I found myself in the midst of a most wonderful revival. The movement spread down the valley and hundreds were converted. Some of the most wicked people in the neighborhood came to Christ and were changed into saints.

Q: What do you believe was the significance of the historical Pentecost?

CHADWICK: At Pentecost the Holy Spirit came as He had never come before. All through the Old Testament the Holy Spirit was creative, directive, energizing, but His manifestations were occasional and special. There was a limitation and incompleteness, foretelling a day of fullness of the Spirit which would come. The signs at Pentecost were not new except in their combination and intensity, enlarged and distributed to a community of believers. The change in the apostles was more wonderful than any of the marvelous happenings of the day. A new power of transformation was at work in them. It brought about a new fellowship: the Church was born. The new thing was not in the wind and fire, or the gift of tongues, but in the possession of the Spirit by each for the good of all. That which happened at Pentecost is the biggest thing that ever happened. Now the biggest question of all is—has it happened to you and me? Have *you* received the Holy Ghost? I have written and preached much on the Holy Spirit, for the knowledge of Him has been the most vital fact of my experience. I owe everything to the gift of Pentecost!

Q: *What did your personal Pentecostal experience do for you in the long range?*
CHADWICK: That experience gave me the key to all my thinking, all my service and all my life. Pentecost gave me the key to the Scriptures. It has kept my feet in all the slippery places and under all sorts of criticism. The things that are stumbling blocks to so many are stepping stones to me. The inexplicable becomes plain when we recognize the Presence and Law of the Spirit. It balances scholarship and gives discernment beyond all human learning. Indeed, learning without the Holy Ghost blinds men to the realities of divine truth. The same Spirit gave me a new understanding and experience of prayer, and with these gifts came a new enduement of wisdom and power.

Q: *Is the baptism of the Holy Spirit the same as regeneration?*
CHADWICK: The baptism of the Holy Spirit is a definite and distinct experience assured and verified by the witness of the Spirit. It is foolish to say that the disciples were not already saved. In our Lord's intercession for

His disciples He calls them His own. This experience is distinct from that of regeneration. It is evident that a man may be born again of the Spirit and not be baptized with the Spirit. In the baptism of the Spirit there is a gift of power, and by it the believer is equipped for service and endued for witnessing. The Spirit fills, vitalizes and energizes with the power of God. Deliverance from sin, efficiency in service and effectiveness in witnessing are given with the fullness of this Pentecostal blessing.

Q: What difference does this experience make in one's prayer life?
CHADWICK: It makes the believer mighty in prayer. Prayer is an impossible task without the Holy Ghost. We know not what we should pray for as we ought, but the Spirit helps our infirmities (Romans 8:26). The Spirit instructs and inspires prayer, gives intelligence and intensity to intercession, and brings reality and joy to communion with God. Spirit-filled people love to pray, and prayer that is in the Spirit must prevail.

Q: You have used the term "abundant life" to describe this experience, as Jesus did. What does that imply?
CHADWICK: Pentecost brings abounding vitality. Our Lord came that we might have abundant and abounding life, and it is found in the Gift of the Spirit of Life. He is the Living Water, springing up into everlasting life and He is the Eternal Source of Life. The Spirit of Life dwells and fills men, permeates their being, sanctifies their nature, quickens their powers, vitalizes their mortal bodies and radiates their life. They live—*they really live!* They live the life that is life indeed. Pentecost turned anemic believers into exuberant saints. People thought they were drunk, and so they were, but not

41

with wine. They were vivacious with abounding vitality. Pentecost wakes people up. It vitalizes latent powers and makes the utmost of every faculty and gift. Those who want life – abounding life, victorious life, satisfying life, glorious life – must get to Pentecost. Life is the best medicine for every kind of sickness. It cures all ills, ends all weariness and conquers death all the time.

Q: What is the significance of the "baptism of fire"?
CHADWICK: It is what Pentecost also brings. Fire is the chosen symbol of heaven for moral passion. It is emotion aflame. God is love; God is fire. The two are one. The Holy Spirit baptizes in fire. Spirit-filled souls are ablaze for God. They love with a love that glows. They believe with a faith that kindles. They serve with a devotion that consumes. They hate sin with a fierceness that burns. They rejoice with a joy that radiates. Love is perfected in the Fire of God.

Jesus Christ came to bring fire upon the earth. The symbol of Christianity is not a cross but a tongue of fire! Whatever this fire may be, it is identified with the Person of the Holy Ghost. Men's souls are charged, saturated, enveloped in the Spirit of God when He enters into and fills them. Fire does not mean ranting or noise or ruthless self-will. It acts differently on different material and in different people, but in all it burns, kindles and glows. It is religion at white-heat.

Q: That seems to scare a lot of people who are more comfortable with quiet, self-controlled worship and lifestyle.
CHADWICK: That is strangely true. Fire in religion awakens a peculiar sense of distrust in the modern mind. There is no objection to it anywhere else. Enthusiasm in politics and recreation, fervor in reform and

business, intensity in work and friendship are among the most coveted qualities of modern life. But in religion they are regarded as bad form! Christian enthusiasts are suspect. Judged in the lump, the saints of the fire-heart are condemned as unlovely, undesirable and unreasonable. For things not fireproof, burning is not a pleasant sensation; but then, only that which can "dwell in everlasting burning" can be saved. We are saved by fire. It is by a holy passion kindled in the soul that we live the life of God. Truth without enthusiasm, morality without emotion, ritual without soul are the things Christ unsparingly condemned.

Q: Is one of the results of the Pentecostal experience that the Spirit gives us fruits?
CHADWICK: Let us be careful to distinguish that *fruits are not gifts.* There are nine gifts of the Spirit and nine graces or fruits of the Spirit, the latter listed in Galatians chapter five. The Scriptures never confuse gifts and graces. Gifts are for service and are bestowed in the sovereign wisdom of the Spirit. Each person may have some gift, some may have more than one, but all gifts of the Spirit are according to the election of grace and are given for the effective working of the divine will in each. Gifts are for work. Work belongs to the workshop; fruit belongs to the garden.

Q: Do fruit and gifts of the Spirit always exist together in the believer who has had a Pentecostal experience?
CHADWICK: Confusion in this area leads often to doubt and distress. It is not uncommon for earnest workers in the church to imagine that if they are filled with the Spirit, they will be endowed with marvelous and miraculous power for service. Examples have been quoted of

wonderful enduement that has turned commonplace men into marvels of power, and they look for like results. But gifts are not fruit. They *may* exist apart from great spirituality. The Corinthians were rich in gifts but unfortunately poor in fruit. Fruit is for all; His gifts He gives to each severally as He wills. The fruit of the Spirit consists of sanctified dispositions. Gifts apart from fruit do not glorify Him. Fruit grows by abiding and is perfected without noise or fuss, without anxiety or care. God glories in fruit. The believer does *not* receive fruit as a gift, nor does fruit come instantly. It grows.

Q: Are the manifestations of the Spirit the same in all Spirit-filled believers?

CHADWICK: They are not. The manifestation of the Spirit is not always the same. There is a manifold variety of the one Spirit. There are varieties according to temperament, according to capability, according to grace, according to function. The failure to remember this ensnares the unwary. They look for the experiences and gifts in others to be given to them. To some it is given to speak with tongues and to others to work miracles of healing and of power, and we are apt to think these are invariable and inseparable from the Holy Spirit baptism and fullness.

Q: What do you mean that the gifts of the Spirit are given according to natural endowments? Do you refer to human talents?

CHADWICK: Spiritual gifts must not be interpreted as natural endowments, but the principle of distribution is the same, and the two are not unrelated. The gifts of the Spirit transcend the gifts of nature, but they function through the sanctified powers of man. There is a new creation, but it is along the lines of natural endow-ment. Not all have the same gifts, and one deciding factor in the will of the Spirit is according to the ability of sanctified nature to receive and function. The scope is not according to our natural talents, but "according to the power that worketh in us." That power works consistently with personality. The natural man cannot receive the things of the Spirit, but it is to spiritual man that spiritual gifts are given according to each man's several ability in the will of the Spirit.

Q: If we all receive the same great power of Acts 1:8 after our personal Pentecostal experience, shouldn't we expect to do the same marvelous evangelistic work as they?

CHADWICK: All have not the gift of healing, neither do all speak with tongues (1 Corinthians 12:30). Neither does the baptism of the Spirit make all into evangelists. This is a snare into which many fall. They read of the mighty Pentecostal experience of the evangelists who have won souls for Christ by the thousands. Many have passed through agonies of disillusionment and disap-pointment looking for the same kind of public results in themselves. God does not make every Spirit-filled man into a Moody or a William Booth. He gives the Spirit to some that they may be ministers of helpfulness; to some that they may be faithful witnesses; and to others that they may be sanctified mothers who are keepers at home working miracles of patience, wisdom and sweet-ness. To each there is a gift of the Spirit, and whatever the kind of gift, there is given to all the gift of power for effective service and testimony. Each receives power. Pentecost swallows up ineffectiveness in power and banishes fear in the victory of courageous faith.

Q: Please give some practical illustrations of the function of the Spirit upon natural gifts.

CHADWICK: Remember that the gifts of the Spirit are distinct from natural talents and from the fruit of the Spirit–related to both and yet distinct from both. Now then, the fullness of the Spirit vitalizes natural powers, quickens dormant faculties and reinforces capabilities. Fire quickens, energizes, clarifies. The brain gets a new quality of alertness, endurance and effectiveness. The mind receives new powers of perception, intelligence and understanding. The heart finds a new clarity of vision, a new simplicity of motive and a new intensity of emotion. The impossible becomes capable of achievement in the sanctified powers of natural man. These are undoubtedly the work of the Spirit. But the gifts of the Spirit are distinct from these, and they transcend the powers of even sanctified natural powers. They are not unrelated, and yet they are in some ways independent.

Q: Would you summarize the relation of fruits and gifts?

CHADWICK: The gifts of the Spirit give a supernatural power to the work of sanctified natural endowments. Viewing these, outsiders are challenged to consider cause and effect, and find there is nothing in the natural man to account for what is manifestly of God. Fruit belongs to character; gifts are enduements of power. Gifts are an evidence of the Spirit; but they are no proof of holiness. Gifts are according to the elections of the sovereign will of the Spirit of God; fruit is the manifestation of cultivated life. Gifts are for service; fruit is for character. Gifts are functional; fruit is a quality of life. Gifts are bestowed; fruit is a manifestation. Gifts may be given immediately and complete; fruit is implanted and of gradual development. They are both of the Spirit and are intimately connected with one another, but they are not inseparable, much less identical. The gifts of the Spirit are given to people who are elect according to the sovereign will of God, who by His Spirit divides to every man severally as He wills.

Q: *Many people speak of the gift of love—why is it not in the list of gifts?*
CHADWICK: Love, in which is included all the fruit, is not in the list of spiritual gifts. All the fruits are for all; gifts are for those for whom they have been prepared. All may not prophesy, but *all must love.* We may covet gifts, but we must bear fruit. Gifts cannot take the place of fruit.

Q: *Is a certain gift given to a believer permanently?*
CHADWICK: That depends on the kind of ministry to be fulfilled. Occasion may determine function. There are seasons when special gifts abound. Some are permanent. Others are given for special vocations and exceptional occasions and the special manifestations of power in times of special visitation.

Q: *Are some gifts operative in one period of history and not available in another?*
CHADWICK: There are no biblical reasons why the gifts of the Spirit should be operative in one dispensation and not in another. They did not cease at the close of the apostolic age. They have been manifest in all ages of the church, and there are abundant proofs that they are still available to the faith and the need of the church. There is no reason why they should not be more manifest, and perhaps there is a greater need for them now than in some other times.

Q: Are there counterfeit gifts?

CHADWICK: The counterfeit outbids the true, but the true is the power that destroys the false. A revival of spiritual gifts in the church would bring to naught the mocking pretensions of the world. Pagan cannot cast out pagan, any more than Satan can cast out Satan; but in the Spirit of God, there is victory over the world.

Q: Then spiritual gifts are really no proof of spirituality?

CHADWICK: That is right. The New Testament nowhere makes spiritual gifts the sign of holiness. There were some greatly endowed of whom Jesus said that at the last it would be declared that He never knew them. There is no suggestion that the gifts were not genuine, but they were perverted to wrong ends or exercised in the wrong spirit. Gifts are not substitutes for grace, and ignorance and carnality have made them a menace to holiness of heart and integrity of character.

Q: How about the gift of tongues?

CHADWICK: The gift of tongues comes last on the list and is usually first in controversy. There is a gift of tongues that is given for a sign, and there is a gift of tongues that is for the perfecting of the saints and the building up of the Body of Christ.

Q: Some say that the gift of tongues means an ability to learn foreign languages with greater ease. What do you believe?

CHADWICK: It means more than a gift for acquiring an unknown language, and it is certainly no substitute for the hard work of learning. A careful study of the New Testament places the gift among the enduements of the church and sets forth adequate safeguards against abuse.

Q: How do some of the other gifts of the Spirit function today?

CHADWICK: Gifts of wisdom and knowledge are related to intelligence and learning, and yet they are so distinct that they are indiscoverable from the natural powers of man and are given to those who have neither natural wisdom nor education. Faith is man's sixth sense. We live by faith, walk by faith, do everything by faith. The gift of the Spirit is faith. By the Spirit, faith sees the invisible and proves the reality of the unrealized.

Q: Is the gift of healing the same as the sanctified skills of medical science?

CHADWICK: Not the same. It is a distinct gift of the Spirit. Those to whom it was given in the early church knew little or nothing of medicine. The sick were instructed to send, not for the doctors, but for the elders, and the appointed means of healing were anointing and the prayer of faith. None could heal indiscriminately. Paul kept Luke, the beloved physician, with him on his journeys, and Trophimus was left at Miletus sick. The Lord, the Healer, still gives to men the gift of healing by His Spirit; and the gift works quite apart from medical knowledge or the use of drugs or herbs.

Q: Has the gift of miracles passed away?

CHADWICK: Miracles are the gift of the Spirit and the age of miracles is certainly not past. As for prophecy as a gift, again it is more than insight or foresight, though the prophet is a seer and a forth-teller, too. By the gift of the Spirit, there is a God-given discernment of spirits. The apostles had it. Many prophets of God had it.

Q: How about abuses?
CHADWICK: Gifts are certainly liable to abuse. In the early church they appealed to unspiritual men who desired them for carnal purposes and thought they had commercial value. They are still commercialized though not always for their cash value. In the Corinthian church they became a source of rivalry, jealousy and disorder. Those possessed of one gift claimed priority in importance and precedence in order. The root of the difficulty lay in the fact that carnal people possessed spiritual gifts and used them for carnal ends.

Q: What are some safeguards against abuse of gifts?
CHADWICK: Safeguards against abuse are in the loyalties of faith. The first is loyalty to the Lordship of Christ. That is the first law of Christian discipleship and the continual standard of Christian life and service. The second line of defense is loyalty to the Word of God. The Word and the Spirit are never at variance, and the Word of Truth attests the Spirit of Truth. The Spirit interprets, corroborates, verifies and confirms the Word. No wisdom is of God that is not according to the Scriptures. There is laid down a plain, practical rule in loyalty to the fellowship in the Body of Christ. Edification is the test and order is the rule. Gifts of prophecy and tongues came into competition, and for these, definite rules were laid down—but the law of love applied to all.

* * *

Writings by and about Chadwick and *books used in research (not intended to be exhaustive):

*The Way to Pentecost
Path of Prayer
*Pioneers of Revival

Lewis Sperry Chafer

[1871–1952]

SPIRITUALITY AND POWER

ORN IN OHIO, THE SON of a Congregationalist minister of British ancestry, Chafer's spiritual birth came as a child of seven. Because of the death of his father when Lewis was 11, he began to assume responsibilities for his family and was self-supporting by age 13. As a youth of 14 he was deeply impressed by an evangelistic sermon on the grace of God, a theme which became a prominent emphasis in his later ministry.

Trained as a musician at the Oberlin College Conservatory, he enrolled in the newly founded Moody Bible Institute, but did not continue his studies there. Chafer opened a music studio, conducted a choral society, gave concerts in nearby communities and led church choirs.

He continued his ministry as musical director and soloist with several evangelists. For a number of years he served as music director for D.L. Moody's Northfield Summer Bible Conferences and taught music and Bible at the Mount Hermon School for Boys there. At Northfield, Chafer was profoundly influenced by C.I. Scofield's expository teaching and established a lifelong connection with him in ministry.

Ordained to the gospel ministry in Buffalo, NY, in 1900, he pastored a church in Lewiston, NY, and then returned to itinerant evangelistic ministry as a preacher. Chafer served on the faculty of the newly established Philadelphia School of the Bible for a time.

In 1919 Chafer was part of the leadership of a World Conference on Christian Fundamentals in Philadelphia from which grew the vision for establishing a conservative theological seminary. Dr. Chafer was serving as interim pastor of the First Congregational Church of Dallas – renamed the Scofield Memorial Church – when the decision was made to locate that institution in Dallas. He was elected the first president of the school in 1924 and served as Professor of Systematic Bible Doctrine and Spiritual Life and Service. Dr. Chafer gave nearly 30 years of leadership to Dallas Seminary.

Chafer served for several years as general secretary of the Central American Mission founded by Scofield.

* * *

APPROXIMATE DATE: 1918

QUESTION: *Dr. Chafer, is spirituality something that rare and especially holy Christians attain?*
LEWIS SPERRY CHAFER: By no means. Neither is spirituality a future idea. We are to experience it *now*. The vital question is: Am I walking in the Spirit *now*? We should

not depend on the presence or absence of some unusual manifestation of the supernatural. We live much of life in the uneventful commonplace. But even there we should have the conviction that we are in right relation with God and enjoying His unbroken fellowship.

Q: Should we expect to spend our lives "on cloud nine," never becoming weary, always wearing a happy face?
CHAFER: Not at all. We still live in bodies with limitations and all of us are subject to the circumstances of life. Neither should we mistake worn nerves, physical weakness or depression for unspirituality. Often we need sleep more than prayer and physical recreation more than heart searching.

Q: Do you mean that we can be spiritual even while doing things unrelated to the Christian life?
CHAFER: Certainly. We are just as spiritual when resting, playing, sleeping, ill or incapacitated, if it is His will for us, as when we are directly serving God. We can maintain an undercurrent of knowing that we are in complete accord with God and pleasing to Him whatever we are doing.

Q: How can ordinary Christians ever attain such an ideal?
CHAFER: Remember that God's provisions are always *perfect*, but our entrance into these provisions is often *imperfect*. When we use terms like "absolute surrender" or "absolute devotion" we are still aware that our compliance with God's conditions is often imperfect. What God provides and gives is in the fullest divine perfection, but our adjustment is human and therefore subject to improvement. We still press on. We shall have as

much at any time as we make it possible for Him to give us.

Q: What does "resting in the Lord and letting Him do the work" mean? Should we be passive?

CHAFER: The spiritual life is not passive. Too often it may look that way when we speak of ceasing from ourselves and our own efforts. The point is that we need to learn to live and serve by the power God has provided, not self-effort. A true spiritual life is even more active, enlarged and vital because the limitless power of God energizes us. Normally the spiritual Christian will occupy himself with effective service for his Lord. We should be yielded and ready to do whatever He may choose. Spirit-filled Christians are quite likely to feel physical exhaustion at the close of the day the same as other people. They are weary *in* the work, but not weary *of* the work.

Q: What is the action of the Holy Spirit on the believer?

CHAFER: Four ministries of the Spirit in relation to the believer happen at the moment he is saved and the Spirit does not repeat them a second time. The believer is born again by the Spirit, indwelt by the Spirit, baptized by the Spirit and sealed by the Spirit. These four operations of the Spirit *in and for* the child of God are not related to some extraordinary experience. The Spirit may, however, actualize all this to the believer some time after his conversion, and it may then become an occasion for most wonderful joy and blessing.

Q: Do you mean that the Spirit baptizes every believer at the moment of his salvation?

CHAFER: The most important point is what the Scripture

says in its context and how it uses that term. According to First Corinthians 12:13, the term "baptized in the Spirit" has to do with the forming of the Body of Christ out of living members. That term applies to one who is being united vitally and organically to Christ.

No Scripture passage uses that term in relation to a believer obtaining power for service. Since the baptism with the Spirit is the organic placing of the believer "in Christ," it is the operation of God which establishes the position and standing of the Christian. Nothing indicates that the Holy Spirit undertakes this baptizing ministry a second time.

Q: Is only one spiritual experience—his conversion—possible for a Christian?
CHAFER: No, I do not hold that. Two great spiritual changes are possible to human experience. But let's back up a little to get a firm foundation in our thinking. No divine classifications divide the *unsaved*—they are all called "natural" men. However, Scripture gives us two classifications of the *saved*. The term "spiritual" man comes before "carnal" man and is in direct contrast with the unsaved. The "spiritual" man is the divine ideal. "He that is spiritual" (1 Corinthians 2:15), is the *normal*, if not the *usual* Christian. But we must consider the "carnal" man and his condition.

Back to your question: The first experience, conversion, changes the "natural" man into the saved man. That is the new birth. The second change is from the "carnal" man to the "spiritual" man. A genuine faith in Christ divinely accomplishes the former. He becomes rightly related to Christ. When a real adjustment to the Holy Spirit takes place in *addition* to his relation to Christ in salvation, the "carnal" man becomes a "spiritual" man.

Q: Could both experiences take place immediately at conversion?

CHAFER: Experimentally, one who accepts Christ by faith *may* at the same time wholly yield to God and enter at once a life of true surrender. However, remember that many Christians are carnal. To these the Word of God gives clear directions as to the steps they should take to become spiritual.

Q: Some teach that the baptism of the Holy Spirit is the way to pass from the carnal state to the spiritual.

CHAFER: Let us make the proper biblical difference between the use of terms and the description of the experience to which the Bible refers. I have already stated what the term "baptism of the Holy Spirit" means in Scripture context. But the Bible calls the passing from the carnal to the spiritual state the "filling of the Holy Spirit." This is a valid and desired and essential experience. But be sure to use the correct Bible term.

This important experience has to do with the quality of daily life of saved people and in no way is it a contrast between the saved and the unsaved. However, we can know the doctrine and yet not enter into its blessings. It is also possible to have entered in some measure into the experience and not know the doctrine.

Q: Experiences and descriptions seem to vary greatly among believers.

CHAFER: It is dangerous to analyze personal experiences apart from the teaching of Scripture. No single experience is ever a true or complete representation of the full purpose of God for every Christian. If it were, nothing short of the infinite wisdom of God could describe it exactly. Because they lack Bible instruction, some people attempt to account for their experience by coining unbiblical terms and phrases which are invariably faulty.

Q: Please describe a valid biblical experience of the Spirit.
CHAFER: When one has found peace, power and blessing through a definite yielding to God and reliance on His strength alone, the Bible clearly identifies it as a larger manifestation of the presence and power of the Holy Spirit. Such a person is "filled with the Spirit."

Q: In point of time, when do the four actions of the Spirit which you mentioned before take place? And when does filling happen?
CHAFER: The four took place at one time *in the past* for the believer. But the filling is a *continuous* action (Ephesians 5:18). The translation of "be filled" should more literally read "be being filled by the Spirit." The revealed purpose of God is to constantly minister the Spirit unto the Christian (Galatians 3:5). The Spirit must fill and then keep filling a Christian for him to be spiritual. An experience may or may not accompany the first entrance into the Spirit-filled life. Even when there is an experience, the need continues for the mighty enabling power of God tomorrow as today. The need never grows less to walk moment by moment in the Spirit-filled life. The utter need of the helpless believer never ceases.

Q: What manifestations of the Spirit can the Spirit-filled believer expect?
CHAFER: First, the Spirit produces Christian character in the Galatians 5 description of the fruits of the Spirit. Second, the Spirit produces Christian service—a direct

exercise of the energy of the Spirit through the believer. "From [within him] shall flow rivers of living water. But this spake he of the Spirit" (John 7:38–39). Human energy could never produce living waters, and certainly not in rivers. The Infinite keys this statement. The human, at best, is no more than the channel or instrument for the divine outflow.

Q: Does every believer have some service to do for God?
CHAFER: According to Ephesians 2:10, God has ordained a very special service for each individual to perform, and the doing of these particular and individual ministries constitutes "good works" according to the divine estimates.

Q: What are other manifestations of the Spirit?
CHAFER: Third, the Spirit teaches us. Therefore the Spirit-filled believer has God's truth revealed to him more than the carnal Christian has (1 Corinthians 3:1–2). Fourth, the Spirit promotes praise and thanksgiving as the direct products of the Spirit in the one whom He fills (Ephesians 5:19). Fifth, the Spirit leads (Romans 8:14). Sixth, the Spirit witnesses with our spirit (Romans 8:16) to actualize every great fact which we take by faith. Lastly, the Spirit makes intercession for us (Romans 8:26) when we do not know how to pray as we ought.

Q: Where do the gifts of the Spirit come in?
CHAFER: Christian service, according to the New Testament, is the exercise of a "gift." We should not confuse the Bible use of the word "gift" with the world's idea of "a gifted person." The latter implies someone who, by physical birth, is especially able to accomplish certain things. The Spirit may use such natural ability. But a

"gift" in the Bible use of the word is a direct undertaking or manifestation of the Spirit working *through* the believer. The Spirit of God does something and uses the believer to accomplish it. This is not the same as when the believer does something and calls on God for help in the task. It is the "work of the Lord" in which we are to "abound." According to the Word, the Spirit produces Christian service as He produces the graces of Christ in and through the believer. He employs every faculty of the human instrument in the work. That human instrument will still experience weariness in the service. Human energy, however, could never produce the divine results which are sure to take place. The Scriptures strongly affirm that true Christian service is a direct manifestation of the Spirit.

Q: How do you view the listing of the gifts of the Spirit in First Corinthians 12:4–11?
CHAFER: Probably those enumerated gifts were the outstanding manifestations of the Spirit according to the conditions and time of the writing of that biblical record. Some have proved abiding to the present hour, other manifestations of the Spirit have evidently ceased. This is not due to failing piety after the first generation of Christians. No evidence of a decrease of piety exists. Those manifestations of the Spirit which have ceased were doubtless related to the *introduction* rather than the *continuation* of the work of the Spirit in this age.

Q: Would you explain that further?
CHAFER: When Christ was born, men saw a star in the east, and heard the voices of an angelic host—these were most unusual conditions. The star did not continue to shine, the angel voices ceased. So it was at the

coming of the Spirit and the introduction of His new work in the world.

Q: Do some Bible teachers differ in opinion about the continuation of these manifestations?
CHAFER: The most devout saints of all past generations have believed that these early manifestations have ceased according to the purpose of God. Yet in these last days when Satan employs every available issue to confuse and divide the Christian body, to divert their energy and prevent their testimony, some demand a return to Pentecostal manifestations as the only realization of the full ministry of the Spirit. Such professing Christians boldly condemn the spirituality of saints of all generations who have not accepted their teachings. They evidently lack in knowledge and regard for those gifts which the Scriptures say are of primary importance in contrast to lesser gifts.

Whatever men do to revive Pentecostal manifestations they should do in view of *all* that is taught in First Corinthians 14. If God is calling His people to a renewal of all the early manifestations of the Spirit, why is it confined to a little sect? Tens of thousands outside that group are yielded and ready to do His will but are never led into such manifestations.

If Satan is using these early manifestations of the Spirit to confuse and divide Christians, he will display all his supernatural power and his most subtle deceptions to produce what might seem the work of God. Many who have been delivered from these "Pentecostal" beliefs and manifestations have since found the more vital things of the Spirit and are deeply concerned for those who are still blinded and self-satisfied in error.

Q: Should believers who are not filled with the Spirit pray for that experience?

CHAFER: There is little Scripture to warrant the believer to pray for the filling of the Spirit. The *normal* work of the Spirit is to fill the one who is rightly adjusted to God. Spirituality, or the filling of the Spirit, does not depend upon patient waiting. The disciples waited 10 days for the coming of the Spirit into the world, and He came according to instructions by Jesus. They were not waiting only for their personal filling, but rather for the beginning of a whole new ministry of the Spirit–as it did on the day of Pentecost. When He came, He instantly filled all who were prepared in heart and life. Since that day no believer has had to wait for the Spirit. Neither prayer nor waiting, therefore, are conditions of spirituality.

Q: *Are there conditions, however, that a Christian must meet to become Spirit-filled?*
CHAFER: Three biblical conditions are set forth, of which two are directly connected with the issue of sin in the believer's daily life, and one with the yielding of his will to God. First, we *grieve* the Spirit by retaining any unconfessed known sin (Ephesians 4:30). We can *quench* the Spirit (1 Thessalonians 5:19) by any unyieldedness to the revealed will of God. By the latter we simply say no to God. The Spirit, however, does not remove His presence. He has come to abide.

On the positive side, the crucial word is *yield* (Romans 6:13). By that we say yes to God. To yield to Him is to allow Him to design and execute the position and effectiveness of our life. Only He knows what is best.

Q: *And the third condition of spirituality?*
CHAFER: It is something the believer must *do*–walk in the Spirit (Galatians 5:16) or more literally, to be walking. This too we cannot do in our own strength. The

Spirit will do the walking in the Christian. Our human responsibility is to wholly depend upon the Spirit. Walking in the Spirit is simply walking in complete reliance upon the ability and power of the One who indwells us. Thus we may prevent sin in our lives.

The major conflict in the believer's life is to *maintain* an unbroken attitude of reliance upon the Spirit. Only in that way can the Spirit possess and vitalize every human faculty, emotion and choice. We cannot meet tomorrow's issues today. To walk is one step after another and this demands a constant appropriation of the power of God. That is spirituality. That is the Spirit-filled life – the unhindered manifestation of the indwelling Spirit.

* * *

Writings by and about Lewis Sperry Chafer and *books used in research (not intended to be exhaustive):

Dallas Theological Seminary: 1924–1974
Dispensationalism
The Early Years of Lewis Sperry Chafer
The Ephesian Letter
Grace
He That Is Spiritual
The Kingdom in History and Prophecy
Major Bible Themes
Salvation
Satan
Systematic Theology, 8 vols.
True Evangelism

Oswald Chambers

[1874–1917]

THE SPIRIT'S CATHEDRAL

HAMBERS WAS BORN IN ENGLAND and gifted in many directions from his youth. A famous art center in Europe offered him a scholarship but he entered Edinburgh University to study business instead. He soon transferred to a small Bible training college in Clapham, England, where he tutored philosophy for many years. Chambers struggled long with his own inadequacy to live the Christian life. He felt he had no power to serve God.

After four years, at a small meeting at Dunoon College, he claimed the power of the Holy Spirit for himself. The experience radically changed his life. His ministry spread to America and Japan where he touched many lives through his teachings on the deeper life in Christ.

He returned to teach at the Dunoon Bible Training College in 1911. In 1915 the Young Men's Christian Association appointed him to overseas service with the British troops guarding the Suez Canal in Egypt. Chambers spent the last two years of his life in the desert with the military men. Every evening he sponsored a meeting in Zeitoun, Egypt, to instruct them on some vital theme. On Sundays he delivered sermons for the soldiers.

He died still in his 40s and his body lies in the military cemetery in Cairo.

Chambers's many writings were compiled and arranged into books. Some were printed simultaneously in Egypt and in England, with growing demand for translation into other languages. Among his publications, the devotional book *My Utmost for His Highest,* is still on best seller lists. It is a compilation of his lectures at the Bible college and in the desert.

* * *

APPROXIMATE DATE: 1914

QUESTION: *What one New Testament truth do you consider the most neglected or unrealized?*
OSWALD CHAMBERS: Without doubt, it is the knowledge and enjoyment that the Christian's body is "the temple of the Holy Ghost." Paul was surprised that the Corinthian converts had not grasped that (1 Corinthians 6:19). It is not an experience; it is a revelation which first takes some believing, and then some obeying.

Q: *Can this knowledge also lead to presumption?*
CHAMBERS: It can. People may say, "Since I have received the Holy Spirit, everything I want to do is inspired by Him." By no means. I must instruct myself, measure my thoughts against the Word of God and ask the Holy

Spirit to interpret my motivations to me. I must never count on my natural wisdom being from the Holy Spirit.

Q: If the fact that believers are really God's temple grips our thinking, how does that change our outlook?
CHAMBERS: Instantly the impossible becomes possible. The things you used to pray about, you no longer pray about, but *do*. As in the natural world, so in the spiritual, knowledge is power. All we need to *experience* is that we have "passed out of death into life." What we need to *know* takes all time and eternity. We must begin to know Him now, and finish never!

Q: Is there also a larger aspect to the Holy Spirit dwelling in us as individual believers?
CHAMBERS: Not only does He dwell in individuals, but corporately in the Body of Christ. God is the Architect of the human body and He is also the Architect of the Body of Christ. There are two Bodies of Christ: the historic body and the mystical body. The historic Jesus was the habitation of the Holy Ghost. The mystic Christ—the Body of Christ composed of those who have experienced regeneration and sanctification—is likewise the habitation of the Holy Ghost.

When we are baptized with the Holy Ghost, we are no longer isolated believers but part of the mystical Body of Christ. Beware of attempting to live a holy life alone—it is impossible. Paul continually insisted on the "together" aspect—"hath quickened us *together*, . . . and hath raised us up *together*, and made us sit *together*" (Ephesians 2:5–6). The Holy Ghost is the one who works out the "together" aspect in the church.

Q: Was the baptism of the Spirit at the historic Pentecost upon individuals?

CHAMBERS: After His resurrection, Jesus breathed on the disciples and said, "Receive ye the Holy Ghost." At that time He imparted the Holy Ghost to them and quickened them. Then on the day of Pentecost the disciples were baptized by the personal Holy Ghost—the *quickening* became an *equipment*. "But ye shall receive power, after that the Holy Ghost is come upon you" (Acts 1:8a). The baptism of the Holy Ghost is the complete uniting of the quickened believer with Christ Himself.

Q: Is the baptism of the Spirit today only upon individuals?

CHAMBERS: The baptism with the Holy Ghost is not only a personal experience, it makes individual Christians one in the Lord. "For by one Spirit are we all baptized into one body" (1 Corinthians 12:13a).

Q: How important is organizational unity among Christians?

CHAMBERS: The only way saints can meet together as one is through the baptism of the Holy Ghost, not through external organizations. The end of all divisions in work for God is when He changes fever into white-heat fervor. Oh, the foolish fever of these days! Organizing this, organizing that—a fever of intense activity for God. The baptism with the Holy Ghost will unite men and answer our Lord's prayer in John 17:21, "that they all may be one; as thou, Father, art in me, and I in thee, that they also may be one in us."

Q: Does the Holy Spirit have unfinished work in the church?

CHAMBERS: The habitation of the Holy Ghost in the church is not yet mature – it is easy to overlook or ignore it. "The habitation of God through the Spirit," (Ephesians 2:22b), which God is building for Himself, refers to the Christian community in this dispensation. And it is an amazing mix-up! But Christ loves the church so patiently that He will cleanse it from every blemish, and "present it to himself a glorious church, not having spot, or wrinkle, or any such thing" (Ephesians 5:27a).

Q: Does the indwelling Holy Spirit make some Christian men great leaders today?
CHAMBERS: *We* make great men and women – God does not. One essential difference between before Pentecost and after Pentecost is that from God's standpoint there are *no* great men after Pentecost. God no longer calls an isolated lonely prophet; the prophets are a figure of the whole Christian church which is collectively separated from the world.

Q: Does Jesus' cleansing of the Jewish temple have any application for our lives as the Spirit's temple?
CHAMBERS: On that occasion we see an absolutely terrifying side of Jesus. He expressed passionate zeal for the desecration of His Father's house. With a whip He drove out men and animals, overturned tables and cleaned the place from commercial enterprise. If we are indeed the temple of the Spirit of God, it shouldn't surprise us when He gives *us* a spring cleaning. We shouldn't try to hide or save anything that is not of Him, because it will have to go. Since my body is His temple it is up to me to honor it and its Occupant, the Spirit, by my bodily practices.

Q: What especially does He want us to get rid of?
CHAMBERS: The one thing He insists on in my spirit, soul and body is purity. We must not dabble in anything else – if we do, the scourge of God will come.

Q: Is that why some people complain that instead of peace and joy after the Spirit came in, they experience a terrible struggle in their personal lives?
CHAMBERS: This *is* the sign that He has come in. He is getting rid of the things that are making the temple into a trafficking place for self-realization. The gospel not only awakens an intense desire in the lives of men, but equally fosters an intense resentment because it threatens to destroy so much of their self-lives. Since I am God's temple, I am not to serve my own ends with my body, but the cause of Jesus Christ as His devoted disciple. I must not use His temple for the convenience of self-love. Covetousness for things, education to realize ourselves, or lust to please ourselves – I must drive them all out. Do I regard His temple, my body, as more mine than His? Do I fill it with my own furniture? Jesus said His temple was to be a house of prayer for all nations, and my personal life is to be the same.

Q: Is self-realization bad?
CHAMBERS: The modern jargon is all for self-realization. We educate ourselves for that purpose; we select our friendships for self-realization. But Jesus says, "whoever will *lose his life* for My sake" – deliberately fling it away – "shall find it." My personal self belongs to Jesus Christ. The counterfeit is to give ourselves to some cause. Thousands of people are losing their lives for the sake of a cause. Many look for self-realization through so-called "Christian work." That is perilously wrong because it is so nearly right.

Anything that motivates us to act on principles or issues instead of a relationship to a person fosters our natural independence. It becomes a barrier to yielding to Jesus Christ. Have we recognized that our body is the temple of the Holy Ghost? Or are we jabbering Christian busybodies, so taken up with Christian work that we have no time for the Christ who started that work? We have no time for Him in the morning, nor at night, because we are so keen on doing the things that are called by His name. What we must watch today is the competition of causes against devotion to Jesus Christ. One life yielded to God at all costs is worth thousands only touched by God.

Q: Is the earth at present the habitation of God?
CHAMBERS: At present the world systems of men have usurped control. But a time is coming when this earth will be the habitation of God. World systems will disappear and then God's "new heaven and new earth" will emerge. Until then, let us realize that the habitation of the Holy Ghost is our own bodies as believers. "For the temple of God is holy, which temple ye are" (1 Corinthians 3:17b).

* * *

Writings by and about Chambers and *books used in research (not intended to be exhaustive):

Approved Unto God
Baffled to Fight Better
Biblical Ethics
Biblical Psychology
Bringing Sons Unto Glory
Called of God
Christian Disciplines, Vol. 1 and 2

Conformed to His Image
Daily Thoughts for Disciples
Devotions for a Deeper Life
Disciples Indeed
*God's Workmanship
*He Shall Glorify Me
Highest Good
If Thou Wilt Be Perfect
If Ye Shall Ask
Knocking at God's Door
Love of God
Moral Foundations of Life
My Utmost for His Highest
Not Knowing Whither (Not Knowing Where)
Oswald Chambers: His Life and Work
Oswald Chambers: The Best from All His Books
Our Brilliant Heritage
Our Portrait in Genesis
Philosophy of Sin
Place of Help
Psychology of Redemption
Run Today's Race
Servant of His Hand
So Send I You
Still Higher for His Highest
Studies in the Sermon on the Mount
*Talks on the Soul of a Christian
Workmen of God

Charles Grandison Finney

[1792–1875]

ENCOUNTERS WITH THE SPIRIT

"OME-SPUN, DRAMATIC, FORCEFUL" were descriptions of the backwoods-born Finney who became in succession a teacher, lawyer, evangelist, pastor, professor of theology and college president.

Born in Warren, Connecticut, he spent his early years in New York state and most of his ministry on the East Coast.

After a dramatic conversion experience while a law student in Adams, NY, he immediately entered evangelistic ministry. Traveling from village to village on horseback as a rural missionary, his preaching sparked fires of revival everywhere. Prominent lawyers, doctors and businessmen were among his converts, especially during the nine peak years of his revivals in major eastern cities. The whole character of communities was said to have been changed after his sweeping evangelistic meetings. During that period, revivals broke out in 1,500 towns and villages.

Later Finney divided his time between teaching, the presidency of Oberlin College, Ohio, and pastoral ministry in New York. Although licensed by the Presbyterians, some of the churches he served were Congregational. His followers built the Broadway Tabernacle in New York for him in 1834. There he preached the famous *Lectures on Revival* that are still studied as models by theological students today.

Finney's methods, regarded as unconventional in his day, employed a frontier revival approach, addressing his audiences as he would a jury. Over 500,000 people were reported to have responded to his public invitations to receive Christ.

Although a common practice in many evangelical churches today, such public invitations were against tradition in sophisticated city churches of Finney's day.

* * *

APPROXIMATE DATE: 1850

QUESTION: *Rev. Finney, your name comes up when anyone mentions evangelistic work.*
CHARLES G. FINNEY: It has pleased God in some measure to connect my name and labors with an extensive movement of the church of Christ. My times are regarded by some as a new era, especially as to revivals of religion. But I am only one of the many ministers and other

servants of Christ who are sharing prominently in promoting them.

Q: Since you are on the cutting edge of a new spiritual movement, what reactions do you meet?
FINNEY: This movement involves the development of views of Christian doctrine which have not been common. Because it has brought about changes in the means of evangelism, it is very natural that some misapprehension should prevail. Even good men called in question the wisdom of such measures and the soundness of certain theological statements. And ungodly men were irritated and strenuously opposed to these great movements. But that was only to be expected.

Q: How have you pioneered in those areas?
FINNEY: I have been considered an innovator both in doctrine and measures. I assailed some of the old forms of theological thought and expression, and stated the doctrines of the gospel in many respects in new language.

Q: Did you have a Christian family background?
FINNEY: I grew up in Oneida county, New York, which, at that time, was almost a wilderness. No religious privileges were enjoyed by the people, and very few religious books were available. Neither of my parents professed religion, and I seldom heard a sermon. Until I went to Adams, NY, as a law student, I was almost as ignorant of religion as a heathen. I had been brought up mostly in the woods.

Q: Were you exposed to Christianity as a law student?
FINNEY: I began to sit under the educated ministry of the Rev. George W. Gale from Princeton, NJ, the pastor

of the Presbyterian Church. He preached hyper-Calvinism, was highly orthodox and of the old school. But I must say, I was rather more perplexed than edified by his preaching.

Q: Why did you attend some prayer meetings?
FINNEY: I used to go just to listen to the prayers from week to week. I was struck by the fact that they were not, as far as I could see, ever answered. I had begun to read the Bible because I found that the old authors frequently quoted the Scriptures, particularly the Mosaic Institutes, as authority for many of the great principles of common law. That excited my curiosity and interest. However, I did not understand much of it, but I did read that God was supposed to answer prayer.

Q: What did those people pray for?
FINNEY: I continually heard them pray for the outpouring of the Holy Spirit, and just as often confess they did not receive what they asked for. Nor were the impenitent converted. This inconsistency was a sad stumbling block to me. I questioned whether these persons either were not truly Christians, and therefore did not prevail with God, or whether I misunderstood the promises and teaching of the Bible on this subject. Or was I to conclude that the Bible was simply not true? At one time it almost drove me into skepticism.

Q: Was anyone praying for your salvation?
FINNEY: At one prayer meeting, I was asked if I desired that they should pray for me. I told them, "I suppose I need to be prayed for, since I am conscious that I am a sinner. But I do not see that it will do any good for you to pray for me, because you are continually asking without receiving. You have prayed enough since I have

attended these meetings to have prayed the devil out of Adams, NY. Here you are—praying on and complaining still."

Q: Did you really feel that way?
FINNEY: I was quite in earnest in what I said, and not a little irritated. Some members of the church proposed in a meeting to make me a particular subject of prayer. Mr. Gale discouraged them saying he did not believe I would ever be converted. From conversing with me, he had found that I was very much enlightened upon the subject of religion but very much hardened.

Furthermore, he was most discouraged because I led the choir and taught the young people sacred music. He feared they were so much under my influence that he did not believe, while I remained in Adams, they would ever be converted either. Another wicked man told his wife repeatedly, "If you Christians can convert Finney, I will believe in religion!"

Q: What turned you toward God?
FINNEY: On further and continually reading my Bible, regardless of the religious inconsistencies around me, I became quite settled that the Bible was nevertheless the true Word of God. Thus I was brought face-to-face with the question of whether I would accept Christ as presented in the gospel, or go on to pursue a worldly course of life. At this period, my mind was so impressed by the Holy Spirit that I could not long leave this question unsettled.

Q: What was holding you back from being converted?
FINNEY: I was very proud without realizing it. I had supposed that I had not much regard for the opinions of others. But I found, when I faced the question, that I

was very unwilling to have anyone even know I was seeking the salvation of my soul.

Q: *Would you share some examples?*
FINNEY: I would only whisper my prayer, after having stopped up the key hole in the door, lest someone should hear and discover me. I kept my Bible, as much as I could, out of sight. If I was reading it when anyone came in, I would throw my lawbook over it, to create the impression that I did not have it in my hand. I found myself suddenly unwilling to converse with anyone on religion. Formerly I loved to argue about it. I did not want my minister to know how I felt because I had no confidence he would understand my case and give me the direction I needed. I was afraid the elders or any of the Christian people would misdirect me. I felt shut up to the Bible alone.

Q: *What were your inner feelings?*
FINNEY: My conviction of sin increased, but I could not shed a tear nor pray. Frequently I felt that if I could be alone where I could use my voice and let my feelings out, I should find relief in prayer. One night a strange feeling came over me as if I were about to die. I knew that if I did, I should certainly sink down to hell.

Q: *Where were you finally converted?*
FINNEY: Alone in the woods. One morning on my way to my law office, it was as if an inward voice said to me, *What are you waiting for? Did you not promise to give your heart to God? What are you trying to do, work out a righteousness of your own?* At that point the whole question of gospel salvation opened to my mind in a manner most marvelous. I saw clearly that I had to submit myself to the righteousness of God through Christ; all

that was necessary on my part was to get my own consent to give up my sins and accept Christ.

I stopped still in the street as the question seemed to be put to me, *Will you accept it now, today?* I replied, "Yes, I will accept today, or I will die in the attempt."

I turned and made my way to the woods where I took frequent walks, feeling that I must be alone to pour out my prayer to God. Yet so great was my pride that I sneaked along under the fence until I got so far out of sight no one from the village could see me. I went a quarter of a mile into the woods, on the other side of the hill, between some large fallen trees. I knelt down for prayer.

Q: Then what happened?
FINNEY: When I attempted to pray, I was dumb; I had nothing to say to God. At least I could say only a few words, and those without much enthusiasm. Any rustling in the leaves made me look up to see if someone was approaching. I was fast verging to despair. I began to feel deeply that it was too late. God must have given me up, and I was past hope. I had no emotion at all. Another rustling of the leaves and opening of my eyes brought me an overwhelming sense of my wickedness in being ashamed to be seen.

This thought took such powerful possession of me that I cried at the top of my voice. I exclaimed that I would not leave that place if all the men on earth and all the devils in hell surrounded me. This at last broke me down before the Lord.

The Spirit seemed to lay upon my heart the text, "When you search for me with all your heart. . . ." I told the Lord that I would take Him at His word because He could not lie. Therefore I was sure He heard my prayer, and that He would be found of me. I continued thus to pray and to receive and to appropriate promises for a long time until my mind was so full that I was on my feet and stumbling up the ascent toward the road.

Brushing through the leaves and bushes, I recollect saying with great emphasis, "If I am ever converted, I will preach the gospel!" The question of my being already converted had not so much as arisen to my thought yet.

Q: You did not know you were converted?

FINNEY: I think I really had not stopped to analyze what had happened to me. Suddenly I realized I was not at all anxious about my soul and about my spiritual state. All sense of sin or guilt had left me, and the repose of my mind was unspeakably great. I never can describe it in words.

The thought of God was so sweet to my mind, and the most profound spiritual tranquility took possession of me. I said to myself, *What is this? I must have grieved the Holy Spirit entirely away. I have lost all my conviction of sin.* This was a great mystery, but it did not perplex or distress me.

Q: The same day of your conversion you received the baptism of the Holy Spirit?

FINNEY: Yes, it happened like this: After dinner we were moving books and furniture to another law office. The thought took possession of my mind that as soon as I was alone in the new office, I would try to pray again.

Later, I made up a good fire in an open fireplace and accompanied Squire W. to the door. As I closed the door and turned around, my heart seemed to be liquid within me. All my feelings seemed to rise and flow out, and the utterance of my heart was, *I want to pour my whole soul out to God.* The rising of my soul was so great that I rushed into the room back of the front office to pray.

There was no fire there and no light; nevertheless it appeared to me as if it were perfectly light. As I went in and shut the door after me, it seemed as if I met the Lord Jesus Christ face-to-face. It did not occur to me then, nor did it for some time afterward, that it was wholly a mental state. On the contrary, it seemed to me that I saw Him as I would see any other man. He said nothing, but looked at me in such a manner as to break me right down at His feet.

I have always since regarded this as a most remarkable state of mind, for it seemed to me a reality that He stood right before me, and I fell down at His feet and poured out my soul to Him. I wept aloud like a child, and made such confessions as I could with my choked utterance. It seemed to me that I bathed His feet with my tears, and yet I had no distinct impression that I touched Him, that I recollect.

Q: How long were you in such a state?
FINNEY: It must have been a good while, because as soon as my mind became calm enough, I returned to the front office, and found that the fire I had made of large wood was nearly burned out. But as I turned and was about to take a seat by the fire, I received a mighty baptism of the Holy Ghost.

Q: Did you have any theological teaching that such an experience was possible?
FINNEY: Without any expectation of it, without ever having the thought in my mind there was any such thing for me, without any recollection that I had ever heard the thing mentioned by any person in the world, the

Holy Spirit descended upon me in a manner that seemed to go through me, body and soul.

Q: Can you describe your feelings?

FINNEY: I could feel the impression like a wave of electricity, going through and through me. Indeed it seemed to come in waves and waves of liquid love–for I could not express it any other way. It seemed like the very breath of God. I can recollect distinctly that it seemed to fan me, like immense wings. No words can express the wonderful love that was shed abroad in my heart.

I wept aloud with joy and love. And I do not know whether I should say, but I literally bellowed out the unutterable gushing of my heart. These waves came over me, and over me, and over me, one after the other, until I recollect I cried out, "I shall die if these waves continue to pass over me!" I said, "Lord, I cannot bear any more!" Yet I had no fear of death. How long I continued in this state, with this baptism continuing to roll over me and go through me, I do not know.

Q: Then what happened?

FINNEY: It was late in the evening when a member of my choir came into the office to see me and found me in this state of loud weeping. He said to me, "Mr. Finney, what ails you?" I could not answer him for some time. He then asked, "Are you in pain?" I gathered myself up as best I could and replied, "No, but so happy that I cannot live!"

He left the office, and in a few minutes returned with one of the elders of our church. This elder was a very serious man, and in my presence had been very watchful. I had scarcely ever heard him laugh. When he came in, I was very much in the same state in which the young man had found me. He asked me how I felt, and I began to tell him.

Q: *Being a church elder, did he understand your experience?*
FINNEY: Instead of saying anything, he fell into the most spasmodic laughter. It seemed as if it was impossible for him to keep from laughing from the very bottom of his heart. I wondered later whether he thought that I was under a delusion or crazy.

Then another young man with whom I had deeply shared many spiritual things came in. He listened with astonishment, and suddenly partly fell upon the floor and cried out in the greatest agony of mind, "Do pray for me!" We all did so, and soon afterward they retired and left me alone.

Q: *Were you tempted later to doubt your baptism in the Holy Spirit?*
FINNEY: In spite of the baptism I had received, immediately a cloud seemed to shut in over me. I had no hold on anything in which I could rest, and after a little while, I retired to bed. I was not distressed in mind, but I was still at a loss to know what to make of my present state. I went to bed without feeling sure that my peace was made with God.

Q: *Did you sleep?*
FINNEY: I fell asleep, but soon awoke on account of the great flow of the love of God that was in my heart. I was so filled with His love I could not sleep. I slept and awoke several times in the same manner. When awake, the love that seemed to be in my heart would abate. But as soon as I was asleep again, it was so warm within me that I would immediately awake again.

When I awoke in the morning, the sun had risen and was pouring a clear light into my room. Words cannot express the impression this sunlight made upon me. Instantly the baptism I had received the night before returned upon me in the same manner. I arose from the bed and wept aloud with joy, remaining for some time too much overwhelmed with the baptism of the Spirit to do anything but pour out my soul to God.

Q: Did you have any doubts about your spiritual state after that?

FINNEY: It seemed as if that morning's baptism was accompanied with a gentle reproof, and the Spirit seemed to say to me, *Will you doubt? Will you doubt?* I cried, "No! I will not doubt. I cannot doubt!" He then cleared the subject up so much to my mind that it was, in fact, impossible for me to doubt ever after that the Spirit of God had taken possession of my soul.

Q: What were the immediate manifestations of your experience?

FINNEY: I began to talk to every person I met about the gospel. I believe the Spirit of God made lasting impressions upon each of them. I cannot remember one person I spoke to of the many that day who was not soon after converted. My whole mind was taken up with Jesus and His salvation, and the world seemed to me of very little consequence. Nothing, it seemed, could be put in competition with the worth of souls. No labor, no thought could be so sweet, and no employment so exalted as that of holding up Christ to a dying world.

Q: What happened to your law career?

FINNEY: I went into my law office that morning still having the renewal of these mighty waves of love and salvation flowing over me. Squire W., my boss, came in, and I said a few words to him on the subject of salvation. He looked at me with astonishment but made no reply. He stood still a few minutes and then left the office.

Later I learned that my brief remark had pierced him like a sword, and he did not recover until he was converted. I had the impression, which has never left my mind, that God wanted me to preach the gospel, and that I must begin immediately.

Q: How could you be so sure?
FINNEY: I somehow seemed to know it. If you ask me how I knew it, I cannot tell, anymore than I can tell how I knew that it was the love of God and the baptism of the Holy Ghost which I had received. I did somehow know it with a certainty past all possibility of doubt. I know the Lord commissioned me to preach the gospel.

I told a client that morning that I could no longer represent him. "I have a retainer from the Lord Jesus Christ to plead His cause and I cannot plead yours." I no longer had any desire to practice law. I had no disposition to make money. I had no hungering and thirsting after worldly pleasures and amusements.

Q: When did you begin your public ministry?
FINNEY: Immediately. In the course of the very same day, a good deal of excitement was created in the village when it was reported what the Lord had done for my soul. At evening, without any appointment, I observed people going to the place where they usually held prayer meetings. They seemed actually to rush to the place of worship.

So I went there myself. No one seemed ready to open the meeting, but the house was packed to its utmost capacity. I did not wait for anybody, but arose and told such parts of my experience as it seemed important to tell.

Q: How did they respond?

FINNEY: What the Lord enabled me to say seemed to take a wonderful hold on the people. Some said I was in earnest; some said I was deranged. Mr. Gale made a confession in a very humble manner. I had never made a prayer in public, but did so with a great deal of enlargement and liberty. From that wonderful meeting we had a meeting every evening for a long time. The work spread on every side, and personal conversions of those with whom I spoke daily were many.

Q: How about those young people under your charge?

FINNEY: As their leader, I immediately appointed a meeting for them which they all attended. I gave up my time to labor for their conversion, and the Lord blessed every effort in a very wonderful manner. They were converted one after another with great rapidity.

Q: What was your view of the Bible after that time?

FINNEY: I found that the Word of God had wonderful power. I was every day surprised to find that just a few words spoken to an individual would stick in his heart like an arrow. I was quite willing to believe whatever I found taught in the Bible, and studied it diligently to check the teachings of men against it. I read my Bible on my knees a great deal in those days of conflict, beseeching the Lord to teach me His own mind. I had nowhere to go but directly to the Bible.

Q: How did your conversion affect your family?

FINNEY: A short time afterward, I visited my parents. My

father met me at the gate saying, "How do you do, Charles?" I replied, "I am well, Father, body and soul. But, Father, you are an old man; all your children are grown up and have left your home; and I never heard a prayer in my father's house."

Father dropped his head, burst into tears and replied, "I know it, Charles. Come in and pray yourself." We did, and my parents were greatly moved. In a very short time both were converted.

Q: Did other converts and those filled with the Spirit act as emotionally as you did?
FINNEY: Let me give you an example. Squire W., a very dignified and reserved man, also came under conviction by the Holy Spirit. He finally went into the woods to pray. Someone saw him pacing to and fro, singing as loud as he could sing. Every few minutes he stopped to clap his hands with his full strength and shout, "I will rejoice in the God of my salvation!" Then he would march around and sing again, stop and shout and clap.

Upon returning to the village, he rushed up to a Christian brother, picked him up in the air, then ran into the office in a profuse perspiration—he was a heavy man. He cried out, "I've got it! I've got it!" Clapping his hands with all his might, he fell upon his knees and began to give thanks to God. He said the Spirit of God came upon him and filled him with such unspeakable joy that it resulted in his reactions.

Yes, others had similar experiences and reactions.

Q: Were there other occasions when you saw visions as you did the night you were filled with the Spirit?
FINNEY: One morning before our usual prayer meeting—we met long before it was light enough to read—I came to the meeting house, and my minister was stand-

ing at the door. As I came up, all at once the glory of the Lord shone upon and around me in a manner most marvelous. The day was just beginning to dawn, but all at once a light perfectly ineffable shone in my soul, and almost prostrated me to the ground. In this light it seemed as if I could see that all nature except man praised and worshipped God. This light seemed to be like the brightness of the sun in every direction. It was too intense for the eyes.

I recollect casting my eyes down and breaking into a flood of tears because mankind did not praise God. I think I knew something then, by actual experience, of that light that prostrated Paul on the way to Damascus. It was surely a light such as I could not have endured long.

I found that Mr. Gale had seen no light. I therefore said little. Indeed, it did not seem to me at the time that the vision of His glory which I had should or could be described in words. I wept it out. Then the vision, if it may be so called, passed away and left my mind calm.

Q: Did you have special experiences during your prayer times?

FINNEY: When I was a young Christian, I had many seasons of communing with God which cannot be described in words. Not infrequently those seasons would end in an impression on my mind like this: *See that thou tell no man.* I did not understand at the time. Several times I paid no attention to this injunction, but tried to tell my Christian brethren what communications the Lord had made to me, or rather, what seasons of communion I had with Him.

But I soon found it would not do to tell my brethren what was passing between the Lord and my soul. They could not understand it. They would look surprised, and sometimes, I thought, incredulous. I soon learned to keep quiet in regard to those divine manifestations, and say but little about them. I spent a great deal of time in prayer, sometimes literally "praying without ceasing."

Q: Have you ever found it profitable to fast?
FINNEY: I have felt very much inclined to hold frequent days of private fasting. On those days I would seek to be entirely alone with God and would generally wander off into the woods, or go into the meeting house or somewhere by myself. Sometimes I would pursue a wrong course in fasting according to the ideas of self-examination then entertained by my minister and the church. I would turn my attention particularly to my own motives and the state of my mind.

But I found invariably that the day would close without any perceptible advance being made because it turned my attention away from the Lord Jesus Christ. My feelings would all subside.

But whenever I fasted and let the Spirit take His own course with me, and gave myself up to let Him lead and instruct me, I universally found it in the highest degree useful.

Q: Have you had times of depression or coolness of spirit or were you always on a spiritual high?
FINNEY: I found I could not live without enjoying the presence of God. If at any time a cloud came over me, I could not rest, I could not study, I could not attend to anything with the least satisfaction or benefit until all was again clear between my soul and God.

I would often come from protracted discussions on theological controversy greatly depressed and discouraged. Several times I was at the point of giving up study for the ministry altogether. God provided an elder of the church who, when I was in a state of great depression, would go with me to my room. Sometimes we would continue till a late hour at night crying to God for light and strength and for faith to accept and do His perfect will.

"Go on," he would say. "Go on, brother Finney; the Lord will give you deliverance." At times he was so burdened for me that he prayed for me day and night. I have reason to believe he prayed for me daily as long as he lived.

Q: Did you ever experience what the Scripture speaks of as the word of faith and the word of knowledge?
FINNEY: Many times. For example, a woman with whom I boarded, not a Christian but her husband was, was taken very sick. She was not expected to live through the night. There came upon me in the sense of a burden that crushed me, the nature of which I could not at all understand, an intense desire to pray for that woman. I could only groan with groaning loud and deep. I got no relief, could not sit still, only walk the room and agonize. Somehow words could not express my prayer.

Eventually the Lord gave me power to prevail, and I was enabled to roll the burden upon Him. I obtained the assurance that the woman would not die, indeed that she would never die in her sins. My mind was perfectly quiet, and I retired to rest.

The next morning the husband reported, smiling, that she was to all appearance better, and I shared my assurance with him. "You may rely upon it," I dared to say. She did recover, and soon after obtained a hope in Christ.

In such matters, I learned not to draw a false inference in respect to the time. In the case of a person's salvation or recovery, it might not be for several months or longer.

Q: When older or more conservative Christians observed how young people who were filled with the Spirit became very zealous in their witness, did they welcome it?
FINNEY: When the Spirit was poured out, I am sorry to say, a mistake was made, or—perhaps I should say a sin committed—by some of the older members of the church. It resulted in a great evil. A considerable number of the older people resisted this new movement among the young. They were jealous of it. They did not know what to make of it, and felt that the young converts were getting out of their place in being so forward and so urgent upon the older members of the church.

This state of mind finally grieved the Spirit of God. It was not long before alienation began to arise among these older members of the church which finally resulted in great evil to those who had allowed themselves to resist this revival.

Q: How did the young people weather this?
FINNEY: The young people held out well. The converts, so far as I know, were almost universally sound, and have been thoroughly efficient Christians.

Q: Now that you have described your early Christian experience allow me to ask you some questions on your beliefs about the Holy Spirit. Can one be a Christian and still not experience a fuller work of the Spirit in his life?
FINNEY: Yes, let me give you an example. The minister, Mr. Gale, under whom I studied theology, had a defect

in his education which I regarded as fundamental. If he had ever been converted to Christ, he had failed to receive that divine anointing of the Holy Ghost that would make him a power in the pulpit and in society for the conversion of souls. He had fallen short of receiving the baptism of the Holy Ghost, indispensable to ministerial success.

Q: What do you regard as the purpose of the baptism of the Holy Spirit?
FINNEY: The baptism poured out upon the disciples on the day of Pentecost was an indispensable qualification for success in their ministry. I did not suppose then, nor do I now, that this baptism was simply the power to work miracles. The power to work miracles and the gift of tongues were given as signs to attest the reality of their divine commission.

But the baptism itself was a divine purifying, an anointing bestowing on them a divine illumination. It filled them with faith and love, with peace and power, so their words were made sharp in the hearts of God's enemies, quick and powerful, like a two-edged sword. This is an indispensable qualification of a successful ministry.

I have often been surprised and pained that to this day so little stress is laid upon this qualification for preaching Christ to a sinful world. Without the direct teaching of the Holy Spirit, a man will never make much progress in preaching the gospel.

Q: Are you speaking of the enduement of the Spirit as a further experience beyond conversion?
FINNEY: Yes. Every Christian possesses a measure of the Spirit of Christ already. In conversion to Christ, the soul has to relate directly and personally to Christ. In the

baptism of the Holy Spirit there is an enduement of power for ministry, for the great work of the world's conversion, which is the commission upon us all.

Q: Is this experience always as instantaneous as it was in your case?
FINNEY: The reception of this enduement of power is instantaneous. I do not mean to assert that in every instance the recipient is aware of the precise time at which the power commences to work mightily within him. It may commence like the dew and increase to a shower.

Q: How does this enduement of power affect those to whom a Christian witnesses?
FINNEY: The gift of the Holy Spirit is given to savingly impress men. It has existed in the church, to a greater or lesser extent, ever since Pentecost. It is a mysterious fact, often manifested in a most surprising manner. Sometimes a single sentence, one word, a gesture or even a look will convey this power in an overcoming manner.

Q: Has that continued to be your experience?
FINNEY: It continues unto today. In the beginning, a few words dropped here and there to individuals were the amazing means of their immediate conversion. Multitudes can attest to the same thing. This power is a great marvel.

Sometimes the most simple and ordinary statements cut men off from their seats like a sword, break the heart like a hammer, take away their bodily strength and render them almost as helpless as dead men. This power seems sometimes to pervade the atmosphere of one who is highly charged with it.

Many times great numbers of persons in a community will be clothed with this power, when the very atmosphere of the whole place seems to be charged with the life of God. Strangers coming into it and passing through the place will be instantly smitten with conviction of sin, and in many instances converted to Christ.

When Christians humble themselves and consecrate their all afresh to Christ and ask for this power—not for their own use—they will often receive such a baptism that they will be instrumental in converting more souls in one day than in all their lifetime before.

Q: *Would you give a specific instance when such a spiritual atmosphere was present?*
FINNEY: In a certain place in Jefferson County, New York, I stopped in a village where there were no religious meetings held at that time, indeed never before in the neighborhood in which one man invited me to preach. I was a total stranger in a very wicked community.

The Holy Spirit began to work through the simple preaching of the Word of God and before long there seemed to fall upon the people an instantaneous shock. I cannot describe the sensation I felt, nor that which was apparent in the people, but the Word seemed *literally* to cut like a sword.

The power from on high came down upon them in such a torrent that they fell from their seats in every direction. In less than one minute nearly every one in the whole congregation was either down on his knees or on his face or in some position prostrate before God. Everyone was crying or groaning for mercy upon his own soul. In fact, they paid no further attention to me or to my preaching.

A marvelous revival henceforth broke out in that place. Those who have lived in that region now testify years later of the permanent results of that blessing.

Q: Is such spiritual power only for ministers or so-called full-time Christian workers?

FINNEY: Just as every member of the church is under obligation to make it his life work to convert the world, so both the promise and the admonition apply equally to all Christians of every age and nation. Christ expressly promised it to the whole church and to every individual.

No one has, at any time, any right to expect success, unless he first secures this enduement of power from on high. I wish most emphatically to add that the lack of an enduement of power from on high should be regarded as a *disqualification* for a pastor, a deacon, an elder, a Sabbath school superintendent, a professor in a Christian college and especially for a professor in a theological seminary.

Q: Do all share your view that the enduement of the power of the Holy Spirit is for all today?

FINNEY: A vast many professors of religion, even ministers, seem to doubt whether this promise is to the whole church and to every Christian. Consequently, they have no faith to lay hold of it. If it does not belong to all, they don't know to whom it does belong! Of course they cannot lay hold of the promise by faith.

It is amazing to witness the extent to which the church has practically lost sight of the necessity of this enduement of power. Much is said of our dependence upon the Holy Spirit by almost everybody; but how little is this dependence realized. Christians and even ministers go to work without it. I mourn to be obliged to say that the ranks of the ministry seem to be filling up with those who do not possess it. May the Lord have mercy on us!

Q: *Who bears the responsibility for more Christians not entering into this deeper experience of power?*
FINNEY: Precisely the leadership of the church! It is a great default not to teach this biblical necessity. I once heard a minister preach upon the subject of the baptism of the Holy Ghost. He treated it as a reality; and when he came to the question of how it was to be obtained, he said truly that it was to be obtained as the apostles obtained it on the day of Pentecost.

I was much gratified, and listened eagerly to hear him press the obligation on his hearers to give themselves no rest until they had obtained it. But in this I was disappointed.

Before he sat down, he seemed to relieve the audience from the feeling of obligation to obtain the baptism, and left the impression that the matter was to be left to the discretion of God. He said what appeared to imply a censure of those who vehemently and persistently urged upon God the fulfillment of the promise. Neither did he hold out to them the certainty of their obtaining the blessing if they did fulfill the conditions.

This was greatly defective. The "what then?" was left out. Many seem to be theorizing, criticizing and trying to justify their neglect of this attainment.

Q: *Mr. Finney, what counsel do you give those in Christian ministry in any generation?*
FINNEY: I must say to many ministers even of the present day that I think their practical views of preaching the gospel, whatever their theological views may be, are very defective indeed. Their lack of unction and of

the power of the Holy Ghost is a radical defect in their preparation for ministry. I say this not censoriously, but nevertheless it is a settled fact in my mind over which I have long had occasion to mourn.

As I have become more and more acquainted with the ministry in America and other countries, I am persuaded that, with all their training and education, they lack practical ways of presenting the gospel to men, and in adapting means to secure that end—but especially in their need for the power of the Holy Ghost!

* * *

Writings by and about Finney and *books used in research (not intended to be exhaustive):

*America's Great Revivals
Answers to Prayer
*Finney Lives On
Finney on Revival
*God Sent Revival
*The Great Revivalists
*Memoirs of Charles G. Finney: Written by Himself
*Power From On High
Principles of Holiness
Principles of Prayer
Principles of Revival
Principles of Sanctification
*They Found the Secret

Jonathan Goforth

[1859–1936]

NO WILD GUST OF WIND

ONATHAN GOFORTH WAS THE SEVENTH CHILD in a family of 10 boys and one girl. Born in Thorndale, Western Ontario, Canada, Jonathan grew up on his father's farm. Jonathan's mother was faithful to teach her children both to read and memorize the Scriptures. Jonathan had to work on the farm for 10 of his early school years and missed much of his formal schooling. But he always caught up and competed with the brightest classmates. When he was only 15, his father put him in charge of a second farm which he successfully ran.

Jonathan's ambition was to study law and become a politician. He walked miles to attend a political meeting, knew the issues well on both sides, and practiced public speaking in a nearby swamp. During his struggle to complete his high school education, he accepted Christ under the preaching of a Presbyterian minister who held Bible studies for the students. He immediately sought to serve the Lord both in the church and in his community.

As he read *The Memoirs of Robert Murray McCheyne* he caught the vision of giving his whole life to the ministry but initially rejected all thought of being a foreign missionary. Later, responding to a missionary speaker from Formosa, Goforth turned his direction to the mission field and graduated from Knox College in Toronto. After a time of home mission work, Goforth, with his young wife, set sail for China in 1888. They were sent out and financially supported by fellow students and alumni of that Presbyterian institution – an unprecedented arrangement.

Based in Honan, China, Goforth evangelized thousands throughout China and trained hundreds of Chinese pastors and evangelists. He identified with the Chinese, even to the extent of dress and diet. During the Boxer Rebellion of 1900 the Goforths barely escaped, and not without suffering. The revival in Korea in 1907 strongly influenced Goforth. God used him in revivals in many provinces of China.

From 1925 the Goforths served in Manchuria until ill health forced their return to Canada eight years later. Although Goforth was blind the last years of his life, he and his wife promoted missions until their deaths.

* * *

APPROXIMATE DATE: 1928

QUESTION: Can you have a spiritual revival without the services of an evangelist?
JONATHAN GOFORTH: As if the Spirit of God is necessar-

ily limited in His workings to a select few! Most emphatically, I am convinced that we may have God's revival *when* we will and *where* we will. I agree with Finney that any body of Christians, provided they wholeheartedly and unreservedly carry out God's will, can have revival. And I agree with Moody that Pentecost was merely a specimen day. This is true anywhere in the world–any group of seeking Christians may receive the full blessing of Pentecost.

Q: What prevents revival from taking place?
GOFORTH: It is inconceivable that the Holy Spirit wants to delay His work even for one day. If men lack the fullness of God, we may be sure it is always due to man's lack of faith and obedience. We are to blame.

Q: What is revival?
GOFORTH: It is simply the Spirit of God fully controlling surrendered lives. Revival must always be possible when man yields. The one sin of unyieldedness can keep us from revival.

Q: What are some other obstacles to revival?
GOFORTH: We must prepare ourselves to receive the Holy Spirit's work. Do we value the Giver and the gift enough? Are we ready to pay the price of Holy Ghost revival?

Q: What is one price we must pay?
GOFORTH: Prayer. Does that sound too simple? The history of revival shows plainly that all movements of the Spirit started in prayer. It is right there that many of us wilt and falter at the cost. Pentecost and all subsequent outpourings of the Spirit resulted from prayer. The same was true during the mighty spiritual upheavals in Reformation times–Luther, Knox and the Moravians at Herrnhut in 1727. Hourly intercession by relays, praying without ceasing, went on for 100 years. It led to the

beginning of modern foreign missions. Why should we not match the Moravian movement today? Has the Eternal Spirit grown weary? Not likely. We may count on it that the blessing is waiting for us if we will only get down on our knees and ask for it. In latter days the same principle of prayer holds—revivals under Wesley, Finney, Spurgeon, Moody, Torrey and the Welsh revival—all resulted from prayer.

Q: And in your own times?
GOFORTH: Prayer by two lady missionaries in 1902 started the revival in India. Intense, believing prayer had so much to do with the Korean revival in 1907. I can trace all movements of the Spirit in China within my own experience to prayer. There is no secret—revival always comes in answer to prayer.

Q: Is there another condition for revival?
GOFORTH: We can never hope for a mighty, globe-encircling Holy Spirit revival without a back-to-the-Bible movement. We dare not cast doubts upon His Word. We cannot lightly esteem it. Unless it is to us in very truth the Word of God, our prayers will be sheer mockery. We must plead the sure promises of God. The Sword of the Spirit, which is the Word of God, is the only weapon which we can ever use mightily in revival. I have always taken for granted that the simple preaching of the Word brings men to Christ. It has never failed me yet.

Q: Is there still one more imperative for revival?
GOFORTH: Finally, the call to revival must be a call to exalt Jesus Christ in our hearts as King of kings and Lord of lords. He is like an Everest peak, rising from the level plain. We must have room only for Him if we want Him to dwell with us at all. We must smash every idol, deny every urge of self.

Q: *Would you give an example of that?*

GOFORTH: The Missionary Conference in Edinburgh in 1910 was an incomparable opportunity for Christian leaders to get rid of their ecclesiastical idols and bring themselves into heart contact with the unsearchable riches of Christ. Great expectations centered on it. Mission leaders came from all parts of the world. It was the confident hope of many that a new era in missions had dawned. It provoked visions of endless possibilities. The home churches, empowered by a mighty Holy Ghost revival, would send out men fitted as were Paul and Barnabas. With their enormous resources in men and means the world would be evangelized in a generation.

Q: *What happened?*

GOFORTH: Alas! It was only a dream. Never have I experienced such keen pain and disappointment as I did that day. Of the many who addressed that great missionary gathering, not more than *three* emphasized God the Holy Spirit as the essential factor in world evangelization! Listening to the addresses that day, one had to conclude that giving the gospel to lost mankind was largely a matter of better organization, better equipment, more men and women. A few more sparks might have precipitated an explosion. But no, the dethronement of the idol of ecclesiastical self-sufficiency was apparently too great a price to pay.

But the Spirit of God is still with us! Pentecost is yet within our grasp. If we are not experiencing revival it is because some idol remains enthroned. We insist on placing our reliance in human schemes. We still refuse to face the unchangeable truth that "it is not by might, but by My Spirit."

Q: *In the revivals in China in which you were in-*

volved, some have criticized abnormal manifestations of the Spirit.

GOFORTH: If the Almighty Spirit moves in sovereign power on the hearts and consciences of men, the outcome must be *above normal.* I agree with Dr. A.T. Schofield that since the days of Pentecost there is no record of the sudden and direct work of the Spirit of God upon men where events more or less *abnormal* have not accompanied it. It should be so. How can we expect an inrush of divine light and power, so profoundly affecting the emotions and changing the lives of men, without remarkable results?

Q: Is it correct to label such expressions abnormal?

GOFORTH: Though some speak of the manifestations at Pentecost as being abnormal, yet we maintain that Pentecost was *normal* Christianity. The results, when the Holy Spirit assumed control in Christ's stead, were according to divine plan. My conviction is that the divine power, so manifest in the church at Pentecost, was nothing more nor less than what we should expect in the church today! Normal Christianity, as planned by our Lord, was not supposed to begin in the Spirit and continue in the flesh. God never builds His temple by might or by power, but always by His Spirit. I believe the Scriptures clearly mean that the Lord Jesus planned that the Holy Spirit should continue among us with as mighty manifestation as at Pentecost. Time has not changed the fact: "Jesus Christ is the same yesterday, today and forever."

Q: Are such marvelous manifestations meant to continue or are they temporary works of the Spirit for certain times?

GOFORTH: Of course, the work will last – if man is faithful. The efficacy of the baptism of the Holy Ghost and

of fire dies down in any soul only when that soul wil-
fully quenches it. Did Pentecost last? Did God will that
it shouldn't? Pentecost was of God. So was the Wesleyan
revival. It is not God, then, but man whom we must
blame for the pitiful way in which the channels of
blessing which originated these great movements, have
become clogged. Can we imagine anyone who is determined to co-work with God to the limit of his being,
asking "Will it last?"

*Q: Have you found that homeland churches and their
leadership enthusiastically accept such marvelous experiences of revival as you have seen in China?*
GOFORTH: That's just where the problem lies. Most seminaries do not teach anything about that. At one place
in Manchuria where the Holy Spirit had descended in
unusual power upon the people, the Chinese evangelists asked the missionary why he had not told them that
the Spirit would work so mightily. He penitently replied
that he himself had not known that it was possible.
How pathetic to come out from "the schools of the
prophets" and not realize that the Holy Spirit could
endue with power to deliver a prophet's message!

Q: Did homeland ministers ever oppose your reports?
GOFORTH: Actually, yes. Even professors from some of
the seminaries and ministerial associations sometimes
refused to listen. Could such schools send out young
prophets filled with a Holy Ghost message? Do we
wonder that spirituality is at such a low ebb throughout
Christendom? Thirty-two percent of the Protestant
churches in the United States report no increase in
membership for 1927. Church attendance in Britain is
not half of what it was 25 years ago. There is no alternative—it is either Holy Ghost revival or apostasy.

Q: Do you think ordinary Christians are in the same condition?

GOFORTH: I am convinced that the majority of Christian people are living on a plane far below what our Master planned for them. Only a few seem to "possess their possessions." Nothing can clothe with victorious might but the baptism with the Holy Ghost and with fire. No one can possess such a baptism without knowing it. Many church members seem only to know water baptism. Alas! I fear that many Christian leaders know nothing more for themselves and their flocks than "John's baptism." In spite of all our ecclesiastical pride and self-confidence, just how much of our building would stand the test of fire?

Q: What is the great hindrance to revival in the church?

GOFORTH: I cannot emphasize too strongly my conviction that all hindrance in the church is due to sin. The Holy Spirit brings all manner of sin to light. The appalling fact is that we find every sin within the church that we find outside the church. That is just as true in the homelands. Sin in individual Christians, whether at home or on the foreign field, grieves and quenches the Holy Spirit. God does not recognize lesser and grosser sins. All sin in the believer, of whatever kind, mars the redemptive work of Christ. True followers of Christ must first have deep conviction of sin and deal with it before they can expect God to move others.

Q: Some have termed the revivals in China as mere emotionalism.

GOFORTH: By my own conservative background I was not prepared for this. I have observed it with amazement. But a power has come into the church we cannot control if we would. The Chinese are most sensitive to public opinion, always afraid to "lose face," and are by nature private, stolid and self-righteous. To see them moved by the Holy Spirit to weep, to confess sin in public, is beyond all human explanation. I agree with my fellow missionaries that we are quite overwhelmed at the wonder of it in our own midst.

One missionary reported to the homeland, "Perhaps you say it's religious hysteria. So did some of us when we first heard of it. But here we are, about 60 Scottish and Irish Presbyterians who have seen it. Much as many of us shrank from it at first, every one who has seen and heard what we have, is certain there is only one explanation—that it is God's Holy Spirit manifesting Himself in a way we never dreamed. We have no right to criticize. We dare not. One clause of the Creed lives before us now in all its inevitable, awful solemnity, 'I believe in the Holy Ghost . . .' "

Q: What was your personal experience of the Holy Spirit in your missionary task?
GOFORTH: When I returned to China in 1901, after having recuperated from the harrowing effects of the Boxer ordeal, I began to experience a growing dissatisfaction with the results of my missionary work. I felt sure there was something larger ahead, if I only had the vision to see what it was and the faith to grasp it. Restless, discontented, I studied the Scriptures more intensely. Every passage that had any bearing upon the price of, or the road to, the power of God became life and breath to me. I read every book in my library on revival over and over. The reports of the Welsh revival especially inspired me.

Q: Did any other publication influence you?
GOFORTH: A friend in India sent me a pamphlet of selections from *Finney's Autobiography and Revival Lectures*. That was the final something which set me on fire. "If Finney is right," I vowed, "then I'm going to find out the laws governing spiritual harvest and obey them—no matter what it costs." Some months later a brother missionary loaned me the full autobiography of Finney. It is impossible to estimate what that book meant to me. Immediately, as I put into practice all that God was teaching me of the Holy Spirit, I began to see evidence of greater power and spiritual results from my ministry. At one of the first meetings, conviction swept over the whole audience. All of us evangelists who were involved in the meeting were too awed to say anything. One of the evangelists spoke for us all: "Brethren, He for Whom we have prayed so long was here in very deed tonight. But let us be sure that if we are to retain His presence we must walk very carefully." Revival began to break out in many areas from that point forward.

Q: Did you see the Korean revival firsthand?
GOFORTH: I traveled there with Dr. R.P. MacKay, the foreign mission secretary of our Presbyterian church. The Korean movement was of incalculable significance in my life because I saw with my own eyes the boundless possibilities of revival. It is one thing to read about revival in books. To witness its working with one's own eyes and to feel the atmosphere of the Spirit with one's own heart is altogether different. Korea made me feel, as it did many others, that this was God's plan for setting the world aflame. Consistent, fervent, believing prayer was again the key.

Q: Would you describe some aspects of the Korean

revival?

GOFORTH: The practical nature of the movement impressed me. I soon saw that this was no wild gust of religious enthusiasm, dying with the wind upon whose wings it had been borne. There were, of course, the usual outward manifestations which inevitably accompany such phenomenal outpourings of spiritual power. But beyond all that was the simple fact that here were tens of thousands of Korean men and women whose lives had been completely transformed by the touch of the divine fire. Churches overflowed. Everyone seemed almost pathetically eager to spread the "glad tidings." The poverty stricken Koreans showed abounding liberality. Everywhere I saw an evident devotion for the Holy Word of God. Everyone seemed to carry a Bible. And permeating it all was that marvelous spirit of prayer.

Q: How did this affect your work in China?

GOFORTH: I had one dominant thought. Since God was no respecter of persons, He was surely just as willing to bless China as Korea. I resolved that this would be the burden of my message wherever I went. And it was. By His Holy Spirit, God swept in revival over China just as faithfully, not only among the Chinese, but among the missionaries.

* * *

Writings by and about Goforth and *books used in research (not intended to be exhaustive):

*By My Spirit
*Goforth of China: A Biography
*Pioneers of Revival
*The Victorious Life

Adoniram Judson Gordon

[1836–1895]

POWER IS
AVAILABLE

B ORN OF CHRISTIAN PARENTS in New Hampton, New Hampshire, Gordon was no stranger to hard work. As a youth he worked in his father's woolen mill, and walked a long distance to country schools. He attended church faithfully with his parents who were old school Baptists. Shortly after his conversion at age 15, Gordon felt called to the ministry.

He attended New London Academy and Brown University, then graduated from Newton Theological Seminary. Ordained a Baptist minister, Gordon pastored a church near Boston for six years. He spent the following 25 years at Clarendon Street Baptist Church in Boston, which became one of the most spiritual and aggressive churches in America.

He edited the *Watchword*, a monthly magazine, became chairman of the Executive Committee of the
American Baptist Missionary Union and founded the
Boston Missionary Training School–now Gordon College and Gordon-Conwell Theological Seminary.

A noted scholar, author and hymnwriter, Gordon was
a frequent speaker and leader in D.L. Moody's great
Northfield Conventions.

* * *

APPROXIMATE DATE: 1885

**QUESTION: *As founder of a noted college and divinity
school, scholar, preacher, author and missionary
statesman, your position on the miracle-working
power of God surprises some people.***
A.J. GORDON: You mean because I believe miracles continue today as in the days of the apostles? The common
answer in my times has been a decided *no!* So my
convictions may not be in accord with the opinions of
the majority of today's theologians.

**Q: *Before we go further, may I ask how the Lord led
you into a deeper walk with Himself?***
GORDON: Questions of experience are much more difficult to answer than questions of doctrine. Questions
about the work of the Holy Spirit in one's own life are
the hardest. While "the testimony of the Lord is sure,"
the testimony of experience varies. But I will try.

**Q: *You were in the midst of a very heavy and hectic
ministerial work load at the time.***
GORDON: Extremely so, but that in itself is a wonder. In
my youth I was known as somewhat indifferent and
seemingly sluggish until my conversion. Even after I

headed for the ministry, an old deacon remarked that I might make a good minister if only I had more energy!

Q: *High speed activity became normal for you after conversion?*

GORDON: Yes, although laboring in God's service eventually turned into drudgery to the point of desperation and disappointment with spiritual results. I worked harder and longer to produce sermons I thought would have more effect. I tried more eloquent delivery, whipped up increased attendance at prayer meetings, tried to improve administration—but the burdens of anxiety increased. Then came discouragement, sleepless nights, physical exhaustion and finally sickness.

One day a still small voice admonished me, *There standeth one among you whom ye know not.* And perhaps I answered, *Who is he, Lord, that I might know him?*

Q: *Did you establish some new relationship with the Lord or the Holy Spirit?*

GORDON: I had known the Holy Ghost as a heavenly influence which I should invoke, but somehow I had not grasped the truth that he is a Person of the Godhead who came down to earth at a definite time, who has been in the church ever since. I had not realized that He is just as real as Jesus was during the 33 years of his earthly life. Many true Christians toil on, bear burdens and assume responsibilities far too great for their natural strength! They are oblivious to the mighty Burden-bearer who is with them to do for them and through them that which they tried to accomplish alone.

Q: *Did your crisis have something to do with Mr. D.L. Moody's Northfield Convention?*

GORDON: Yes, it was there in 1882 that I reached a climax

in my seeking. I had believed there was something beyond and desired to secure what I lacked as a believer and servant of Christ. One midnight hour of great heart-searching the Lord filled me with His Spirit.

Q: Did you have an ecstatic emotional experience?
GORDON: No, it didn't happen through some sudden burst of revelation nor through a thrilling experience of instantaneous sanctification. My discovery was quiet, sure and steady, increasing more and more. Jesus in the Spirit stood with me in a kind of spiritual epiphany. Just as definitely and irrevocably as I once took Christ crucified as my sin bearer, so I now took the Holy Spirit for my burden bearer.

Q: Would you say you received the baptism of the Holy Spirit at that time?
GORDON: Well, I prefer not to use an expression which I don't think is strictly biblical. The great promise "Ye shall be baptized in the Holy Ghost" was fulfilled on the day of Pentecost once for all, it seems to me. Then Jesus sent the Paraclete for the entire dispensation for the whole church, present and future, to bring it into the economy of the Spirit. It is written,"For by one Spirit are we all baptized into one body" (1 Corinthians 12:13). But for God to give is one thing; for us to receive is quite another. The difference is between the Holy Spirit for renewal and the Holy Spirit for ministry. One can receive the Holy Ghost to qualify for service.

Q: Could not the two experiences happen at one time?
GORDON: Many have this blessing in immediate connection with their conversion, from which we need not necessarily separate it. Only understand that as the Scripture speaks plainly of the giving of the Spirit by the

Father, so it speaks distinctly about the disciples receiving the Spirit. Many thoughtful students of Scripture maintain that the same order still holds.

Q: *What is the biblical basis for a further experience of power from the Holy Spirit?*
GORDON: On the whole, and after prolonged study of Scripture, I have come to this conviction: As Christ, the second person of the Godhead, came to earth to make atonement for sin and to give eternal life, and as sinners must receive Him by faith to have forgiveness and sonship, so the Holy Spirit, the third person of the Godhead, came to earth to communicate the "power from on high." As believers we must similarly receive Him by faith to qualify for service.

God gave both gifts, but we have not necessarily *appropriated* both by conscious faith. It is not what we have, but what we *know* we have which determines our spiritual wealth. Why should "the forgiveness of sins, according to the riches of his grace" (Ephesians 1:7b) satisfy us when the Lord also wants to give us "according to the riches of his glory, to be strengthened with might by his Spirit in the inner man" (Ephesians 3:16)?

Q: *Dr. Gordon, some teach that the enduement of the Spirit is not any special or higher experience, but already the condition of every child of God.*
GORDON: I do not believe that. It seems clear from the Scriptures that the duty and privilege of believers is to receive the Holy Spirit by a conscious, definite act of appropriating faith, just as they received Jesus Christ. To say that when we received Christ we necessarily in the same act received the gift of the Spirit seems to confuse the distinction which the Scriptures make. I believe that logically and chronologically the gift of the Spirit comes

after repentance. We must appropriate the Spirit as sons in the same way as we appropriated Christ as sinners.

Q: Some teach that our relationship to the Holy Spirit and His gifts in this dispensation differs from the apostolic age. What is your position?
GORDON: Whatever relationship believers had to the Spirit in the beginning, I believe they have a right to claim today. I believe the exegesis is inconsistent which would make the water baptism of apostolic times still rigidly binding, but would relegate the baptism in the Spirit to a bygone dispensation. I hold indeed that Pentecost was once for all, but equally that the appropriation of the Spirit by believers is always for all.

I believe that the confining of certain great blessings of the Holy Ghost within that ideal era called "the apostolic age," however convenient an escape from fancied difficulties, may rob believers of some of their most precious covenant rights. I agree with Dr. J. Elder Cumming that a great mistake into which some have fallen is to suppose that the results of Pentecost were chiefly miraculous and temporary. The effect of such a view is to keep spiritual influences out of sight.

Q: One more differing viewpoint: Some do not teach the need for any definite crisis; they say that the Christian life is one of gradual spiritual growth only.
GORDON: If we conceive of the Christian life as only a gradual growth in grace, we fall into the danger of regarding this growth as both invisible and inevitable and so take little responsibility to accomplish it. Let the believer receive the Holy Ghost by a definite act of faith for his consecration, as he received Christ by faith for his justification, and he will be sure he acts in a safe and scriptural way. I know of no plainer way to state the

matter than to say it is simple acceptance by faith. It is a fact that Christ has made atonement for sin; in conversion faith appropriates this fact to our justification. It is a fact that the Holy Ghost has been given; in consecration faith appropriates this fact for our sanctification.

Q: *What is the main purpose of this experience of the Holy Spirit?*
GORDON: The great end for which we receive the enduement of the Spirit is to qualify us for the highest and most effective service in the church of Christ. Other effects will certainly attend the blessing – a fixed assurance of our acceptance in Christ and a holy separateness from the world. But these results will be conducive to the greatest and supreme end – our consecrated usefulness.

Q: *Can we expect such an experience only once in our lives?*
GORDON: I do not hold that this is an experience once for all. We receive the Spirit once for all, but repeated fillings may follow. To conclude that since our capacity keeps increasing, our need is constantly increasing is reasonable.

Q: *What steps must a believer take to obtain this enduement of power?*
GORDON: Although I believe it is every Christian's privilege and duty to claim a distinct anointing of the Spirit to qualify him for his work, I am careful not to prescribe any stereotyped exercises which one must do to possess it.

I can easily cite cases of decisive, vivid and clearly marked experiences of the Spirit's enduement as in the life of Finney and others. But let us not confuse the issue by too detailed theological definitions on one hand, nor by a too exacting demand for striking spiritual exercises on the other. Nevertheless, I cannot emphasize too strongly the divine crisis in the soul which fully receiving the Holy Ghost may bring.

Q: What changes took place in your personal life after the enduement with power?
GORDON: The change may be described thus: Instead of praying constantly for the descent of a divine influence, I now surrendered, however imperfectly, to a divine and ever-present Being. Instead of making a constant effort to use the Holy Spirit for doing my work, I felt a clear and abiding conviction that the true secret of service lay in yielding to the Holy Spirit in such a way that He might use me to do His work.

Q: What does such a spiritual step cost?
GORDON: This power comes at great cost. It costs self-surrender, humiliation and the yielding of our most precious things to God. It costs the perseverance of long waiting and the faith of strong trust. But when we really experience that power, we find this difference: where before we found it hard to do the easiest things, now we find it easy to do the hardest! As we understand more of this matter, we learn to pray less about the details of duty and more about the fullness of power. The source of our power is what should concern us most, not the results.

Q: My original question was whether miracles continue in this present age. Please tell us more about your teaching.
GORDON: I realize I expose myself to the arrows of theological archers when I declare my position. I desire

nothing but the advancement of the truth. Human opinion does not matter; scriptural testimony does. I wish my argument to lean its heaviest weight, therefore, on the Word of God.

To state it clearly, I believe the church in every direction needs to reshape itself on the apostolic model and be reinvested with its apostolic powers. The indignant clamor of skeptics against primitive miracles has frightened the Lord's people out of their faith in the supernatural. The church is drifting into an inappropriate cautiousness concerning the miraculous.

Q: You said that not only those of the world and false professors dislike to admit miracles, but so do many real, true-hearted and sincere disciples. Why?
GORDON: With any mention of their possible occurrence in our time, many are afraid of them and inclined to push them away with quick impatience. In most cases this aversion comes from a wholesome fear of fanaticism.

Q: What is fanaticism?
GORDON: Fanaticism in most instances is simply the eccentric action on doctrines that are loosened from their connection with the Christian system. Every truth needs the steadiness and equipoise which comes from harmony with all other truths. If the church by her neglect or denial of any real doctrine of the faith thrusts that doctrine out into isolation and contempt, thus forcing some special sect to take it over, she should not be surprised if she loses her balance. The church deprives that doctrine of the conserving influence which comes from contact and communion with other and central doctrines. She has doomed it inevitably to irregular manifestations.

If the whole body of Christians had been faithful to such truths as the second coming of Christ and scriptural holiness, for example, the fanaticism of adventism and perfectionism would not have arisen. There is nothing wrong with a doctrine that has caused fanaticism. I am not defending fanaticism, just putting it in perspective.

Q: Regeneration itself is a miracle, isn't it?

GORDON: We would not think to question regeneration, the work in which God comes into immediate contact with the soul for its renewal. That is no less a miracle than healing in which God comes into immediate contact with the body for its recovery. In one case a direct communication of the divine life comes to the spirit, which Neander calls "the standing miracle of the ages." In the other a direct communication of divine health comes to the body which in the beginning was called "a miracle of healing." An able writer said, and I believe it was the truth, "You ask God to perform as real a miracle when you ask Him to cure your soul of sin as you do when you ask Him to cure your body of a fever." Yet who thinks we encourage fanaticism if we preach and pray for man's regeneration? Remember, fanaticism is not heresy. Heresy is an error—a false doctrine not substantiated by the Scripture.

Q: Do you teach, as some do, that First Corinthians 13:10, "when that which is perfect is come," is proof that certain gifts have passed away?

GORDON: This passage has been used as an attempt to shut up all miracles within the apostolic era, as belonging to the things which were in part and therefore destined to pass away. In the first place, note that only prophecies, tongues and knowledge are specified—not

116

healings. Put no more within this limitation than the Word of God puts there. In the second place, the boundary set to the exercise of these gifts is "when that which is perfect is come," which scholarship generally holds to mean when the Lord Himself shall return to earth.

It does not seem therefore that the gifts of tongues and of prophecy should be confined within the first age of the church. We cannot forget, indeed, that the utterances of prophecy and knowledge culminated and found their highest expression when the Canon of the New Testament was completed. So some thoughtful expositors have conjectured that concerning prophecy and knowledge this may have been "the coming of that which is perfect." In either event, this does not affect the gifts such as healing. These cannot have culminated so long as sickness and demoniacal possession are unchecked in the world, nor until the great Healer and Restorer shall return from above.

Q: What essentially is a miracle?
GORDON: Definitions vary widely and those who argue evade facts by hiding behind them. I prefer to appeal to examples of acknowledged miracles and then ask whether any like them occurred through the ages and in modern days.

Q: Are miracles abnormal or contranatural?
GORDON: If miracles were abnormal manifestations of divine power, against nature as well as above nature, they might indeed be expected to cease—the abnormal is not as a rule perpetual. Miracles of healing, for instance, are manifestations of nature's perfect health and wholeness, lucid intervals granted to our deranged and suffering humanity. They are not catastrophes, but exhi-

bitions of that divine order which shall be brought in with our complete redemption.

We cannot for a moment admit the complaint of skeptics that miracles are an infraction of the laws of nature. Though we call them "supernatural," they are not contranatural. If miracles of healing are exhibitions of divine recovery and order in nature, and not rude eruptions of disorder, once begun, should they entirely cease? We are under the dispensation of the Spirit which we hold to be an unchangeable dispensation so long as it shall continue.

Q: Do you believe that healing is in the atonement?
GORDON: The atonement of Christ seems to have laid a foundation for faith in bodily healing. I do not want to be dogmatic about it, but Christ as the sickness bearer as well as the sin bearer of His people is a suggestive truth. If our Redeemer and Substitute bore our sicknesses, we may reason that He bore them that we might not bear them.

Christ's ministry was twofold, constantly affecting both the souls and bodies of men. The ministry of the apostles, under the guidance of the Holy Spirit, is the exact facsimile of the Master's—preaching the kingdom and healing the sick, redemption for the soul and deliverance for the body. Certain great promises of the gospel have this double reference to pardon and cure.

Q: In your view, should we expect for today the whole of Mark 16:17–18, with its listing of signs to follow them that believe?
GORDON: I don't want to put limitations where the Lord has not put them. The only safe position is to emphasize the perpetuity of the promise, and equally to admit the general weakness and failure of the church's faith to

appropriate it. I agree with the writer Bengel that the reason why many miracles do not take place now is because *unbelief reigns*. I conclude that this text teaches that God gives miraculous gifts to abide in the church to the end, though He does not confer them on every believer.

Q: Might the oil for anointing in James 5:14-15 have had medicinal properties?
GORDON: That does not seem reasonable. Oil is a symbol of the communication of the Spirit, by whose power healing takes place. Observe that they called elders of the church, not doctors, to apply it. They accompanied the application with prayer, not manipulations and medications.

Q: How would you summarize your reasons for the continuation of miracles to our own time?
GORDON: In the first place, if they should cease, they would form a distinct exception to everything else which the Lord introduced by His ministry. The doctrines He promulgated and which His apostles preached—atonement, justification, sanctification and redemption—have never been abrogated or modified. Likewise He never suspended the ordinances and the divine operations. These all belong to the dispensation of grace which Jesus Christ introduced and which is to span the whole period between His first and His second advents. All orthodox Christians hold these as perpetual and unchangeable.

We are to expect an enlargement of knowledge and a development of doctrine under the ministry of the Holy Spirit rather than a decrease, for "He will guide you into all truth." In the "greater works" of John 14:12-17 we anticipate a reinforcement of power for service rather than an abatement. The law of Christianity is from less to greater and not from greater to less. Two streams of blessing started from the personal ministry of our Lord, a stream of healing and a stream of regeneration. One is for the recovery of the body, the other for the recovery of the soul. These two flowed on side by side through the apostolic age. Is it reasonable to suppose that God's purpose was for one to run on through the whole dispensation of the Spirit, and the other should fade and utterly disappear within a single generation? I cannot think so.

Q: Should we ask God to perform a miracle of healing on our own or someone else's behalf?
GORDON: Someone has said that to ask God to act at all, and to ask Him to perform a miracle, are one and the same. A miracle is the immediate action of God as distinguished from his mediate action through natural laws. Why should we hesitate to pray for the healing of our bodies any more than for the renewal of our souls? Both are miracles; the same clear word of promise covers and provides for both.

Q: Is it important to recognize God's healing power today?
GORDON: We do not need to give the highest place in Christian doctrine to faith in supernatural healing. We readily admit that grace is vastly more important than miracles. But miracles have their place as shadows of greater things. We urge that they may hold this place to help us better apprehend the substance.

Q: Doesn't faith in the sovereignty of God discourage prayer for healing?
GORDON: While we recognize the doctrine of divine

sovereignty, this should no more keep us from asking in faith for the healing of our bodies than the doctrine of election should prevent our asking with the fullest assurance for the salvation of our souls. We must not bear so hard upon divine sovereignty as practically to deny man's freedom to ask or expect miraculous healing.

Some even push God almost into an iron fixedness where even the Almighty is not at liberty to work miracles any longer—as though God was under bonds to restrain this office of His omnipotence since the apostolic age. We must keep these two great elements of prayer in equilibrium: *believing strongly but asking submissively.* We should present our request with one hand holding up "Thus saith the Lord," and the other hand holding up "The will of the Lord be done."

Q: *Does the general state of the church today have anything to do with the little evidence of healing that we see?*
GORDON: In an age in which the church enjoys much prosperity in an earthly direction, we may miss great triumphs of faith and intercession. Our prosperity and our rest from persecution and trial are sources of weakness and enervation. Therefore faith for healing cannot rise above the general level of the church's faith.

We should pray always and earnestly that the Lord would restore to His church her primitive gifts, her primitive endowments of unworldliness, poverty of spirit and separation unto God. If any organ of the body is weak and sickly, the only sure method of restoration is to tone up the whole system to the normal standard of health.

If the entire body of Christ were revived and reinvested with her first spiritual powers, we would see much more exercise of these special gifts and functions

---

121

of which we have been speaking–to the glory of God.

* * *

Writings by and about Gordon and *books used in research (not intended to be exhaustive):

*Adoniram Judson Gordon: A Biography
How Christ Came to Church
In Christ: The Believer's Union with His Lord
*The Ministry of Healing
*The Ministry of the Spirit
*They Found the Secret
The Twofold Life: Christ's Work for Us and Christ's Work in Us

Samuel Dickey Gordon

[1859–1936]

POWER
CONNECTIONS

S AMUEL GORDON WAS BORN IN PHILADELPHIA and educated in the public schools there.

He was the assistant secretary of the Young Men's Christian Association in Philadelphia from 1884 to 1886. Later he spent eight years as the Ohio state secretary of the Y.M.C.A. while devoting much time to Christian ministry.

He was much sought after as a public speaker in churches and conferences, and closely associated with the Keswick Deeper Life movement both in England and in America. For four years, Gordon traveled abroad in a speaking ministry throughout the Orient and Europe.

He is well known as the author of the *Quiet Talks* series of devotional books.

* * *

APPROXIMATE DATE: 1899

QUESTION: Mr. Gordon, many Christians admit their need for more power in their lives. How can we experience that?
S.D. GORDON: In recent years people speak and write much about the Holy Spirit. I read and listened to a great deal myself without acquiring a simple workable understanding of how to receive the much-talked-of baptism of power. That may quite likely have been because of my own dullness of comprehension. But now I am eager to put the truth as simply as I can so others won't blunder along and lose precious time as I did.

Q: Can we rely on personal testimonies?
GORDON: Personal experiences are intensely interesting and often helpful. But there are apt to be as many different experiences as persons. That is why they are often misleading. We are so likely to desire the same experience as someone else. Some written accounts, too, have clouded rather than cleared the issue.

Q: How can a person sort out the many different views about that experience?
GORDON: First, we should build upon a clear understanding of God's law of dealing with men. We should conform to that even though circumstances might differ in our case. We may then profit from the experience of others.

Q: Even the terminology seems confusing.
GORDON: We should look for scriptural terms. The New Testament uses five leading words to refer to the Holy

Spirit's relation to us: "baptized," "filled," "anointed," "sealed" and "earnest."

Q: Are they all part of the same experience?
GORDON: Each reflects a different side. "Baptized" is the historical word – an act completed once for all on the day of Pentecost. It tells God's side. I am not speaking now of the manner or mode of water baptism. The phrases in Acts which describe the baptism of the Holy Spirit on that historical Pentecost all suggest an act from above.

Q: Isn't "filling" the same?
GORDON: No, "filled" and "full" are used at the time of actual occurrence and afterward. It tells what persons experienced at Pentecost and afterward. It describes *their* side. Baptism was the *act*; filling was the *result*. It is an *experience* word.

Q: And "anointed"?
GORDON: That indicates the *purpose* of this filling. It is the *power* word to indicate that the Holy Spirit comes specifically to set us apart, to qualify us for right living and acceptable and helpful service.

Q: Does "sealed" describe our assurance of salvation?
GORDON: No, it is more a *personal-relation* word. The Holy Spirit is Jesus' ownership mark stamped upon us to indicate that we belong to Him. He is our sole owner. And if any of us do not give Him full control of His own property, we deal dishonestly.

Q: "Earnest" occurs three times in Paul's writing, doesn't it?
GORDON: Yes, it is a *pledge* given in advance as an

125

evidence of good faith. The Holy Spirit who fills us now is Jesus' pledge that He has purchased us, and that some day He is coming back. It is a partial advance payment which insures a payment in full when the transaction is complete. It is a *prophetic* word.

Q: Are these not separate experiences?
GORDON: No, it takes all five words to understand the entire truth about our Friend the Holy Spirit and what His coming into one's life means. In sequence, the words point us backward, inward, outward, upward and forward.

Q: Haven't all Christians received the Holy Spirit? Why do some of us still lack power?
GORDON: It is true that the Holy Spirit's presence in us makes us Christians. His work begins instantly at conversion when the Spirit enters. Here is the distinction: The Holy Spirit is *in* every Christian but many do not allow Him free and full *control*. Therefore they experience little or none of His power. Only as He has full sway is His power manifest.

Q: Could we experience that power from the time of conversion?
GORDON: If at the time of conversion or decision someone gives clear instruction and the person makes a wholehearted surrender, the Spirit's presence will be immediately evidenced. And if the new life goes on without break, His power will continue in ever-increasing measure. But many times, through ignorance or lack of instruction, or some disobedience or failure to obey, a break occurs, or a cog slips somewhere and interrupts the flow of power.

Q: What should we do when that happens?

GORDON: A new start is necessary. Then a new experience or rather a reexperience of the Spirit's presence often follows the full surrender. This new experience sometimes is so sharply marked as to begin a new epoch in life. Some of the notable leaders of the church have gone through just such an experience.

Q: A second experience is not really necessary then?

GORDON: I think it may be said quite accurately that in God's plan the person needs no second experience. But in our experience, a second state—and sometimes more than a second—occurs. In so many of us the connections break and make a fresh act on our part necessary.

Q: How can a Christian maintain power continuously?

GORDON: John 7:37–39 states it most simply. The four verbs describe four steps into a new life of power. Sometimes a person takes these steps so quickly that they seem in experience like only one.

Q: The first must be "thirst"?

GORDON: Thirst means desire, *intense* desire. No word in our language is as strong. Physical thirst will completely control your actions. You are in agony. Jesus uses the word that way. If you are not thirsty for the Master's power, are you thirsty to become thirsty? No step comes before that.

Q: I understand that "glorified" was not part of the words of Jesus in that passage.

GORDON: No, John apparently added it long afterward when the Spirit had enlightened his understanding. It has two meanings: the first is a *historical* one; the second is a personal or *experimental* one. The historical meaning is this: When Jesus returned home all scarred in face and form from His trip to earth, He was received with great enthusiasm. He was glorified in the presence of myriads of angel beings and enthroned at the Father's right hand. Then the glorified Jesus sent the Holy Spirit down to the earth as His personal representative for His new peculiar mission.

The personal meaning is this: When Jesus is enthroned in my life, the Holy Spirit fills me. The Father glorified Jesus by enthroning Him. That act of enthroning Him implies the dethronement of self.

Q: Is this costly and serious?

GORDON: Let me say plainly that here is the searching test of the whole matter. *Why* do you want power? For the rare enjoyment of ecstatic moods? For some hidden selfish purpose like Simon of Samaria? So that you may move men? These motives are all selfish. Better stop before you begin. But if your uppermost and undermost desire is to glorify Jesus and let Him do in you and with you whatever He chooses, then He will flood the channel-ways of your life with a new stream of power.

Q: "Drink" seems to be an easier act.

GORDON: It is one of the easiest actions imaginable. Drink simply means *take*. It is saying, "Lord Jesus, I take from Thee the promised power. I thank Thee that the Spirit has taken full control."

Q: Is that all?

GORDON: Yes, even if you do not feel anything as a result. It was the same when you were urged to take Jesus as your Savior. You were told not to wait for feeling, only to trust. When you did, the light came.

That leads us to the fourth word, "believe." The law of God's dealing with you has not changed. Jesus says, "Out of his belly shall flow rivers of living water" (John 7:38b). You are to believe His word.

Q: But how shall one know he has the power?
GORDON: First *believe* that Jesus has indeed done what He agreed. He promised the Spirit to those who obey Him. The Holy Spirit fills every surrendered heart. The second way is that you will experience the power *as the need arises.* Power is always manifest in action. That is a law of power. Faith acts first and steps out in obedience to God's command. As the need arises, you will find the power rising within you to meet it. You will at that time sense His power in control. To believe means to expect.

Q: It does not seem so mysterious or difficult after all.
GORDON: It is simple. The four words could be restated "desire," "enthrone," "accept," "expect." Are you thirsty? Will you put Jesus on the throne? Then accept and go out with your eyes open—expecting, *expecting, EXPECT-ING.* He will never fail to reveal His power.

Q: Surely no one would want to break the connection once it was made. But it still happens.
GORDON: *You* may not want to break your power connection with the Holy Spirit, but *someone* does.

Q: Who is that?
GORDON: Satan is intensely interested in breaking that contact because you have established an intimate relationship with Jesus. Satan is more than a match for any of us, but greater is He who is now in you than he who is in the world. Satan will do his best by bold attack and cunning deceit to tamper with your couplings. One of

the saddest sights, and yet not uncommon, is to see a man whom God once mightily used eventually lose his usefulness. Many lives become spiritually blighted and dwarfed and some forever lose their opportunity of service.

Q: Can we lose the Holy Spirit?
GORDON: The Spirit of God never leaves us. We do not lose His presence. But whatever grieves Him prevents Him from manifesting His presence. You may lose the *evidence* of His presence through wrongdoing. We cannot store up power apart from God's presence. It passes through us only when He has control. Once you disturb the connection between Him and you, it interrupts the flow of power.

Q: How can we insure His continued power?
GORDON: How I wish someone had told me long ago. It might have saved me many a break. Three laws guarantee that. First, *obey.* Disobedience means disaster. Every heart is a battlefield where Jesus and Satan wage a hot contest. Satan cannot enter without your consent and Jesus will not. An act of obedience to God slams the door in Satan's face and opens it to Jesus' control. Even slight disobedience does the opposite.

Q: How do we know what and whom to obey?
GORDON: An important point. Sometimes the voices coming to our ears seem to confuse us; they do not agree. Pastors do not all agree; churches are not in accord on some matters; my best Christian friends think differently. How shall I know?

The second law guides us in this matter: *Obey the Book of God as interpreted by the Spirit of God.* Not the Book alone—that will lead into superstition. Not the

Spirit without the Book–that will lead to fanaticism. God speaks by His Spirit through His Word.

Q: *Does God ever speak directly without the written Word?*
GORDON: Yes, but very, very rarely. The Spirit guides frequently through mental impressions. I am speaking now of His audible inner voice. He is sparing with that.

Q: *How can we distinguish between these impressions?*
GORDON: When God speaks, the test must be that the voice of God always agrees with itself. The spoken word is never out of harmony with the written Word. Since He gave us the written Word, it becomes our standard to know His will. God's Book *was* inspired and it *is* inspired. God spoke in it before; He speaks in it today. It will surprise you to find how light on every question will come through this in-Spirited Book.

Q: *And the third law?*
GORDON: *Time alone with the Bible daily is essential.* It should be unhurried time. You should have time enough not to think about time. This may seem very difficult for some but it is a necessity. The first two laws depend on this one for their practical force.

Q: *Do you have a final word of counsel on living in God's power?*
GORDON: Maintain good connections in two directions–inward toward the Source of power and outward for use. We do not run on the storage battery plan but on the trolley plan. Constant communication with the Source of power is essential for the life of power.

* * *

Writings by S.D. Gordon and *books used in research (not intended to be exhaustive):

*Quiet Talks on Power
*Quiet Talks on Prayer

James Henry McConkey

[1858–1937]

A CLOVER LEAF
OF POWER

CCONKEY WAS BORN in Wrightsville, Pennsylvania, where he spent his early years. He loved to play the violin and fish as a child. Although he attended Sunday school and church, he did not profess Christ in public until the age of 20.

At 18 he entered Lafayette College, transferring to Princeton the following year. His father died during his college years and James became head and sole support of a large household with an invalid mother, seven sisters and a brother. He struggled to support the family while continuing his studies at home. He returned to Princeton only to take examinations. McConkey graduated in 1880 and was president of his class, in which he graduated fourth. He was not particularly noted for his

Christian testimony at Princeton.

Although McConkey was admitted to the bar in York, PA, he never practiced law. He went immediately into the wholesale ice business in which he continued for 15 years.

When he was 24, McConkey was made an elder of the Presbyterian church of Wrightsville, an office he held until his death. He also served as superintendent of the Sunday school.

Broken in health from the pressures upon him, he went abroad, and upon his return did not continue in business. He began his lifelong ministry of teaching the Bible for which he is noted. His ministry was not denominationally bound, nor limited to churches. Some of his greatest influence was among the executives of large business firms, laymen in the professions and the Young Men's Christian Association.

One of his most noted books is *The Three-fold Secret of the Holy Spirit* written in 1897, translated into many languages and distributed worldwide. He was associated with the Pennsylvania Bible Institute in Philadelphia and the Africa Inland Mission.

In 1914 he moved to Pittsburgh where he founded the Silver Publishing Company, incorporating it as a society in 1922. Its distinctive was no sales and no solicitation of funds. Books and tracts were provided freely to all who requested them worldwide, which voluntary offerings made possible. In his later years McConkey extended his literature ministry by establishing a Braille library.

McConkey was a celebrated teacher of the Bible in Georgia, Alabama and Virginia during the winter months where he resided for his health.

* * *

APPROXIMATE DATE: 1897

QUESTION: What are the secrets of the Holy Spirit to which you refer?
JAMES H. MCCONKEY: They are three – the secret of His incoming, the secret of His fullness and the secret of constant manifestation.

Q: Is the reason many Christians remain spiritually powerless and barren because they do not have the Holy Spirit?
MCCONKEY: No, every child of God has received the gift of the Holy Ghost. Since that is so, it is a fatal mistake for the believer to keep waiting and praying to receive the Holy Ghost, or to have the baptism. He must now yield and surrender to Him. We are not waiting *on God* to do something; God is waiting *on us* to do something. God's Word clearly teaches this.

Q: Should we follow the example of the apostles to be baptized by the Holy Spirit?
MCCONKEY: No, the conditions were different. We confine ourselves too closely to the apostolic *experience* instead of the apostolic *teaching* at Pentecost. The apostles lived before Christ came, while He walked the earth, and after He left it. They had one experience of the Holy Ghost as Old Testament believers, another when the risen Christ breathed upon them and said "receive ye the Holy Ghost," another when the ascended Christ poured out the Holy Ghost upon them at Pentecost. You might say they lived through the dispensations of Father, Son and Holy Ghost.

But that is not true of us. The experience that matches ours is not that of the apostles, but that of the apostles' converts who believed on Him exactly as we do, after Christ had finished His work and sent the Holy Ghost.

Q: What did the apostles teach?

MCCONKEY: The teaching was clear from the very day of Pentecost. Peter instructed, "Repent and be baptized every one of you in the name of Jesus Christ for the remission of sins, and ye shall receive the gift of the Holy Ghost" (Acts 2:38). Those two conditions bring us into the kingdom of God and give us the Holy Ghost. Having received Him, we should never ask to receive Him again.

Q: How can we be sure we have received Him?

MCCONKEY: By the witness of the Spirit Himself, and by our own experience of His incoming when we fulfilled those conditions. Some remember the day and the hour, others do not. God's Word constantly gives us assurance in passages like First Corinthians 3:16 and 6:19, also Second Corinthians 6:16 and 13:5. His indwelling does not depend upon our emotions, but upon our union with Christ. Acts 19:2 should have been more clearly translated, "Did ye receive the Holy Ghost *when* ye believed?" The apostle expected all children of God to receive the gift at the time of repentance and belief in Christ. Marvelous and impressive experiences may or may not accompany a man's conversion, but no man should expect the experience of others to be the same as his own.

Q: Are the receiving of the Holy Spirit in regeneration and the baptism of the Holy Spirit the same experience?

MCCONKEY: They are absolutely synonymous, as the Bible uses these terms. I do not recall a single instance where "baptism" with the Holy Ghost was a subsequent experience of the believer. The apostles were again and again "filled" with fresh anointing of the Spirit but they

136

were never baptized again. Nor were any converts who received the Spirit in regeneration ever said to have been baptized with the Spirit. It was clearly an initial rite administered upon entrance into the kingdom of God.

Q: *Is there a second experience for the believer after his conversion when he receives the Holy Spirit in greater power and abundance?*
McCONKEY: There is a fullness of the Holy Ghost that does not come to most Christians at conversion and, in point of time, is usually a second experience. But let us keep to scriptural teaching: this is not the gift of the Holy Ghost, not the receiving of the Holy Ghost, not the baptism of the Holy Ghost. He is a person who comes into the believer *once* and to *stay.* This second experience is a fullness in response to our consecration. We should not throw back on God the reason we do not have this fullness. There are certain conditions of this fullness different from those at regeneration.

Q: *How may we receive the Spirit's fullness?*
McCONKEY: By the absolute, unqualified surrender of our life to God to do His will instead of our own. At this surrender the Spirit, already entered, takes full possession.

Q: *Since the believer has two natures within, how can he be filled with one of them?*
McCONKEY: A new life, a divine life, the life of God comes into the believer when he is born again. He now has what the sinner does not have—a new nature. But when the new life, the Spirit, came in, did the old life, the "old man" go out? Alas, no! Otherwise, when we received the Spirit we would at once have been filled

137

forever with Him. The believer continues to have a dual nature. Both "the flesh" and "the Spirit"—the old life and the new—co-exist and struggle within him. Each wants possession; each wants to fill him. He can only be filled by yielding himself wholly to the one which he wants to fill him.

Q: Is it all up to us as believers?

MCCONKEY: We have the power of choice; we can yield to either nature, and then that one will fill us and control us (Romans 6:19). In teaching new converts, we often send them on a detour from the main path of victory. We tell them to study the Bible; to be diligent in prayer; to abound in good works; to be good stewards of their gifts; to be faithful in church services and to busy themselves in countless church activities. But we omit the most important instruction—to surrender themselves to God for His fullness.

Q: Is there no place in this experience for praying, agonizing, wrestling and waiting?

MCCONKEY: In all of those you would be calling on *God* to do something instead of obeying His command to do something *yourself.* It is a question of your receptiveness, your surrender. You may have all the fullness you will make room for. No use to attempt to believe, to struggle at reckoning it done. Those are substitutes for simple obedience. Prayer is all right *with* obedience, but not *instead* of it. We should not petition God for this fullness; He is petitioning us to yield to Him.

Q: Perhaps some are afraid of God's will.

MCCONKEY: No cruel fate awaits the believer who fully yields to God. The Christ who asks your surrender is the Christ of love who desires to fill you with His own fullness of love and guide you in His perfect ways. Don't be afraid of His will. When you have honestly laid your life at His feet, "He will give thee the desires of thine heart" (Psalm 37:4b).

Q: How can we be sure we have truly surrendered and received His fullness? Will we have manifestations?
McCONKEY: You must distinguish between *the indwelling* of the Holy Ghost and *the manifestation* of His fullness. Indwelling is His presence in us; manifestation is the consciousness of that presence. The former depends upon our *union* with Christ through faith; the latter depends upon our *obedience* to His commandments (John 14:21). If you are an obedient child of God, the Spirit manifests Himself in you. Your walk depends upon yourself. Your sonship is irrevocable, and so is His indwelling. But obedience and communion, being largely in our hands, are variable—so is manifestation. We must not make manifestation the test of indwelling!

Q: How about emotion?
McCONKEY: Do not dictate to Him the kind of feeling of fullness you desire. Do not insist upon a sudden rush of emotion. Do not expect another believer's experience. Leave all that to God or else you will be disappointed. The Lord knows just what form and degree of fullness to give each of us, to keep us from spiritual pride or exaltation. Sudden or gradual, quiet or jubilant, great peace or great power—it doesn't matter. When we are concerned about meeting the *conditions* of promise, God will always take care of the *fulfillment* of the promise. Let us not spend our time awaiting tongues of fire and the sound of rushing, mighty wind. It is damaging to be constantly inspecting our inner lives to see if God is fulfilling His promise in our experience. The less we

concern ourselves about the manifestation of His full-ness, the sooner it will come.

Q: It seems to be a common experience for the full-ness of God's blessing to eventually diminish.
McCONKEY: Yes, for many there comes a change. The brightness of the experience seems to dim; its power begins to wane; its manifestation to subside. A believer may still continue to "claim" what he feels is gone; to profess what he does not possess, in the hope that this may bring back the "blessing." But despair comes at last and he must admit to a lost experience.

Q: What happened? Has the Spirit gone away?
McCONKEY: No, but He has ceased to reveal Himself in His former fullness. It is lost manifestation, not lost indwelling. The Blesser has not left, but the blessing has. It failed in continuousness. Christ stated the specific conditions of the manifestation of the Spirit in John 14:21, "He that hath my commandments and keepeth them . . . I will manifest myself to him." These are not the commandments of the Law, but those of Grace, which fulfill the Law. Constant manifestation can come only from a continual doing, a daily living in the will of God. The surrender of the life is only the beginning of a life of surrender. We must follow the act of consecration with a life of consecration if begun blessing is to be continued blessing. Consecration is the threshold not the climax of the Spirit's fullness—a gate-way which we need to constantly open.

Q: Is the third secret of the Spirit abiding?
McCONKEY: Yes, and another way to say it is "walking in the Spirit." Every time we yield to the flesh and walk in the flesh, we frustrate, grieve and check the manifesta-

tion of the Spirit. God cannot put His seal on a life of non-conformity to His will. With every act of yielding to the flesh a sense of darkening begins to come, as though a cloud had passed between the believer and God. Daily we must maintain unbroken communion with Christ. That communion is like a delicate mirror—even the breath of the flesh-life on it will condense enough to shadow God's presence. We dare not rely today on yesterday's fullness. Jesus illustrated the relationship as the vine and the branch. The branch dare not draw on the vine one day and fail to draw on it the next—it would produce no fruit by such intermittent abiding.

Q: Do we improve as time goes on while living a life full of the Spirit?
McCONKEY: The believer's old nature is no better after conversion, or even after an extended time of experiencing the fullness of God's Spirit. It is just as dead a thing as before. So his new life is not an improved "I" but it is "no longer I, but Christ that liveth in me, and that life I now live in the flesh I live in faith" (Galatians 2:20 RV).

Q: What is the nature of that faith?
McCONKEY: This faith of abiding is a habitual attitude. One who is spiritually dead in himself is constantly looking to, and daily and hourly drawing upon the life of another—the fullness of life of Jesus Christ within him. A walk is simply a reiterated step.

Q: Please give some practical illustrations.
McCONKEY: Do we desire power or love? We must look to Him for it each time it is needed. Do we desire anointing for service? We must look to Him at each

recurrence of such service. Do we believe that Christ meant exactly what He said, "Apart from Me ye can do *nothing*?" Dare we lead that meeting; write that paper or letter; deliver that address; witness to someone about Christ; make that decision; take that next step – dare we do *anything* without that swift uplift of faith to Him in whom alone dwells spiritual life?Words spoken, prayers uttered, acts done in the energy of self alone have no power of spiritual germination. God does not fill us with His Spirit on the storage-battery principle, but on the trolley principle. We are not charged with independent power, but united in dependent faith to Jesus Christ who is the One charged with power. The Lord wants to keep us in a place of dependence. He will not fill us with the Spirit so we may run for a year, a month or even a day by ourselves. Our spiritual life is simply not our own, but drawn from another.

Q: You stated that there are two aspects of abiding?
MCCONKEY: The Spirit not only wants us to let Him *in*, but also to let Him *out* to others. The believer is a *channel* for the Spirit who is, in figure, a stream or river (John 7:38). That which has been received must flow out. A good channel is always receiving, always full, always outflowing. Two gateways of faith and love must be kept constantly open. Inflow without outflow means stagnation; outflow without inflow means emptiness. Communion without ministry is one-sided.

Q: Is there a danger in ministry without communion as well?
MCCONKEY: The life of some is one continual round of meetings, societies, conventions, addresses and services. Hours of prayer are unknown; communion is a meaningless term; waiting on God a waste of precious

time; the guidance of the Spirit and the life of trust are outside one's experience. Such lives lack a radical something. They fret and fume, worry, complain of lack of power, absence of joy, peace and blessing.

The chamber of prayer is the only true power-house. Ministry without anointing is lifeless; we must touch Christ before we touch men. We cannot pour out if we have not received from Him. The two in perfect harmony result in an abiding fullness of the Holy Ghost.

* * *

Writings by and about McConkey and *books used in research (not intended to be exhaustive):

Believing is Seeing
Chastening
The Dedicated Life
The End of the Age
Faith
The Fifth Sparrow
*Give God a Chance
The God-Planned Life
Guidance
*James H. McConkey: Man of God
The Ministry of Suffering
The Practice of Prayer
The Spirit-Filled Life
*The Three-fold Secret of the Holy Spirit

Frederick Brotherton Meyer

[1847–1929]

TAPPING INTO POWER

B. MEYER WAS BORN IN LONDON, ENGLAND, and received his early education at Brighton College. He became a Baptist minister and held several successful pastorates in Britain.

He met D.L. Moody on the evangelist's mission to England in 1872, and was instrumental in introducing him to churches in Britain at a time when Moody was little known even in America.

Meyer was strongly interested in the practical influences of the gospel on society, and led a number of social work projects to clean up the moral climate of cities.

In 1904–1905 Meyer was president of the National Federation of Free Churches and also its evangelist, conducting meetings in South Africa and the Far East.

For many years he was closely involved with the Deeper Life Conferences at Keswick, and carried on an extensive speaking and writing ministry.

* * *

APPROXIMATE DATE: 1897

QUESTION: When Mr. Moody invited you from England recently to preach at Northfield, what did you think of the spiritual climate in America?
F.B. MEYER: I noticed that sensational preaching from the pulpit has increased. Instead of textual, expository preaching, prominent preachers seek to develop topics of current interest either in the political or social world. I also find a growing worldliness in churches. Fairs, social parties for raising the minister's stipend and elements which should be taboo and unworthy in churches are also in vogue.

Q: Do you find any evidence of revival?
MEYER: There is some counterfeit revivalism. When church membership drops, and when the life of God in the churches seems to diminish, we should go back to God Himself–to His Word and prayer–to revive the churches. Instead, the tendency is to call in revivalist preachers and use other methods like newspaper advertising to start a revival. I believe this direction is disastrous. But these influences have caused a great yearning on the part of ministers and people for a deeper, richer and more scriptural life.

Q: Do you feel that America is more open than England to new methods and new spiritual concepts?

145

MEYER: Very much so. Such things grow like mushrooms in America and prejudice the minds of thinking people, especially ministers, against what we call the movement for the deepening of spiritual life. One man who knew America well told me that if I came here I must never mention a word about holiness if I desired to make people really holy. Certain schools of teaching have had great power in America and prejudiced people's minds. I find a revulsion toward that special teaching which some of us love and preach.

Q: *What did you preach on at Mr. Moody's Northfield conferences?*
MEYER: Dr. A.J. Gordon and others of us began to teach the necessity of entire consecration, faith in the keeping power of God and the urgency of receiving the enduement of the Holy Spirit of Pentecost.

Q: *What was the response toward your teaching on the Holy Spirit?*
MEYER: People enthusiastically received it. The ministers who attended this conference in large numbers went to all parts of the States like people who had passed through a baptism of fire. Mr. Moody heard, as we did also, that all over America there was a great crying out for the enduement of the Holy Spirit.

Q: *Was your teaching on the Holy Spirit questioned by any?*
MEYER: It was indeed. It was not unusual to have a reserved area in some of my meetings for 500 ministers. After one such meeting in Boston, about 400 ministers asked to question me closely about my teaching. I had been very careful to affirm that the Holy Spirit is in us if we are believers, but that we could also receive Him as

an anointed power. I was able to answer all their questions satisfactorily, I think. At the close of that very memorable meeting, they accepted what I taught. Then we knelt together and received from God an overwhelming baptism of His most blessed Spirit. I believe that meeting was the beginning of an era in the life of many of our beloved brethren in Boston.

Q: Did that happen anywhere else?

MEYER: In New York at a vast gathering in one of the large Presbyterian churches, the ministers questioned me again. They asked me to distinguish between dying to self and the death of self, and whether the enduement of the Holy Spirit is intermittent or permanent—questions of that sort. Just as soon as my brethren found that the teaching was consistent with theology, and above all with the Bible, I received their Godspeed and again we sought the enduement of the Holy Spirit.

Q: Are you optimistic about the direction of the church in America at this point?

MEYER: The interest of the moment within the church is for revival. Ministers and people are coming back to God, to Pentecost, to the Holy Spirit. In my judgment, people in England desire this as much as in America. I would certainly say to every evangelist and to every Christian worker that nothing is more urgent than to get back to the enduement of the Holy Spirit. This is all the more critical as we near the end of this age and enter a new era.

Q: Do you think that some great movement of the Spirit is on the way?

MEYER: I have great faith that God is going to bless us—I don't know when or how or where, except that it will be along this line of the enduement of the Holy Ghost. The church has had her former rain and God is about to give her the latter rain also. But it must begin with us.

Q: Does the church need any changes in its attitude?
MEYER: Let us put away sectarianism—the curse of the church! Put away back-biting, this merciless criticism of one another's methods, this perpetual jealousy. Sweep it all away before the tide of the love of God, and then we will soon be able to reach the great world of men.

Q: What is your personal experience related to a special enduement of the Holy Spirit?
MEYER: As a young minister I attended many meetings where people discussed and taught about the Holy Spirit. None of them brought me triumphant faith until I went to the Keswick Deeper Life Convention in England in 1887.

Q: Please share what happened.
MEYER: I had my own deeper experience on a memorable night when I left that little town with its dazzling lamps to climb a neighboring hill. A few of us had been debating far into the night at a prayer meeting. Some of the men agonized for the Spirit, but because I was too tired to agonize I left. As I walked I said, "My Father, if there is one soul more than another within the circle of these hills that needs the gift of Pentecost, it is I. I want the Holy Spirit but I do not know how to receive Him— and I'm too weary to think or feel or pray intensely."

Then a voice said to me, "As you took forgiveness from the hand of a dying Christ, take the Holy Ghost from the hand of the living Christ. Reckon that the gift is thine by a faith that is utterly indifferent to the presence or absence of resultant joy. According to thy *faith* so shall it be unto thee." So I turned to Christ and said, "Lord, as I breathe in this whiff of warm night air, so I breathe into every part of me Thy blessed Spirit."

Q: Did you feel anything different right at that moment?
MEYER: I felt no hand laid on my head, there was no flame, no rushing sound from heaven. But by faith, without emotion, without excitement, I took for the first time, and I have kept on taking ever since.

As I turned to leave the mountainside, the tempter whispered that I had nothing—that it was all my imagination. But I answered, "Though I do not feel it, I reckon that God is faithful."

The next morning all was peace. That was the high water mark! From that time I have had no doubt about my experience. I have been increasingly concerned about my fellow ministers that they should share the grace that has come to me, and that they might seek and find a fuller enduement of the power of the Holy Spirit for themselves and their brethren.

Q: Do you think the majority of Christians today are living in the power that is available to them in Christ?
MEYER: I think many suffer from different forms of spiritual weakness, all of which are directly attributable to the lack of the Holy Spirit.

Q: Do you mean that they don't have the Holy Spirit?
MEYER: No, they are not completely destitute of Him. If they were, they would not be Christians at all. But the Holy Spirit is like a shallow brook within them. Why should this satisfy us? Pentecostal fullness, the enduement of power, the baptism of fire—all are within our

reach. Let a holy ambition inspire us to get all that our God wills to bestow.

Q: *What symptoms express this weak spiritual state?*
MEYER: Some lack assurance at times. Others don't have a settled peace in Christ. Some lack victory over sin—which is no wonder since they neglect the Holy Spirit. Christ is not real nor near to others. If He is only an occasional vision to us, we lack the first mark of the Pentecostal gift.

Q: *Can believers today expect the constant presence of the Holy Spirit?*
MEYER: We can, since the day of Pentecost. That inaugurated an era in which the weakest and least of believers may possess Him in the same measure as only some did in Old Testament days. Before Pentecost, only a few experienced His fullness. They were the elite, the Elijahs and Isaiahs and Daniels. But since that day God gives the Spirit in all His fullness to the many: to men, women and children; to obscure thinkers and hidden workers; to handmaids and servants; to all and any who fulfill the conditions and abide by the results.

Q: *Are the New Testament gifts of the Holy Spirit also for us today?*
MEYER: I am willing to admit that special gifts of the Holy Spirit belong to the apostolic age. God gave them for a special purpose and they are now withdrawn—though it is a serious question whether they might have continued if the church had been more faithful to her sacred trust.

Q: *How does your position on the gifts apply to the*

manifestation of the fullness of the Holy Spirit in us today?
MEYER: The special gifts of the Holy Spirit are altogether separate from His blessed fullness. His fullness is not the exclusive right of any age. God did not confine it to a limited era or epoch in the history of the church. The only condition is that we keep the channel of communication cleansed and open.

Q: Is the filling of the Holy Spirit optional for believers?
MEYER: "Be filled with the Spirit" is a command as wide-reaching in its demands as "Husbands, love your wives," which we find on the same page of the Bible. It is a positive injunction which we must obey. Yet God enables us to keep all of His commands. In other words, He prepares to make us what He tells us to become.

Q: What are some of the conditions to receiving the Spirit's fullness?
MEYER: We cannot expect to have it if we are quite content to live without it. Our Father is not likely to entrust this priceless gift to those who are indifferent to its possession. Where the flame of desire burns low, we cannot expect to realize the Holy Spirit's fullness. And it is not enough to have occasional and inconstant desire, which flames up today but will remain dormant for months and years. There must be a steady purpose, able to stand the test of waiting – if need be for 10 days – and to bear the rebuff of silence or apparent denial.

Q: What is the proper motive for seeking this fullness?
MEYER: If you want it for experience' sake, or to attract people to yourself, or to transform some difficulty into

a stepping stone, you are likely to miss it. You must have the single purpose to magnify the Lord Jesus in your body, whether by life or death. Destroy all inferior motives and let the desire burn strong and clear within you. God will not supply water for us to use for turning our own water wheels. He will do nothing to minister to our pride. He will not give us the Holy Spirit to enable us to gain celebrity, to procure a name or to live an easy, self-contented life. If we seek the Holy Spirit merely for our happiness, comfort or liberty of soul, we will not likely receive it.

Q: *Once we have this fullness, will we receive special revelations?*
MEYER: That brings up a problem that we need to guard against. A subtle danger, taught by some earnest people, is to magnify the inner light and leading of the Holy Spirit to the neglect of the Word which He gave, and through which He still works on human hearts. This is a great mistake and the prolific parent of all kinds of evil. As soon as we put aside the Word of God, we lay ourselves open to the solicitation of the many voices that speak within our hearts. We no longer have a test, a criterion of truth, a standard of appeal. How can we know the Spirit of God in some of the more intricate cases which our conscience brings into court unless our judgment is deeply imbued with the Word of God? We must not content ourselves with the Spirit without the written Word or with the Word without the Spirit. Our life must travel along these two, as the train along the parallel tracks. The Word is the chosen vehicle of the Spirit. Only by our devout contact with it are we able to detect His voice. It is by the Word that the Spirit will enter our hearts, as the heat of the sun passes into

our rooms with the beams of light through the open
windows.

Q: Does it cost to experience the Holy Spirit's fullness?

MEYER: We must prepare ourselves for all that it involves. We must be willing for the principle of the new
life to grow at the expense of the self-life. We must
consent for the one to increase, while the other decreases, through processes which are painful to the
flesh. The perpetual filling of the Holy Spirit is only
possible to those who obey Him, and who obey Him in
all things. There is nothing trivial in this life. By the
neglect of slight commands, a person may speedily get
out of the sunlit circle and lose the gracious fullness of
Spirit power.

Q: In simple terms, how may believers receive this fullness?

MEYER: As once you obtained forgiveness and salvation
by faith, so now claim and receive the Holy Spirit's
fullness. Fulfill the conditions already named; wait
quietly but definitely before God in prayer—for He gives
His Holy Spirit to them that ask Him. Then reverently
appropriate this glorious gift, rise from your knees and
go on your way, reckoning that God has kept His word,
and that the Spirit has filled you. Trust Him day by day
to fill you and keep you filled. According to your faith,
so shall it be done to you.

Q: Will there be manifestations?

MEYER: At first there may not be the sound of rushing
wind, or the coronet of fire, or the sense of His presence. Do not look for these, any more than the young
convert should look to feeling as an evidence of accept-

153

ance. But *believe*, in spite of feeling, that God has filled you. Say over and over, "I thank Thee, O my God, that Thou hast kept Thy word with me. I opened my mouth, and Thou has filled it—though as yet I am not aware of any special change."

Q: Will feelings eventually come?

MEYER: The feeling will sooner or later break in upon your consciousness, and you will rejoice with exceeding great joy; all the fruits of the Spirit will begin to show themselves.

Q: Is this filling once for all?

MEYER: No, like the apostles we must seek perpetual refilling. Those whom God filled in the second chapter of Acts He filled again in the fourth. Happy is that man who never leaves his room in the morning without definitely seeking and receiving the fullness of the Spirit! He shall be a good student in God's school because of the anointing which God gives him like fresh oil. It shall abide in him and teach him all things. Above all, Christ will teach him the secret of abiding fellowship with Himself.

Whenever you are conscious of leakage or greater need, you need refilling. It may be that service has exhausted you and you have not received fresh spiritual supply. Some new avenue of ministry may have opened before you, or you discovered a fresh talent. Go again to the same source for a refilling, a recharging with spiritual power, a reanointing by the holy charisma.

Q: What is the scriptural basis for repeated or continuous fillings?

MEYER: The book of Acts uses three tenses concerning the filling of the Spirit which still have their counterparts today. "Filled" denotes a sudden decisive experience for a specific work (Acts 4:8). "Were being filled" is the imperfect tense, as though the blessed process were always going on (Acts 13:52). "Full" is the adjective, indicating the perpetual experience (Acts 6:8).

Q: Is it possible there is still more in the experience of the Holy Spirit than believers experience today?
MEYER: Of course there is more in the doctrine of the Holy Spirit than I realize. The fiery baptism of the Holy Spirit may be something far beyond. Let us not content ourselves with what we have experienced. Let us not miss anything that is possible to redeemed men, but leaving the things that are behind, let us press on to those before, striving to apprehend all for which Christ Jesus has apprehended us.

Q: Dr. Meyer, you have taught much about letting God work in and through us. Would you illustrate that?
MEYER: When I was staying in a hotel in Norway, a little girl was among the families staying as guests. She was obviously only a beginner in playing the piano. But she insisted upon practicing in the drawing room whenever she chose. She played with one finger and one note, usually discordant. Everyone bolted for open air whenever they saw her coming.

It happened that one of the finest musicians in Norway was also a guest. Instead of vanishing with the others, he took a stool and sat beside the child. For every note she struck, he struck the most exquisite chord of music, introducing a most lovely accompaniment. As the notes floated outside, the people streamed back to enjoy the music. When the child made a more terrible mistake than usual, he improvised a still finer-outburst of music. After 20 minutes, he took the child by the hand and led her around the company introducing her as "the young lady to whom you are indebted for the music this afternoon." The child knew well enough that she had not done it, but everyone paid their compliments.

The truth this story illustrates has deeply touched my heart through the years. I have been as that child at the piano of God's truth. I have tried my level best to make music with my one finger. Again and again and again I have come away feeling that I am a terrible failure and play nothing but discord. But, oh, I have also found the Holy Spirit sitting by my side. For every note of discord I have made, He has struck a nobler note. Whatever you try to do for the Lord, small or great, and feel you are only making mistakes and failures and false notes, believe that the blessed Holy Spirit is by your side turning your discords into the Hallelujah Chorus!

Q: Is there any danger in an over-emphasis upon the Holy Spirit?

MEYER: We must carefully avoid making the Holy Spirit the figurehead in any movement, however sincere and well intentioned its promoters may be. It is surely a profound mistake to make any special experience of the Spirit the objective or aim of a religious movement. In the present dispensation, the one aim of the blessed Paraclete is to glorify our Savior. He must surely shrink from any attempt, however well intended, to divert one thought from Him, who must ever be the Alpha and the Omega of our faith.

* * *

Writings by and about Meyer and *books used in research (not intended to be exhaustive):

Abraham: The Obedience of Faith
Blessed Are Ye: Talks on the Beatitudes
Choice Notes on Joshua and Second Kings
Christ in Isaiah
David: Shepherd, Psalmist, King
Devotional Commentary on Exodus
Devotional Commentary on Philippians
The Directory of the Devout Life
Elijah and the Secret of His Power
Ephesians
Expository Preaching: Plans and Methods
The Five Books of Moses
*F.B. Meyer: A Biography
*Frederick Brotherton Meyer: A Biography
*Five Musts of the Christian Life
Gospel of John
Israel: A Prince with God
Jeremiah: Priest and Prophet
John the Baptist
Joseph: Beloved, Hated, Exalted
Joshua
*Meet for the Master's Use
Moses: The Servant of God
Paul: A Servant of Jesus Christ
The Prophet of Hope: Studies in Zechariah
Samuel the Prophet
Saved and Kept
The Shepherd Psalm
The Secret of Guidance
Tried by Fire: Expositions of the First Epistle of Peter
Way Into the Holiest

Dwight Lyman Moody

[1837–1899]

POWER UNLIMITED

ORN IN NORTHFIELD, MASSACHUSETTS, Moody experienced a difficult childhood with the loss of his father when he was four. He had to terminate his formal education at age 13. His Sunday school teacher led him to Christ while he was working in his uncle's shoe store in Boston.

After moving to Chicago, Moody became a traveling salesman for a wholesale shoe company, and in his spare time was active in the Young Men's Christian Association and local Sunday schools. He married Emma Revell in 1862 after resigning from business to devote himself to Christian work.

Moody served in the Civil War in somewhat of a chaplain position and ministered to troops on both sides, often at the front. After the war he became president of the Y.M.C.A. in Chicago, and built an independent church at the urging of his converts.

Still an unknown preacher, Moody teamed with Ira D. Sankey for successful revival meetings in England. He returned as an acclaimed evangelist. Although he conducted evangelistic services throughout the United States, he made Northfield his home. That became the site of the Northfield Bible Conventions, which became world known. Moody established the Northfield Seminary for Young Women and Mount Hermon School for Young Men.

In 1889 he founded the Chicago Bible Institute (now Moody Bible Institute), which has prepared Christian workers for ministry throughout the world. He was a rough, folksy preacher known for his homespun anecdotes and stories, but the educated respected him as well. It is claimed that over one million people accepted Christ during Moody's ministry.

* * *

APPROXIMATE DATE: 1890

QUESTION: Mr. Moody, you are living in an exciting and changing era of history. Do you sense any renewed interest in the ministry of the Holy Spirit today?
DWIGHT L. MOODY: There has been much inquiry lately on the subject of the Holy Spirit. In America and other lands thousands of persons have been giving attention to the study of this grand theme.

Q: Toward what is this leading?
MOODY: I hope it will lead us all to pray for a greater manifestation of His power upon the whole church of

God. How much we have dishonored Him in the past! How ignorant of His grace and love and presence we have been! True, we have heard of Him and read of Him, but we have had little intelligent knowledge of His attributes, His offices and His relationship to us. I fear He has not been a reality to many professing Christians. I was a Christian a long time before I even found out the Holy Spirit was a Person.

Q: You have spent your lifetime preaching the gospel in America and abroad. One hundred thousand persons have heard the gospel through your ministry. Where does the power come from for your effectiveness?

MOODY: The gospel proclamation cannot be divorced from the Holy Spirit. Unless He attends the Word in power, vain will be the attempt to preach it. Human eloquence or persuasiveness of speech are mere trappings of the dead if the living Spirit is absent. Besides, if we look only to ministers, if we look only to Christ's disciples to do this work, we shall be disappointed. But if we look to the Spirit of God and expect it to come from Him and Him alone, we shall honor the Spirit, and the Spirit will do His work.

Q: Would you tell us about the beginning of your Christian life?

MOODY: When I was 17, I decided to accept Christ in response to the witness of my Sunday school teacher, Mr. Kimball, when I was a shoe salesman in Boston. The first work of the Spirit is to give spiritual life. He gives it and sustains it. But I had so little natural and educational endowment and such inadequate scriptural knowledge that I failed even to be accepted as a church member at that time. I didn't know enough to find the gospel of John in the Bible.

Q: Did anyone in your church encourage you in your spiritual life?
MOODY: On the contrary, when I tried to speak up for Christ at a midweek prayer meeting, a deacon told me that I might serve the Lord better by keeping quiet. But when the Spirit imparts life, He does not abandon us to droop and die, but constantly fans the flame. I had to make my own opportunities.

Q: How did you do that?
MOODY: When I moved to Chicago to seek my fortune in business, I rented a pew in church, and went out with zeal into the streets to persuade young boys of poverty and mischief to fill it on Sunday.

Q: Did you succeed?
MOODY: So well that I soon filled four pews, and many of those street gamins were soundly converted and changed. I did not teach those youngsters; I just brought them in. I did the same in another little mission Sunday school. Because there were more teachers than scholars, I had to go out and recruit my own class – again, hoodlums from the streets. Soon the building was crowded. I repeated this in another part of Chicago on a larger scale, and the building again overflowed. We moved into a larger hall, which eventually became one of the largest churches in Chicago.

Q: Were you preaching by then?
MOODY: Not much yet because I spoke very awkwardly in public. A Christian brother advised me, "You make too many mistakes in grammar." I replied, "I know that,

and I lack many things, but I'm doing the best I can with what I've got." He then paused and inquired of another man. "Look here, friend, you've got grammar enough–what are *you* doing with it for the Master?" I was counselled to recognize my limitations, stick to bringing people into church, concentrate on my business success–and leave the preaching to others.

Q: How old were you at that time?
MOODY: All the above happened before I was 23. I was doing extremely well in business and took pride in making better and larger sales than my fellow clerks. My ambition was to succeed in a business career and be worth $100,000. That was considered a fortune then. I was promoted to represent the firm as a commercial traveler and was well on my way toward my goal. My boss suddenly died and his wife insisted I should settle her husband's business–his estate was worth $100,000. Being such a youth, I was awed and honored by that heavy responsibility. I fully expected to be a businessman the rest of my life.

Q: What changed your direction?
MOODY: I accompanied a dying teacher of one of our Sunday school classes of girls to the home of each of his students. He explained the way of salvation to every one of the very frivolous girls, and with tears and prayers, each personally responded to accept Christ then and there. I never witnessed such a thing before! I had worked hard to fill buildings with people for others to preach to, but I had never spoken individually to anyone about his soul. That was the work of the elders, I thought.

I considered numbers to be the measure of success, so I worked for numbers. When the attendance ran to

1,200 or 1,500, I was elated. Still, none were converted; there was no harvest. God used that dying teacher's example to show me that souls could indeed be converted in an instant by the Spirit of God, if people were presented with the clear gospel and urged to accept it right away.

Q: What resulted from that experience?
MOODY: I took the $7,000 I had carefully saved, quit my good job, economized in every way and decided to live on that sum as long as it lasted. I spent all my time in Christian work, and began to visit my students in their homes, personally urging them to accept Christ. I felt now that God was calling me into His work. Beginning with the children, I gained access to the homes and the parents. Rather unintentionally, I entered regular evangelistic work. I still secured other speakers for the evangelistic meetings, but I also began speaking myself.

Q: You have been acclaimed as one of the most prominent evangelists of all time. Your meetings are among the greatest the world has ever known. You have swept tens of thousands of people into the kingdom of God. How do you account for your spiritual power, since you admit your limitations were so serious?
MOODY: I did have a measure of success, yes, but I was hungry and thirsty after a deeper Christian experience and effectiveness in serving the Lord. During my first visit to Britain for the purpose of studying the methods of Christian work there, I was inspired by Spurgeon, Muller and others. But it was Mr. Henry Varley, a well-known evangelist, who challenged me as we sat together on a public park bench in Dublin, "The world has yet to see what God will do with and for and through and in and by the man who is fully consecrated

to Him." He said "a man." He did not say a great man, nor a learned man, nor a smart man—but simply "a man." I am a man, and it lies with each man himself whether he will or will not make that entire and full consecration. I decided I would try my utmost to be that man.

Q: Was that the time you entered into the deeper experience you longed for?
MOODY: No, it was one of the steps toward it. There were many more steps before that spiritual hunger was satisfied. I had been greatly used of God, but still I felt there were much greater things in store. I realized more and more how little I was fitted by personal abilities for God's work, and how much more I needed to be qualified for service by the Holy Spirit's power.

Q: What was another step toward that experience?
MOODY: When I was traveling from Boston to New York to preach, I was confronted by an unknown person in an incident which probably influenced me more than any other single experience in my life. As I was getting into the carriage to hurry from the Sunday school to another service, I was touched on the shoulder by an old man whose white hair was blowing in the wind. With his finger pointing at me, he said, "Young man, when you speak again, honor the Holy Ghost."

I got into the carriage and drove away, but the voice continually rang in my ears, yet I did not understand it. It was six months afterward before God revealed to me the meaning of that message—that I was entirely dependent upon the Holy Spirit. From that day to this, I seldom stand before a great audience without seeing that old man, with his outstretched finger, and hearing his voice, "Honor the Holy Ghost."

Q: What did God use next in your life to lead you deeper?

MOODY: There were two godly women, Mrs. Cooke and her friend Mrs. Hawkhurst, who used to come to my meetings in Farwell Hall in Chicago. When I began to preach, I could tell by the expressions on their faces that they were praying for me. At the close of the evening services, they would say to me, "We have been praying for you." I would say, "Why don't you pray for the *people?*" They answered, *"You* need power!" I said to myself, *Why, I thought I had power. Didn't I have a large Sunday school and the largest congregation in Chicago?* There were some conversions at that time, and in a sense I was satisfied. But right along, these two godly women kept praying for me, and their earnest talk about "the anointing for special service" set me thinking.

I finally asked them to come and talk with me, and we got down on our knees. They poured out their hearts for me to receive the anointing of the Holy Ghost. A great hunger came into my soul. I did not know what it was. I began to cry as never before. The hunger increased. I really felt I did not want to live any longer if I could not have this power for service. I kept crying all the time for God to fill me with His Spirit.

Q: Did you finally receive your heart's desire?

MOODY: Unfortunately, my seeking was interrupted by the great Chicago fire of 1871, when one third of the city was laid to ashes and thousands were left homeless. All of the institutions I founded were also in ruins, and I went East to appeal for funds to restore God's work. But my heart was not in fund raising. It was upon my crying need to be filled with His Spirit and power.

Q: *Then it happened?*

MOODY: Yes, and oh, what a day! In New York City I was walking along Wall Street. I cannot describe it; I seldom refer to it. It is almost too sacred an experience to name. The apostle Paul had an experience of which he never spoke for 14 years. I can only say that God revealed Himself to me, and I had such an experience of His love that I had to ask Him to stay His hand.

Q: *What changes took place in you or your ministry?*

MOODY: I went to preaching again. My sermons were not different. I did not present any new truths, and yet hundreds were converted. I would not now be placed back where I was before that blessed experience. If you should give me all the world, it would be as the small dust of the balance.

Q: *Would you tell us clearly what you believe and teach on the filling of God's Spirit?*

MOODY: I do want this point clearly understood: If any man has been cleansed by the blood of Jesus, redeemed by His blood, and then sealed by the Holy Ghost, the Holy Ghost *is* dwelling in him. But I want to call your attention to this—that God has a good many children who have just barely received life but have no power for service. You might safely say, I think, without exaggeration, that 19 out of every 20 professing Christians are of no earthly account so far as building up Christ's kingdom. On the contrary, they are standing in the way. They have eternal life but have settled down and not sought for power.

Q: *Do we receive this power of the Holy Spirit at the time of our new birth?*

MOODY: No. The Holy Ghost coming upon us with

power is distinct and separate from conversion. If the Scripture doesn't teach it, I am ready to stand corrected. There are a great many sons and daughters of God without power. I believe we would accomplish more in one week than we could in years, if we only had this fresh baptism. The Holy Spirit dwelling *in* us is one thing; the Holy Spirit *upon* us is another.

Q: Do you mean there are different kinds of Christians?

MOODY: Yes, I believe this is affirmed in Scripture. The first class, in the third chapter of John, are those who get to Calvary and receive life. They believe on the Son and are saved. They rest satisfied. They do not seek anything higher. Then in the fourth chapter of John, we come to a different class of Christians. They have a well of living water bubbling up. There are fewer of these, but they are not a hundredth part of the first class. But the best class is in the seventh chapter of John, "out of his belly shall flow rivers of living water." That is the kind of Christians we ought to be.

Q: What are the conditions for the Holy Spirit to fill us?

MOODY: I firmly believe that the moment our hearts are emptied of pride, selfishness, ambition, self-seeking and everything else that is contrary to God's law, the Holy Ghost will come to fill every corner of our hearts. But if we are full of those things and pleasure and the world, there is no room for the Spirit of God. I believe many a man is praying to God to fill him, when he is already full—of something else. Before we pray that God would fill us, I believe we ought to pray for Him to empty us. When the heart is turned upside down, and everything is turned out that is contrary to God, then the Spirit will come.

Q: If the Spirit already indwells us at the new birth, is it scriptural to sing such a hymn as "Come, Holy Spirit, Heavenly Dove"?
MOODY: I believe that if we understand it, it is perfectly all right. But if we are praying for Him to come out of heaven down to earth again, that is wrong—because He is already here. He has not been out of this earth for 1800 years. He has been in the church, and He is with all believers who are the called-out ones, called out from the world. Every true believer is a temple for the Holy Ghost to dwell in.

Q: Is the experience you are talking about a significant need in the church today?
MOODY: A great many people are thinking that what we need are new measures, that we need new churches, new organs, new choirs and all kinds of new things. That is *not* what the church of God needs today. It is the old power that the apostles had—that is what we want. And if we have that in our churches, there will be new life. Then we *will* have new ministers—the same ministers renewed with power, filled with the Spirit.

Q: Is there much church activity with little regard for spiritual power?
MOODY: Some Christians are interested only in working. They seem to think they are losing time if they wait on God for His power, and away they go to work hard without unction. They are working without any anointing and without any power. There is no use in running before you are sent. There is no use attempting to do God's work without God's power. A man working with-

out this unction, this anointing, without the Holy Ghost upon him, is losing time after all. I don't believe anyone breaks down from hard work—it is because he is using machinery without oil, without lubrication. It is not hard work that breaks down ministers—it is the toil of working without power.

Q: Is this wonderful filling of the Holy Spirit a one-time experience?

MOODY: A great many think that because they have been filled once, they are going to be full for all time. But oh, we are leaky vessels! We have to be kept right under the fountain all the time in order to stay full. What we need is a fresh supply, a fresh anointing, fresh power. And if we seek it, and seek it with all our hearts, we *will* obtain it.

Q: If the filling of the Spirit is for service, then why should the ordinary Christian need it?

MOODY: Oh, not only the ministry needs to be anointed! Every disciple! Do not suppose pastors are the only laborers. There is not a mother who does not need it in her home to manage her family, as much as the minister needs it in the pulpit, or the Sunday school teacher needs it in her class. We *all* need it, and let us not rest day or night until we possess it. If that is the uppermost desire in our hearts, God will give it to us when we hunger and thirst for it. We must say, "God helping me, I will not rest until I have been endued with power from on high!"

Q: How do you view the future of America in connection with spiritual life?

MOODY: There is nothing I am more concerned about just now. May God revive His church in America! I believe it is the only hope for our republic. I don't believe a republican form of government can last without righteousness. It seems to me that every patriot, every man who loves his country, ought to be eager for the church of God to be quickened and revived.

Q: Should we expect revivals in the years to come?
MOODY: I think you will find that revivals are perfectly scriptural. Perhaps the term "awakening" is a better word, but "revival" seems more familiar. In all ages God has been quickening His people.

Q: Why do some Christians not welcome spiritual awakenings?
MOODY: Every true work of God has its bitter enemies—not only from the outside, but also from the inside—just as in the days of Nehemiah. There are usually some good people who join with the ungodly, and lift their voices against the work of God. The best work usually meets the strongest opposition. But I cannot for the life of me see how any man or woman who knows the Bible can throw his influence against a revival. I am amazed to find that in the history of the church, denomination after denomination has set its face against what I call the work of God. The older the church, the more it needs to be revived, because of the tendency to formalism. Yet many people are afraid of awakenings and bring up objection after objection against them.

Q: What is one example of an objection to awakenings?
MOODY: One argument that seems to carry great weight with so many people right now is that there is too much excitement in an awakening. I wish I could see as much excitement in the church of God, in the work of God,

as I see in other areas. If you want to see excitement, go to some place of amusement! The moment there comes a breath of interest in spiritual things, some people cry, "Sensationalism, sensationalism!" But I tell you that I would rather have sensation than stagnation any time. Don't be afraid of a little excitement. It seems to me that almost anything is preferable to deadness. Where there is life, there will always be a commotion. What we need is *life*! People *ought* to get stirred up over eternal life and death.

Q: *Are some revivals counterfeit?*
MOODY: I believe that if we ask God for a real work, He won't give us a counterfeit. If we ask God for bread, He isn't going to give us a stone. If we have counterfeit dollars, there must be genuine dollars somewhere. And if there are counterfeit revivals—and the devil tries to counterfeit everything—we are not going to give up the real ones.

Q: *What is a good climate for an awakening?*
MOODY: When there is great need. And when there is great darkness. It is surely getting darker. There is no doubt about that. It is darkest just before dawn. But don't think for a moment that I am a pessimist. I haven't any more doubt about the final outcome of things than I have of my existence. I believe Jesus is going to sway His scepter to the ends of the earth—that the time is coming when God's will is to be done on earth as it is done in heaven, and when man's voice will be only the echo of God's. I believe the time is coming when every knee will bow and every tongue confess Christ.

Q: *Do you think another awakening is coming soon?*
MOODY: God is coming very near us. I believe we are on

the eve of a mighty work, if we will just rise and claim it. Before I go hence, I would like to see the whole church of God quickened as it was in 1857, and a wave going from Maine to California that shall sweep thousands into the kingdom of God. Why not? Pentecost isn't over yet! The revival of 1857 isn't over yet by a good deal. Why shouldn't we have now, at the close of this old century, a great shaking up and a mighty wave from heaven? Are *you* doing anything to hinder it?

* * *

Writings by and about Moody and *books used in research (not intended to be exhaustive):

*America's Great Revivals
*The Great Revivalists
*The Life of D.L. Moody
*Moody's Latest Sermons
Prevailing Prayer
*Secret Power: The Secret of Success in Christian Life and Work
*They Found the Secret

George Campbell Morgan

[1863–1945]

FULL POWER

ETBURY, ENGLAND WAS THE BIRTHPLACE of G.
Campbell Morgan and a godly family was his
heritage. A child prodigy in religious circles,
he began to preach regularly in country
chapels at the age of 12. Rallying from a two-year period
of spiritual doubt at the age of 19, he began to live for
one goal–the faithful exposition of the Scriptures.

When he was 23 he left the secular teaching profes-
sion to devote his full time to teaching the Word of
God. All England soon heard of his dynamic preaching
and teaching, and his fame spread to the United States.

D.L. Moody invited Morgan to America to teach the

Word of God to many thousands of new converts resulting from his own ministry and that of other evangelists. Five successful years later, he returned to England and became pastor of Westminster Chapel, London. After 14 years in that position, he returned to America for the next 14 years of itinerant ministry. He resumed his former pastorate in England until his retirement.

Those who sat under Morgan's ministry or who now read his books have been taught how to diligently study the Scriptures for themselves.

* * *

APPROXIMATE DATE: 1910

QUESTION: *Dr. Morgan, what place does the ministry of the Holy Spirit have among Christians today?*
G. CAMPBELL MORGAN: Within the church a marked and wonderful revival of such interest is being expressed. During the last quarter of this 19th century, men in all parts of the Christian church have spoken and written about the ministry and work of the Holy Spirit. Dr. Scofield of Northfield said, "More books, booklets, and tracts about the Holy Spirit have issued from the press during the last twenty years than in all the time since the invention of printing."

Q: *With what result?*
MORGAN: The proclamation of this truth has resulted in new life within the churches. Everywhere eager souls are inquiring after fuller, more definite, more systematic knowledge of this great ministry of the Spirit. Ministries accomplishing great results in the kingdom of God today are those which put the whole burden of their work upon the Holy Spirit of God. He is finally becoming thought of as a Person rather than an influence.

Wherever the Spirit of God is being enthroned in preaching and in all Christian work, and given His rightful place as the Administrator of the things of Jesus Christ, apostolic results follow.

Q: Are all the expressions genuine?

MORGAN: As always in the history of fallen man, the divine movement has its counterfeit. The devil has two strategies regarding the living truth of God. First, he seeks to hide the vision. When that is no longer possible, when truth with its inherent brilliance and beauty is driving away the mists, then the devil's procedure is falsification. Taking the truth out of proportion, he turns it into deadly error.

The greatest peril which threatens the truth of the Spirit's personal ministry today arises from an emphasis on a certain truth by those who are not careful to discover the mind of the Spirit. With this revival of interest people have launched a number of wholly unauthorized systems. These have brought bondage where the Spirit would have brought liberty.

Q: Is this partly because of error in terminology?

MORGAN: Yes, men have been misapplying phrases connected with this subject. The baptism of the Spirit, the anointing of the Spirit, the indwelling of the Spirit, the sealing of the Spirit, the filling of the Spirit—all these are based upon Scripture. But people take them out of their context and make them the current phraseology of a new system of thought, a new form of legalism.

Q: Please illustrate.

MORGAN: For instance, they teach that a man who is already converted may be baptized of the Spirit *if* . . . – and then after the *if* comes the statement of certain conditions. And these constitute a legalism as disastrous as that of Judaizing teachers among the churches of Galatia. They say that if a man will abandon this, that or the other—and in many cases will cease to observe the laws of life which are purely natural—God will fill or baptize him with the Spirit. All of this is contrary to the teaching of the New Testament.

The New Testament always uses the term baptism of the Spirit with reference to regeneration, and never with what they often speak of today as the *second blessing*.

Q: *What do you believe is the true teaching about the fullness of the Holy Spirit?*
MORGAN: The filling of the Spirit through the fuller faith of the believer is often, but not necessarily, a second blessing. All that one needs for fuller realization of the divine life becomes the birthright and property of the believer as soon as he is born again of the Spirit of God. Nothing is worse than the habit of making up systems upon disjointed Scripture phrases apart from their connection with the context.

Q: *What are the guidelines to keep us from error?*
MORGAN: One sure and infallible guide to truth, and therefore one, and only one, corrective for errors is the Word of God. It is our only court of appeal. In approaching the subject, our mind should be cleared of all previous conclusions and prejudices. No revelation of the activities of the Spirit of God, or of the spiritual world, comes to us except as the revelation through the Bible.

Q: *Please explain the work of the Spirit in relation to Christians.*

MORGAN: The children of God do not need to pray for God to *give* them the Holy Spirit. John 14:16–17 assures us that Jesus gave Him to be with us forever. Then the Master proceeds to emphasize the method in which He will abide: "He dwelleth with you, and shall be in you." The first mission of the Spirit is to abide with the church by taking up His abode in the individual. The Spirit is no longer a transient guest, but the indwelling life of the believer. He creates and maintains – in spite of all apparent breaking up – the one catholic church of Christ.

His works with regard to believers are, as Jesus stated, to teach us all things, to bring to our remembrance all that He said, and to bear witness of Jesus (John 14:26). He shall guide us into all the truth (John 15:26); He shall declare unto us the things that are to come; He shall glorify Jesus (John 16:13–14).

Q: What is the significance of the historic Pentecost?

MORGAN: God poured out the Holy Spirit on the day of Pentecost as a gift. Man had no claim upon God for that great gift. He did not pour Him out in answer to any prayer of man, nor because of any merit in man. He was, as was the gift of Jesus, a gift of grace which God gave to all. Pentecost, in the economy of God, was the occasion of the outpouring of the Spirit in answer to the completed work of the Christ and that God might realize His purpose in the character of men.

Pentecost, for the disciples, was the change from being merely followers and learners, into a living union with the living Christ.

Pentecost, for the world, was the coming into the world of a new temple consisting of living men, women and children indwelt by the Spirit of God for purposes of praise, prayer and prophecy.

Q: *What is your view on the baptism of the Spirit?*
MORGAN: In dealing with these important matters of the Spirit, it is wise to keep, as far as possible, to the terms of the New Testament. It would be enormous gain if we use them only as Scripture does. We generally misunderstand and therefore misapply the term "the baptism of the Spirit." People use it as though it were synonymous with "the filling of the Spirit." Consequently, some speak of the baptism of the Spirit as "a second blessing." They teach that believers must ask for, wait for and expect this baptism as something different from and beyond conversion. That view is utterly unauthorized by Scripture. The baptism of the Spirit is the primary blessing—it is, in short, the blessing of regeneration.

Q: *Does the Spirit baptize us at the time we are born again?*
MORGAN: Yes. There is, however, an essential difference between that initial blessing and the blessing into which thousands of God's people have entered during recent years—the difference between the baptism of the Spirit and the filling of the Spirit. The majority of believers experience the filling of the Spirit *after* the baptism. Both are the same in the purpose of God, but different in experience.

When we review all the passages in the New Testament that refer to the baptism of the Spirit, in every case the reference is not to some blessing after regeneration, but to regeneration itself. That is the supernatural miracle by which a person passes from darkness into light, out of death into life, from the power of sin and Satan into the glorious liberty of a child of God.

Q: *Then you believe Christians today should not ask for or wait for the Holy Spirit?*

MORGAN: That is correct. Nothing warrants this popular and prevalent idea. Neither is it a second blessing. The Holy Spirit came in response to *the asking of Jesus* and upon the ground of His finished work. He never gives the Spirit in answer to *human* asking. He gives the Spirit upon the ground of repentance and faith. He baptizes man with the Spirit and from that moment the Spirit of God takes possession and dwells within him. The believer may check Him, hinder Him, quench Him and grieve Him. Nevertheless, from the moment of his new birth he is the temple of the Holy Spirit. It is in the initial miracle of regeneration that God baptizes persons with the Holy Spirit.

Q: What about the need for "tarrying" or waiting?
MORGAN: That does not apply at all to Christians today. If men have to tarry until endued with power today, it is not because God did not give them the Spirit, but because there is something in their lives which will not let the Spirit work. Every believer is already a temple of the Holy Spirit. If there is tarrying, it is because of some disobedience and not because of any unreadiness on the part of God to bestow full blessing upon all His children. Such tarrying is not the waiting of man for the Spirit, but the waiting of the Spirit for man.

Q: What does the Bible teach about the "filling of the Spirit"?
MORGAN: The expression occurs in the Acts of the Apostles eight times and once in Ephesians. To summarize: the Spirit-filled life is the normal condition of the believer; a believer may lose it; it can be restored. God immediately fills newly born-again people at the time He baptizes them by the Spirit into union with Christ.

179

But very often for lack of clear teaching and full understanding of the law of the Spirit, they lose the fullness of
the blessing.

**Q: *Are you saying that we not only* receive *the Spirit
at conversion, but God* fills *us with the Spirit at the
same time?***
MORGAN: On the day of Pentecost, in a moment when
God transformed the group of Jewish disciples into the
church, He not only gave the Spirit to them, He filled
them. Therefore the will of God for His people is that
He should fill them *at once.* God does not give a man
the Spirit today and then require him to wait for perhaps a number of years before He fills him with the
Spirit. The supreme miracle by which a man is born of
the Spirit, and baptized of the Spirit into new relationship with Christ, is also the miracle by which He fills
him with the Spirit of God.

Q: *Do any fillings come later?*
MORGAN: God gives special fillings of the Holy Spirit for
special service. When Peter or Paul or any present servant of Christ has a special work to do for the Lord,
God may specially fill him with the Spirit to accomplish
that special work.

**Q: *Does the use of the imperative verb in Ephesians
5:18, "be filled with the Spirit," have any significance?***
MORGAN: Because it signifies a command, it lays responsibility not upon God but upon the believer. We see that
responsibility expressed in the words, "Grieve not the
holy Spirit of God, whereby ye are sealed unto the day
of redemption" (Ephesians 4:30). Here is a solution for
the mystery that gathers around the experience of thou-

sands of Christians. They are born of the Spirit and none will deny that they are Christians.

The Spirit does not fill them because their lives do not manifest the fruit of the Spirit. They must have grieved the Holy Spirit of God in some way in the past. God clearly marked the path of obedience but they have disobeyed. Christian people whom the Spirit has baptized into a new relationship with Christ have obviously grieved the Spirit by disobedience, lukewarmness, indifference to the claims of Christ, worldliness or frivolity. The Spirit therefore does not fill them.

Q: *Is the expression "one baptism and many fillings" correct?*
MORGAN: That is a very helpful statement. It is borne out by New Testament teaching and history. One baptism—at the moment of the new birth at which time the Spirit comes upon the repenting and believing person and unites him to Christ. Christians may be disobedient and lose the *filling* of the Spirit. They may restore it by repentance and obedience. In the experience of multitudes of believers this formula proves correct—one baptism, but many fillings.

Q: *What proportion of Christians do you think actually live filled with the Spirit?*
MORGAN: Indeed, that experience is far beyond the majority of Christians. Nevertheless, God's purpose is to fill every child of His not a year, not two years, not 10 years after conversion, but at the *moment* of conversion, and *perpetually* until the consummation of his life on earth.

Q: *If a Christian sincerely wants to be Spirit-filled, what steps should he take?*

MORGAN: That is the most important question a believer can ask if he really wants to be what God would have him be, if he is tired of all the merely formal and mediocre, and if he is eager to live in the will of God at all costs. God gives clear conditions by which the believer, born of the Spirit, may live a Spirit-filled life.

These conditions are twofold, the initial and the continuous—how to obtain the blessing and how to maintain it. The first is *abandonment*; the second is *abiding*.

Q: Is "abandonment" the same as consecration, surrender or dedication?

MORGAN: I use *abandonment* intentionally. Consecration is a great word, but so much abused that it has lost much of its deepest significance. Abandonment is perhaps not an ordinary theological term, but is full of force. Whenever we make whole-hearted, absolute, unquestioning, positive, final abandonment of our life to God, filling with the Spirit results. Abandonment is twofold—abandonment to purification by the Spirit (Ephesians 4:30–31), and abandonment of the whole being to Jesus Christ so that He may offer it to God (Romans 6:13).

Abandonment may be easy to talk about, yet all men shrink from it. They would rather do anything else. But nothing can take the place of abandonment. Some people attempt to put prayer where God has put abandonment. Others profess to wait until God is willing to fill them. Both are wrong! While they think they are waiting for God, God is waiting for them. At any moment, if they yield to the Spirit, He will sweep through every gate and avenue and into every corner of the life.

Q: How do we maintain the fullness of the Spirit?

MORGAN: Abiding in Christ keeps us filled with the

Spirit. People talk a great deal about abiding, and many have endeavored to define the term. Some give beautiful definitions, mystical and poetic, but mostly out of reach to the ordinary life of the believer. Let us stay with definitions in Scripture: "He that keepeth His commandments dwelleth in Him, and He in him" (1 John 3:24). The definition is so clear. I will state it simply: To abide is to obey.

Q: Will we feel something when the Spirit fills us?
MORGAN: A word of warning is necessary. People make a vital mistake if they formulate a code of sensations and wait for them as evidences of the Spirit's filling. Some expect a magnetic thrill, some overwhelming ecstasy. Some may experience these, some may not. Others wait for an experience like that of someone else. They will never have it. Many read stories of great Christian leaders and expect what they had. Disappointment will result.

We may safely say that the experience of the filling of the Spirit is in no two cases exactly the same, any more than the consciousness of ordinary life can ever be the same in any two persons. Points of resemblance, yes, and great fundamental facts are the same; but in the light and shade there is variety. If this is true of ordinary life, it is also true of the higher spiritual blessing. The Holy Spirit fills all believers. The experience of the one differs from that of the other. "There are diversities of operations, but it is the same God" (1 Corinthians 12:6).

Q: What are the common denominators?
MORGAN: Those who are Spirit-filled have a common consciousness—the consciousness of Christ. When the Holy Spirit comes in His fullness, He gives men the knowledge of the Lord as they never knew Him before.

Even the consciousness of Christ in the experience of believers will still vary.

Remember that it takes the whole church to realize the full consciousness of the Head. His greatness is such that He cannot give Himself wholly and utterly and finally to one individual. He needs the whole church to display His perfect glory, to unfold the majesty of His Person. Let no one narrow his consciousness of Christ to the consciousness of any single person. He is one thing to one man; He is another thing to another. But believers are united in the realization that it is the Master of whom they are all conscious by the Spirit. The Lordship of Jesus as a reality is a primary result of the Spirit-filled life.

Beside this, His people share in Christ's victory over evil and the Holy Spirit will reproduce in them a likeness of Jesus.

Living as a Spirit-filled Christian is a matter of personal responsibility. Is He indwelling *in you* in all His fullness? Or are you grieving and quenching Him? Believer, abandon your whole life to Him.

* * *

Writings by and about Morgan and *books used in research (not intended to be exhaustive):

*The Acts of the Apostles
Answers of Jesus to Job
The Corinthian Letters of Paul
The Crises of Christ
The Expository Method of G. Campbell Morgan
God's Last Word to Man
Hosea: The Heart and Holiness of God
The Letters of Our Lord: A First Century Message to Twentieth
  Century Christians

Malachi's Message for Today
The Ministry of the Word
The Minor Prophets: The Men and Their Messages
The Parables and Metaphors of Our Lord
Peter and the Church
Preaching
The Prophecy of Isaiah, 2 Vol.
*The Spirit of God
Studies in the Four Gospels
Studies in the Prophecies of Jeremiah
The Teaching of Christ
The Ten Commandments
The Voice of the Devil
The Westminster Pulpit, 5 Vol.

Handley Carr Glyn Moule

[1841–1920]

REACH OUT
FOR POWER

HANDLEY MOULE GREW UP IN A MANSE under the godly training of his parents who had been strongly influenced by the evangelical awakening of 1859. Moule dated his own conversion during his 25th year. He was the youngest and best known of a family of eight remarkable brothers.

After earning a brilliant classical degree at Cambridge, Moule became successively a teacher at Marlborough School; fellow dean of Trinity College, Cambridge; first principal of Ridley Hall; Norrisian professor; and Lord Bishop of Durham. His personal influence was profound and far reaching on his students.

In outward appearance Moule was refined and distinguished. In his capacity as bishop he wore splendid episcopal robes. His position gave him the privilege of standing at the right hand of the King of England at his coronation. Although he was ordained in the Church of England and served as curate with his father, and was a lifelong Anglican, it was not until later in his career that he experienced the greater spiritual power for which he longed.

In 1882 while in his third year as principal of Ridley Hall, Dwight Moody and Ira Sankey came to Cambridge to conduct meetings at the university. Although apprehensive at first, the dignified principal himself was among those who knelt at the altar. His experience was further deepened the following year under the ministry of other Keswick speakers at Cambridge.

Moule took a leading part in introducing the common-speaking American, Moody, to the more sophisticated English audiences and lent credibility to his evangelistic meetings. He was also instrumental in sending out the famous Cambridge Seven to the mission field. From 1884 he identified himself with the Keswick movement and for the rest of his life was one of its most acceptable speakers. His great strength lay in his personal and spiritual appeal and the platform his bishopric gave him to address the Christian world. His expository volumes on certain books of the Bible are considered classics.

* * *

APPROXIMATE DATE: 1890

QUESTION: *You have taught much about the Holy Spirit. Is the filling of the Holy Spirit the same experience as the new birth?*
H.C.G. MOULE: It is not the same in idea with the initial

work of the Spirit as the Life-giver—whether or not it coincides in time. The filling always takes place where the Holy Spirit is *already* present by the new birth. The possession of that new birth causes a holy desire and longing to obtain that filling.

Q: *What is the baptism of the Holy Spirit?*

MOULE: That is not precisely a Pauline term. We only approach it in his words, "by one Spirit are we all baptized into one body" (1 Corinthians 12:13). But it has a close and important connection with the subject of the fullness of the Spirit. It occurs in each of the gospels and twice in the Acts. The Lord Jesus is always the Baptizer. Notice also that while the Scripture frequently mentions filling, it only mentions two occasions of the baptism: on the day of Pentecost and the closely parallel occasion in the house of Cornelius. Nowhere in the epistles does the precise phrase "baptism of the Spirit" occur.

We conclude that the baptism is not the same as the filling, and is not, like the filling, presented to us as a blessing for which the Christian is to seek. The two occasions of the baptism are not only historical events but great representative occasions. Each of them was a kind of birth time of the true church by the power of the Spirit. Each may typify and signify on a great scale the true birth process and birth time, by the same power, in the individual believer.

It is remarkable and significant that the developed teaching of the epistles contains no appeal to the man already in Christ to seek the baptism of the Spirit. As those who have already received Him, we are to be filled and to be full of Him.

Q: *Is it biblical to wait for a special baptism of the Spirit?*

MOULE: With tenderness and deep spiritual sympathy for those who believe we must wait, I am convinced that a mistake underlies that practice. It is not uncommon among earnest Christians to feel that they must wait for a special "baptism of the Spirit" to be more effectual in service for the Lord. It is true, by one Spirit we *have been* baptized into one body. And now our part, First Corinthians 12:13, is to open in humblest faith all the avenues and regions of our soul and life that the Spirit may *fill* us with what we *already have*. We should not cry "enter" but "possess."

Q: How can the Spirit fill us?
MOULE: Paul gives the answer: "That we might receive the promise of the Spirit *through faith*" (Galatians 3:14). God has promised that if we open our mouth, He will fill it (Psalm 81:10). For God to fill us with His Spirit is for us to open and receive. We take our stand upon His promise, not by some mighty spiritual effort on our part to receive it.

We are to take the Lord at His word, to trust Him to bless us fully as He keeps His word. We should open all of our inner doors just as we open the main front door. We are to use the same key, the key of promise, the key of our simplest and most confiding faith. Believing, we receive. Then we will have the blessed manifestations of the holy Gift in one special direction or another.

Q: Will we always have a conscious, well-defined crisis to distinguish when the Spirit has filled us?
MOULE: Many people are not clear if the Scripture teaches that every Christian should come to some stage of his spiritual progress and take a solemn step from a lower to a higher experience, from an ordinary to an extraordinary state of communion with his Lord. I have

not found in the New Testament any formed and deliberate doctrine that every convert must seek such a single and ruling crisis.

It could certainly take place with the initial acceptance of Christ, at the new birth. It is possible that in countless instances that filling is already truly present. Its arrival and its development may have been unnoticed by the believer—it took place through a process which he cannot even analyze. Let no Christian judge another in this matter.

But let no Christian who has such an undefined experience think that his friend or brother doesn't need one either. Remember that the Indweller wants to *arrive* in order to *reside* in the heart in His fullness no matter when it happens.

Q: How much importance should we give to personal testimonies of deeper experiences of the Holy Spirit?
MOULE: Many reputable Christians testify to the arrival of Jesus Christ in their hearts, followed by a residence of the Spirit in a new and blessed experience. Such people discover that their occasional and exceptional communion with their Lord has now become a continuous and habitual experience.

Remember that one uniform description of how the Holy Spirit arrives in the heart and how He takes up His full residence does not fit all believers. Even the most experienced in spiritual matters continues to have new experiences in the Spirit as he progresses spiritually, which make the experiences seem almost as if the Spirit had just arrived. Let no Christian judge another in this matter.

Q: Does the Holy Spirit act in more than one way in our lives?

MOULE: The Spirit expresses His fullness in two main aspects or phases. A special, critical phase is during a great crisis when His fullness comes out in evident, and perhaps wholly abnormal manifestation. At such times, the man or woman is able to utter supernatural prediction or proclamation.

The second aspect is what we may call the habitual phase, where we use the term to describe the condition of a believer's life day by day and in its normal course. Such believers are described as being "full." Apparently where the Scriptures use these terms the same man might in one respect be full while in another he needs to be filled.

Q: Is there a connection between the filling of the Spirit and miraculous powers?
MOULE: From one view, there is a close connection, particularly the miraculous work of infallibly "inspired" speaking. The immediate result at Pentecost was an instantaneous speaking "with other tongues, as the Spirit gave them utterance" (Acts 2:4b). Peter, Paul and Stephen all spoke supernatural words of testimony or authority or vision when thus "filled with the Spirit." Some may think we should expect a similar manifestation of the fullness. But it seems clear that this inference is by no means necessary.

I believe the emphasis of Scripture is on the nobler and more perfect kind of operation by the Spirit–on the moral, the transformation of the will, the heart and the soul. Whatever the fullness has to do with tongues and prophecies, it has its very highest concern with the believer's spiritual knowledge of his glorious Lord in the life of faith and its true manifestation in the loveliness of a holy walk. To be filled with the Spirit is a phrase

191

intensely connected with the fullness of our consecration to the will and work of God in human life.

Q: Does the Ephesians 5:18 instruction refer to the crisis or the process aspect of being filled?

MOULE: Not for a crisis but for the whole habit of the Christian's life. Notice that Paul does not refer in the least to works of wonder in the context. "Psalms and hymns and spiritual songs" are the manifestation of the fullness, along with the habit of thankfulness and the readiness to forget self in the interest of others. Then follow all the lovely details of the life of a sanctified home.

The preceptive verb in the Greek is in the present or continuing tense. It indicates a course, a habit, not a critical effort or attempt. This puts the responsibility upon the believer. He must use the open spiritual secrets of his life in the Lord to enter upon and walk in such a state of fullness that he will bless others around him in his daily life.

Q: Is the filling of the Spirit only for exceptional Christians?

MOULE: The promise is not for great or exceptional Christians, but for any Christian who yields himself to God. Paul addressed everyday Christian believers at Ephesus: husband, wife, parent, child, master, slave. He encouraged all to live lives divinely full, full from within. What this command to be filled with the Spirit meant in Ephesus, it means in England, it means to the one who writes these words in his study at Cambridge, and to his brother in Christ who reads them wherever God has bid him dwell.

Q: Some have cautioned against addressing, praying

to or worshipping the Holy Spirit. What is your view?
MOULE: The truth of the personality of the Holy Spirit
as the third person of the Trinity brings Him into our
experience with more reality. Scripture teaches little
about direct adoration of the Holy Spirit. The Author of
the Book, the Spirit Himself, is reticent about His own
nature and glory. The Holy Spirit's special function is
not only to speak to and deal with and intercede for
men, but also to speak and work through the men He
renews and sanctifies. That helps us understand even
more why He does not present Himself for our articu-
late adoration.

On the other hand, knowing from the Scriptures that
He is divine and personal, we cannot refrain from an
attitude of worship. Our Lord presented the Spirit to us
as coordinate with Himself in glory and grace as "another Comforter."

So, while watchfully and reverently seeking to remember the laws of Scripture proportion, let us trust-
fully and thankfully worship Him and ask blessing of
Him as our spirits are moved under His grace. Let us
not only pray *in* the Holy Ghost but also *to* Him. We
may do so in the words of some ancient hymn or in the
many songs of supplication which have been given us,
surely not without His leading, in these latter days of
His gracious dispensation.

* * *

Writings by and about Moule and *books used in research
(not intended to be exhaustive):

Christ and the Christian
Christ is All
Colossians and Philemon Studies: Lessons in Faith and Holiness
Ephesian Studies: Lessons in Faith and Walk

The Epistle to the Romans
The Old Gospel for the New Age
Philippian Studies: Lessons in Faith and Love
The Resurrection of Christ
The Second Epistle to the Corinthians
Studies in II Timothy
*They Found the Secret
**Veni Creator: Thoughts on the Person and Work of the Holy
  Spirit of Promise*

Andrew Murray

[1828–1917]

FLASH FLOODS
AND QUIET
FOUNTAINS

THE SON OF A DUTCH REFORMED MINISTER of Scottish ancestry, Andrew Murray was born in South Africa. When Andrew was nine, his parents sent him and his elder brother to Aberdeen, Scotland, for their education. In 1845 both received master's degrees from Aberdeen University and enrolled together in Utrecht University to pursue their theological education.

While at Utrecht they excelled academically, formed a Students' Missionary Society, and in 1848 the Dutch Reformed Church ordained them to the ministry. Returning to South Africa, Andrew accepted a pastorate in Bloemfontein.

While convalescing in England from an attack of fever, he met and married Miss Rutherford of Capetown, South Africa. In 1860 Murray accepted a pastorate in Cape Colony and at the same time began the writing of his many devotional books. The theme of most of his 240 books and tracts was the deepening of the spiritual life of Christians. They have been published in 15 languages.

In addition to pastoring churches, Murray spent half of his time in itinerant evangelism. A prominent missionary statesman, Murray was moderator of the Dutch Reformed Synod three times. He started a branch of the Young Men's Christian Association in Capetown, established the Huguenot seminary at Wellington in 1874, organized a missionary training school and founded the South African Keswick.

Murray spent the last 12 years of his life speaking in conventions and evangelistic meetings in the United States, Canada, England, Ireland, Scotland, Holland and South Africa.

* * *

APPROXIMATE DATE: 1888

QUESTION: *Mr. Murray, you teach and write a great deal about the work of the Holy Spirit. Is your teaching something new for the church today?*
ANDREW MURRAY: Not new. But the emphasis is long overdue. In the church in the past the Holy Spirit did not have the recognition He ought to have had as the equal of the Father and the Son. He is the divine Person through whom alone the Father and Son can be truly possessed and known.

Q: *Why didn't the Reformation emphasize that?*

196

MURRAY: In that era the gospel of Christ had to be vindicated from the terrible mistaken idea which made man's righteousness the ground of his acceptance with God. The freeness of divine grace had to be made clear. To the ages that followed was committed the trust of building on that foundation and developing what the riches of grace would do for the believer through the indwelling of the Spirit of Jesus. The church rested too content in what it had received. The teaching of all that the Holy Spirit will be to each believer in His guiding, sanctifying, strengthening power has never yet taken the place it ought to have in our evangelical teaching and living.

Q: Do you mean God is giving us a new revelation?
MURRAY: No. The finality of God's revelation is in the Scriptures. A quotation from Dr. A. Saphir's book, *The Lord's Prayer*, may help us: "If we review the history of the church, we notice how many important truths, clearly revealed already in Scripture, have been allowed to lie dormant for centuries, unknown and unappreciated except by a few isolated Christians, until it pleased God to enlighten the church by chosen witnesses. Then He bestowed on His children the knowledge of hidden and forgotten treasures. For how long a period, even after the Reformation, were the doctrines of the Holy Ghost, His work in conversion, and His indwelling in the believer, almost unknown!"

Q: Should a Christian pray for the Holy Spirit to come into his life?
MURRAY: No. That is not according to Scripture. Every believer *has* the Holy Spirit already dwelling in him. He ought to know this and believe that the Spirit will work in him what he needs for further growth and strength.

197

Q: What accounts for the differences of spiritual depth, power and usefulness among Christians?
MURRAY: Not all believers have attained the same full experience of all that the indwelling of the Spirit implies.

Q: Is the filling of the Spirit restricted to a very few—like apostles or ministers—and on special occasions?
MURRAY: Indeed not! That misunderstanding has been the cause of much powerless living among believers on this side of Pentecost. Before Pentecost, in Old Testament times, this limitation did prevail. But since then, this should be the ordinary, consistent experience of every true-hearted believer. Only this will enable him to live the life for which he has been redeemed. It is not a high aspiration, but the normal expectation of every believer.

Q: Why is there such controversy, especially among ministers and Bible teachers, as to the means of being filled with the Spirit?
MURRAY: I would say there are two diverse views, both claiming to be biblical. The first maintains that since every believer receives the Holy Spirit in regeneration, no baptism of the Spirit should be sought for. The promise was already fulfilled to the church at Pentecost, and every believer gets his share when he believes in Christ. The opposite view holds that, as in the several cases in Acts, certain men were true believers and yet needed specially to receive the promised Spirit. So now every believer must seek and may expect this baptism subsequent to his conversion.

In fact, a third view takes somewhat middle ground. While agreeing that the Holy Spirit dwells in every believer, such people maintain that the believer may from time to time receive very special conscious renewals of the Spirit's presence and power from on high. These may justly be regarded as fresh baptisms of the Spirit.

Q: How do those holding the first view attain to the fullness we are talking about?
MURRAY: They consider that this fullness is a glorious fact already, but the believer needs to enter more thoroughly into an intelligent and spiritual perception of what at present actually exists. They teach that you have all of the Holy Spirit you will ever have. The other viewpoint teaches the necessity of waiting before God for this filling as a special distinct gift, the fulfillment of the Father's promise.

Q: And what do you believe, Mr. Murray?
MURRAY: If the second view insists that every believer *must* consciously seek and receive *as a distinct experience* such a baptism, I do not think that is what the Word teaches. But if it is put in this way, that in answer to believing prayer many believers have received—and those who seek it will often receive—such an inflow of the Spirit of God as will to them indeed be a new baptism of the Spirit, then I believe this is in harmony with the teaching of Scripture. At the same time, I cannot agree with the first position that we should not still pray for the Spirit. This view must be supplemented.

Q: But how can you ask for what you already have? Shall we pray for more of the Spirit?
MURRAY: Look at it this way: Our lungs are full of breath, yet call for a fresh supply every moment; our fingers pulse with the fullness of blood, yet continually

call to the heart for a fresh supply. We should praise God for the Spirit that has been received, and yet always desire His fuller inflow. It would indeed be sad if a believer, once having received the Spirit, were to feel that he has now outgrown his need for this chief of blessings. As the anointing with fresh oil is a daily need, just so Jesus baptizing with the Spirit is not just a memory of a *past* thing, done once for all, but a promise of what may and should be a daily, *continuous* experience. The faith that we have the Spirit within us, even when it has come almost like a new revelation and filled us with joy and strength, will lose its freshness and its power unless the inflow is maintained in living fellowship with the Father and the Son.

Q: *Is the filling an outpouring into us from outside or from within us?*

MURRAY: When the flood came of old, the windows of heaven and the fountains of the great deep were together opened. It is still so in the fulfillment of the promise of the Spirit. The deeper and clearer our faith in the *indwelling* Spirit, and the simpler the waiting on Him, the more abundant will be the renewed *downcoming* of the Spirit from the heart of the Father directly into the heart of His waiting child. You have already received the Spirit—the fountain is within you. It has to be opened up and it will spring up and fill your being. "He that believeth on me, . . . out of his belly shall flow rivers of living water" (John 7:38). At the same time that there is the ceaseless inflow of the sap from Him who is the living vine, it is met by the upspringing of the fountains within. The baptism with the Spirit has as distinct a commencement as His cleansing with the blood. But it must be maintained by a continuous renewal so that the inflow will grow ever stronger until it is overflowing.

Q: Isn't it true that some believers experience great changes in their lives when they are filled with the Holy Spirit, even greater than when they were born again?

MURRAY: There may be, and in the great majority of Christians is, a great difference before and after an experience of filling with the Holy Spirit, just as was the state of the disciples before and after Pentecost. Pentecost was certainly not the bestowal of the Spirit for regeneration; Pentecost was the definite communication of the presence in power of their glorified Lord. This difference between the bare knowledge of His presence and the full revelation of the indwelling Christ in His glory causes those great changes or responses.

Q: Why isn't every believer filled with the Holy Spirit?

MURRAY: I believe it is either because of ignorance or unfaithfulness. When a believer distinctly understands what the indwelling of the Spirit was meant to bring and is ready to give up all for it, he may ask and expect what may be termed a baptism of the Spirit. He may receive such an inflow of the Holy Spirit as will consciously lift him to a different level from the one on which he has been living.

Q: How then can we be filled with the Spirit?

MURRAY: The *way* in which the baptism comes may differ from one person to another. To some it comes as a glad and sensible quickening of their spiritual life. They are so filled with the Spirit that all their *feelings* are stirred. They can speak of something they have distinctly experienced as a gift from the Father. To

201

others it is given, not to their feelings, but to their *faith*. It comes as deep, quiet, but clearer insight into the fullness of the Spirit in Christ as really being theirs. This faith feels confident that His sufficiency is equal to every emergency that may arise. In the midst of weakness they know that the Power is resting on them. In their case they know that the blessing has been given from above, to be maintained in obedience and deep dependence on Him from whom it came.

Q: That must be an exhilarating experience.

MURRAY: Indeed. But the focus should not be on its *enjoyment*. Such a baptism is specifically given as *power for work*. It may even be received before the believer fully understands his calling to work, and while he is chiefly occupied with his own sanctification. But it cannot be maintained unless the call to witness for the Lord is obeyed. The baptism at Pentecost, and thereafter as we experience it, was and is given as preparation for witness.

Q: Since God's Spirit is power, shall we always feel strong and powerful after we are filled?

MURRAY: Receiving the power of the Holy Ghost takes place in a way quite contrary to all our natural expectations. It is a divine power working in weakness. The sense of weakness is not taken away; the power is not given as something we possess. We only have the power as we have the Lord Himself. He exerts the power in and through our weakness.

Q: What are the manifestations of having been filled with the Spirit?

MURRAY: We must beware of laying down fixed rules as to the manifestations of that baptism. God's gifts and love are larger than our hearts. But one thing is always manifested. It will prove its own power to open the mouth and bring forth testimony for God. "But ye shall receive power, after that the Holy Ghost is come upon you: and ye shall be witnesses" (Acts 1:8a). "Be filled with the Spirit, speaking to [one another]" (Ephesians 5:18–19). The fountain must spring up; the stream must flow. Silence is death.

Q: Is there no uniform way that a believer must respond when filled with the Holy Spirit?
MURRAY: The natural temperament of a person has something to do with the kind of response. Also, the Holy Spirit sovereignly comes upon individuals and groups of believers in different ways at different times.

Q: What was your own experience in South Africa relating to the outpouring of the Holy Spirit upon a group?
MURRAY: During the mighty revival that God brought to us in the mid 1800s, there were many unusual manifestations of the Spirit among us which we had not been taught nor had expected. Strange scenes were witnessed with this rising tide of blessing. A person close to this revival remarked, "An outsider, unacquainted with the working of the Spirit of God, would have called it undiluted fanaticism."

Even I was not prepared immediately to recognize what God was doing by His Spirit. We heard the mighty rushing sound come upon our meeting place on more than one occasion. People sometimes fell as if unconscious to the floor during meetings and were not hurt. Without efforts made to stir the emotions—for we of the Dutch Reformed Church are very conservative— even without preaching, whole congregations were moved to simultaneous audible prayer and tears and confessions and repentance unto salvation. The Spirit even moved among those in isolated villages and on farms in the wilderness.

Q: *Was there any common denominator in such moving of the Spirit?*
MURRAY: Again, it was the opening of the mouth in praise and prayer and bold witness. Everywhere those whom the Lord had touched shared the gospel without fear or shyness, resulting in still more conversions and fruit that remained.

Q: *Please counsel us regarding the diversity of experiences resulting from this filling.*
MURRAY: Those who receive the experience variously must be careful not to criticize those who differ or discount their experiences as being ungenuine or incomplete. Let me illustrate. In South Africa we often suffer from drought. There are two kinds of reservoirs for catching and storing water. On some farms you have a spring or well but with a stream too weak to use for irrigation. A reservoir is made for collecting the water, and the filling of the reservoir is the result of the gentle, quiet, continual inflow from the fountain day and night. In other places, the farm may not have a spring; a reservoir must be built in the bed of a stream or in a hollow where, when rain falls, the water can be collected. In such a place, the filling of the reservoir is often by the sudden heavy fall of rain in a very few hours. There it is accompanied by a rush and violence not free from danger.

This is a parallel to the receiving of the fullness or baptism of the Spirit and also the response to it. On the day of Pentecost, or at times of crisis, when new beginnings are made, or the outpouring of the Spirit of conversion in unevangelized lands, or of special revival among Christian people, suddenly, mightily, manifestly, men are filled with the Holy Spirit. In the enthusiasm and joy of newly found salvation, the power of the Spirit is undeniably present.

Q: It would seem that the spectacular way would be more desirable than the quiet way.
MURRAY: This is entirely of God's appointment, not our choosing. For those who receive it in such a striking way, there are special dangers. The blessing may often be too dependent on fellowship with others, or extend only to the outward and more easily reached currents of the soul's life. The sudden experience is often, though certainly not always, more superficial, with the danger that the depths of the will and the inner life may not have been reached.

Q: If a believer's experience of filling has been comparatively calm and conservative, might he doubt that he has received a full experience?
MURRAY: One should not doubt. It often happens that Christians who have never been partakers of any such marked experiences, nevertheless have the fullness of the Spirit no less distinctly. In them it is expressed in their deep and intense devotion to Jesus, in a walk in the light of His countenance and the consciousness of His holy presence. Theirs is a life of simple trust and obedience, and the humility of a self-sacrificing love to all around.

Q: Do you mean there is really no single way of being filled or baptized with the Spirit?
MURRAY: The same illustration applies. There are farms

on which *both* the above kind of reservoirs are to be found at the same time, auxiliary to each other. There are even reservoirs in which both the modes of filling are made use of. The regular, quiet, daily inflowing keeps them supplied in time of great drought; in time of rain they are also ready to receive and store up large supplies. There are some Christians who are not content unless they have special, mighty visitations of the Spirit—the rushing mighty wind, floods outpoured and the baptism of fire—these are their symbols. There are others to whom the fountain springing up from within and quietly streaming forth appears to be their genuine response to the Spirit's work.

We should recognize God in *both* and hold ourselves always ready to be blessed in whichever way He chooses to come!

Q: Mr. Murray, please summarize for us what you personally believe is the biblical teaching on the filling of the Holy Spirit.
MURRAY:

I *must* be filled. It is absolutely *necessary.*
I *may* be filled. God has made it blessedly *possible.*
I *want* to be filled. It is eminently *desireable.*
I *will* be filled. It is so blessedly *certain.*

* * *

Writings by and about Murray and *books used in research (not intended to be exhaustive):

Abide in Christ
Aids to Devotion
Andrew Murray: Apostle of Abiding Love
Andrew Murray and His Message
The Believer's Absolute Surrender

The Believer's Call to Commitment
The Believer's Daily Renewal
*The Believer's Full Blessing of Pentecost
The Believer's New Covenant
The Believer's New Life
The Believer's Prayer Life
The Believer's School of Prayer
The Believer's Secret of Holiness
The Believer's Secret of Living Like Christ
The Believer's Secret of Obedience
The Believer's Secret of the Master's Indwelling
The Believer's Secret of a Perfect Heart
The Believer's Secret of Waiting on God
The Blood of the Cross
Day by Day
Daily Thoughts on Holiness
*Divine Healing
God's Best Secrets
The Inner Chamber
Jesus Christ: Prophet-Priest
Key to the Missionary Problem
*The Life of Andrew Murray of South Africa
*The Spirit of Christ
The Spiritual Life
*The State of the Church
*They Found the Secret
Working for God

Ruth Paxson

[1876-1949]

IN SEARCH
OF RIVERS

R
UTH PAXSON WAS BORN in Midwestern United
States and little is known of her early years
and education. She became a traveling secretary of the Young Women's Christian Association assigned to evangelistic work in eminent wom-
en's colleges on the East Coast. Among the schools in
her circuit were Smith, Mt. Holyoke, Vassar and Welles-
ley.

Ruth actively participated in the Student Volunteer
Movement and also traveled on its behalf speaking in
colleges and churches. Although already 35, she felt
God's call to missionary service and set sail for China in
1911 sponsored by the "Y." Later she severed any organizational connections and served as an independent
missionary ministering wherever opportunities presented themselves.

Her primary ministry was to newly-founded missionary schools for Chinese girls. Her personal work among

them resulted in many becoming Christians and assuming influential positions in China and in Christian leadership.

Ruth also felt God's special call to minister the deeper Christian experience to missionaries of many denominations and mission boards in China. She established a summer home in North China as a spiritual retreat for missionaries.

At age 49 Ruth wrote the book *Life on the Highest Plane* from which her smaller book, *Rivers of Living Water* was excerpted. She based most of her Bible messages on the theme of those books. One of the few American women invited to address the famous Deeper Life Conferences at Keswick in England and in America, she was much in demand for personal counselling.

Ruth never married and retired in Massachusetts where she died at the age of 73.

* * *

APPROXIMATE DATE: 1925

QUESTION: Miss Paxson, Christians seem to differ greatly in their success in living the Christian life. Why?
RUTH PAXSON: As a background to your question, let us recognize that we can't talk about Christians in a general way. There are *two* kinds of Christians clearly named and described in Scripture. It is of utmost importance for every Christian to know which kind he is and then determine which kind he wishes to be. Paul, in 1 Corinthians 3:1-4 speaks of Christians as either carnal or spiritual.

Q: What is the difference?
PAXSON: An unregenerate person, one who has not ac-

cepted Christ, has only one nature—the flesh, unable to please God and bent toward evil. He is called the natural man. When he is born again, a new nature, Christ's nature, comes also into him—that is of the spirit and desires to please God. Every believer then has two diverse laws warring against one another in the same personality. These two forces are absolutely contrary to each other, contesting for control. Sometimes the spiritual nature is in the ascendancy, and the believer enjoys momentary joy, peace and rest. But more often the fleshly nature is in control and there is little enjoyment of spiritual blessings.

Q: Why do believers continue to live as carnal Christians? Can't they determine to be spiritual?
PAXSON: The trouble is not with the will, for you may be very sincere in the decisions made and fully determine to carry them out (Romans 7:18). Who has not made countless resolutions at the dawn of a new day or of a new year regarding things we would or would not do? But our hearts have been repeatedly heavy with the humiliating sense of failure (Romans 7:15,19). It is a life of repeated defeat, of protracted infancy. The Bible says that such Christians remain "babes in Christ," barren and fruitless. Their walk does not correspond with their witness.

Q: Are we stuck with this inner conflict of two natures all our earthly lives?
PAXSON: There will still be conflicts in the life of the spiritual Christian, because growth comes through conquest in conflict. But there is deliverance. It must be a deliverance out of the condition of Romans 7 and into the experience of Romans 8. Then there is peace through conscious victory in Christ. The spiritual Chris-

tian does not continue in the practice of known, wilful sin, so he lives in the unclouded sunshine of Christ's presence.

Q: What is the life of the spiritual Christian like?

PAXSON: It is a life of habitual victory (1 Corinthians 15:57). If God has ever given you a victory over one sin, He can give you victory over all sin. He who has kept you from sin for a moment, can with equal ease keep you from the same sin for a day or a month (Romans 8:37; 2 Corinthians 2:14).

Q: Do you mean that the spiritual Christian is not able to sin?

PAXSON: No, not that he is not able to sin, but that he is able not to sin. Continuous sinning will not be the practice of his life. And it does not mean mere outward control over the expression of sin, but a definite dealing with the inner disposition to sin.

Q: Is this a kind of "holiness" teaching?

PAXSON: Every Christian is called to a holy life (1 Peter 1:15-16). But many Christians do not want to be holy. They may want to be spiritual but they are afraid to be holy. This may be due to misunderstanding of what holiness is through false teaching on this subject. Holiness is not sinless perfection, nor eradication of the sinful nature, nor is it faultlessness. It neither places one beyond the possibility of sinning nor removes the presence of sin.

Scriptural holiness is *blamelessness* in the sight of God. We are to be "preserved blameless" unto His coming, and we shall be "presented faultless" at His coming (1 Thessalonians 5:23; Jude 24). Holiness is Christ, our

Sanctification, enthroned as Life of our life. It is Christ, the Holy One, in us, living, speaking, walking.

Q: *Many Christians occasionally experience glorious freedom from some sin, but it doesn't seem to last. Is there really such a thing here on earth as habitual victory over all known sin?*
PAXSON: God says there is (Romans 8:12). On Calvary's cross Christ died to set us free from sin. To make that perfect victory permanent He has sent the Holy Spirit to indwell and control.

Q: *The spiritual life seems to be biblical and logical, but is it practical? It does not match most people's experience, almost too perfect in an imperfect world.*
PAXSON: God doesn't give any command or hold out any promise that is impossible to achieve. Whoever has Christ's life in any measure, may have it in its fullness, abundantly (John 10:10; Colossians 2:9–10). Basically, we are talking about the possibility of the fullness of the Holy Spirit in our lives, in other words, the Spirit-filled life.

Q: *Is the Holy Spirit a special gift for which the believer is to pray?*
PAXSON: No, the believer of the present age already receives the Holy Spirit when he is born again. Christ's twofold work was to take away sin and to baptize in the Spirit. Christ promised to bestow a gift upon the one who received Him as Savior, which would bring perfect satisfaction and sufficiency to him and then through him overflow in rich blessing into other lives. We are explicitly told what the gift was, "But this spake he of the Spirit, which they that believed on him were to receive . . ." (John 7:37–39).

Q: Don't believers today have to go through the same sequence as the disciples did—to pray for, wait for and receive the Holy Spirit?

PAXSON: No, because the Holy Spirit was sent into the world at a point in time when Jesus was glorified. After the resurrection when Christ returned to glory, He fulfilled His promise and sent back the Spirit. On the day of Pentecost the disciples in the upper room were baptized in the Spirit. From that day every one who has been organically and vitally united by faith with the living Lord has received the gift of the Holy Spirit. It is impossible to accept the Son and refuse or not have the Spirit (Romans 8:9).

Q: Is the Spirit-filled life only for special holy people who don't live in the mainstream of life?

PAXSON: It is God's purpose that every Christian should live a life of deep spirituality. It is not the privilege of a few but the prerogative of all and the need of all. One hundred and twenty were filled at Pentecost, and only 11 of them were apostles. Some were women who went back home to cook, to sew, to care for a family. Others were men who returned to the field and the shop. No one is too young or too old to be filled with the Spirit. It is not optional but obligatory. It is an express command for all believers to "be filled with the Spirit" (Ephesians 5:18).

Q: Since the Holy Spirit is dwelling in the believer, isn't that enough?

PAXSON: Not enough. The Spirit must be given full right of way to fill you from center to circumference. Permit Him to energize you with His mighty power through filling you with Himself. As refusal of life in Christ is the greatest sin of the unbeliever, so refusal of the

213

abundant life through the Spirit is the greatest sin of the
believer.

Q: *Does the filling of the Holy Spirit take place gradually as we learn more about Christ and grow spiritually?*
PAXSON: We must understand the distinction between
"filled," "full" and "fullness." "Be filled with the Spirit" is
a *crisis*; "Full of the Holy Spirit" is a *state*; "Filled unto all
fullness" is a *process*. The apostles were with Christ for
three years, but they were not filled with the Holy Spirit
until the day of Pentecost. This was a crisis. But they
were filled more than once, until we read of Stephen
and of Paul that they were "full of the Holy Ghost." This
was a state. But there was an inexhaustible, infinite
fullness from which they might draw according to their
receptive capacity, so there was a continuous infilling.
This was a process.

As for believers today, there should be a definite time
when we are "filled" for the first time. But there should
be repeated infillings to keep us habitually full and yet
ever taking in more and more of the fullness of God. To
be spiritual, one must *be* filled and *kept* filled.

**Q: *How do we know we have been filled? What are the
manifestations?***
PAXSON: Sometimes there is great confusion at this
point because one expects a spectacular manifestation
of so wonderful an experience. There is also much
unscriptural teaching on this subject which is leading
many astray. Scripture clearly teaches a threefold manifestation. First, the realization of Christ's abiding presence. The lives of the early Christians seemed charged
with a vivid, joyous consciousness of the presence of
their glorified Lord. He was very real to them. Second,

the reproduction of Christ's holy life by the fruit of the Spirit. Third, the re-enactment of Christ's supernatural power (Acts 1:8). As He sent His disciples forth to do a supernatural task, He promised to endue them with a supernatural power. Wherever He is in fullness, He manifests Himself in power.

Q: This seems to answer the original question of why Christians differ so much in power for living and witness. Is it because the powerless ones are carnal Christians?
PAXSON: Yes, and the fullness of the Holy Spirit is the only thing that will change a carnal Christian into a spiritual one. After the day of Pentecost when the apostles were filled with the Holy Spirit, even a casual comparison of their lives before Pentecost reveals a marvelous change.

Before, in spite of having been with Jesus for several years, they were characterized by failure, defeat, sin, jealously, ambition, selfishness, pride, cowardice, self-will, self-love and self-seeking. After the filling with the Holy Spirit, we see power, humility, love, courage, heavenly-mindedness and transformed lives. Rivers of living water began coursing through them into Jerusalem, Judea, Samaria and to the uttermost parts of the earth. Such is the evident change in a believer today who passes from the carnal life into the spiritual life.

Q: Would you please illustrate the difference between these two conditions?
PAXSON: It is the difference between having a water pot as did the Samaritan woman at the well, having to get it continually filled up, contrasted with having the well. The Spirit-filled life is one of satisfaction and sufficiency. The Holy Spirit is a well of Living Water, a

215

continuously upspringing fountain in every Christian. Jesus promised, you "shall never thirst!" If there is a divine inflow, there is always a divine outflow. Drink until you are satisfied, until you are full, until you overflow. The fullness of the Holy Spirit is for every one who thirsts.

Q: Suppose that a believer is thirsty for the abundant life. How does one actually become filled with the Spirit?

PAXSON: When you are physically thirsty, how do you get water into yourself? You drink. God has made the provision, but you must make the decision whether you will be Spirit-filled or not. There is a boundary line, the right of every person to choose, beyond which even God cannot go. God has set a feast before you, but He cannot compel you to eat. He has opened the door into the abundant life, but He cannot compel you to enter. He places in the bank a spiritual deposit that makes you a spiritual multimillionaire, but He cannot write your checks. God has done His part, now you must do yours. The responsibility for fullness or lack of fullness is now in your hands. God is hindered by one thing only – the room that you give Him to fill. You have a clearly defined part in becoming spiritual.

Q: Please explain further.

PAXSON: The basic principle in a spiritual life lies in its control. The Holy Spirit works to bring the Christian to refuse the further reign of self and to choose the sovereignty of Christ over his life by yielding to Him as Lord (Romans 6:16). To yield the life unconditionally to Christ is the first step to be filled with the Spirit and thereafter to walk in the Spirit.

216

Q: *Would you define yielding?*
PAXSON: It is the definite, voluntary transference of the undivided possession, control and use of the whole being—spirit, soul, and body—from self to Christ, to whom it rightfully belongs by creation and purchase. It is not *in order to be His,* but *because we are His* that we yield our lives to Him. Purchase gives title to property, but it is only delivery that gives possession.

Q: *Don't most believers take for granted they have already done that when they accepted Christ?*
PAXSON: Too many of us stop short with merely "giving our heart to the Lord" or "the saving of our soul." It is the easiest thing in the world to use the phraseology of consecration while missing the reality of it. It is necessary to understand the full measurement of a yielded life. Many of us think that God wants *things* from us. God is a Person. What He desires most is fellowship with a person, so He wants *us.* He asks first that we yield ourselves (2 Corinthians 8:5). He asks for the body as well as the spirit and soul (Romans 12:1). That includes every member of our body (Romans 6:13).

Q: *So then yielding or surrendering is like opening the door to Christ?*
PAXSON: That's it! (Revelation 3:20) Yielding to Christ is a definite act. It is not an oft-repeated wish that stops in mere desire, but a decisive act of the will. Desire becomes decision and decision crystallizes into action. You must say, "I do here and now yield myself unreservedly to Christ." It is always a voluntary act. God will never force you to it. With a smile and a song He wants you to open the door!

Q: *It would seem that this yielding could never be*

final because who can know what is ahead for the rest of his life?

PAXSON: *It is a final act.* If your yielding is such as I have described, then the act need never be repeated. If done honestly, it is for time and for eternity. It is a transaction of ownership. To repeat this initial act implies dishonesty and falseness in ever having done it.

Q: What should you do when you realize that something in your life is still not under His control?

PAXSON: You don't need to yield your life all over again. Simply say, "Lord, this thing was part of that whole which I yielded to Thee. It, too, belongs to that initial surrender. I did not see until now that it is still unyielded. Just now I yield this particular thing to Thee." Thus the initial act of yielding becomes a *continuous* attitude. Surrender is a crisis that develops into a process. The point is, once you have yielded, consciously keep every door unlocked and open to Christ as Lord.

Q: Some may say, as far as I know, I have yielded my life wholly to Christ; yet I still seem to be living on the plane of the carnal Christian. Is it possible to be yielded and yet not filled with the Holy Spirit?

PAXSON: Yes, the emptied, yielded life waits for *faith* to claim the fullness. Surrender says, "Lord, I am not my own. I present my body a living sacrifice." Faith says, "Christ liveth in me." Surrender says, "Lord, what wilt Thou have me to do?" Faith says, "I can do all things through Christ which strengthens me." Surrender crowns Christ Lord. Faith appropriates Christ as Life. Faith in itself has no power whatsoever to save or to keep us, but it links us with Christ who has that power.

Q: How can we apply this in a practical way to the Spirit-filled life?

PAXSON: Are you God's child? The Holy Spirit is already within you. Then, by virtue of your sonship, you may be filled with the Spirit. Why, then, do you not possess your birthright? It must be received as a gift. What does one usually do with a gift? He receives it and thanks the giver. That is precisely what God wants you to do with this wondrous gift of the Holy Spirit's fullness.

Don't make the mistake of continuing to pray for this fullness after you know that it is available, and after you know that you desire it. Don't keep refusing the gift until you think yourself worthy of it. Don't foolishly attempt through self-effort to make yourself full of the Spirit. And don't wait for some ecstatic feeling as proof of the infilling of the Spirit of God.

Q: *Yes, in view of your biblical explanation that would seem foolish.*
PAXSON: If you tell God that you long to be filled with the Holy Spirit and yet persist in doing these foolish things, either you are not honest and really do not want to be filled or else you do not believe that God is honest when He offers you the gift of the Spirit's fullness.

Are you honest? Do you truly want to be filled with the Holy Spirit? Then *acknowledge* the presence of the Holy Spirit within you, and *claim* His fullness as your birthright. Take the gift, thank the Giver, and use the gift immediately in winning souls to Christ. By an act of faith you may receive the Spirit's fullness. By a constant succession of acts of faith, the Spirit's fullness becomes habitual.

* * *

Writings by Paxson and *books used in research (not intended to be exhaustive):

RUTH PAXSON

*Life on the Highest Plane
*Rivers of Living Water
*The Wealth, Walk and Warfare of the Christian

Evan Roberts

[1878–1951]

FOOTBALL FEVER
AND
SPIRIT FERVOR

ORN AT LOUGHOR on the Glamorgan and Carmarthenshire border in Wales, Roberts never traveled far during his lifetime. His brief public ministry came into prominence, burned fiercely under the power of God, and diminished as quickly in the short months of the 1904–05 Welsh revival.

Roberts came from a poor but devout Christian family and was brought up in the Calvinistic Methodist Church. He worked in the coal mines in his youth. From his teen years he was burdened for the spiritually lost and wept and anguished for 11 years for revival in Wales.

Lacking formal education, he studied the Bible diligently and spent much time in prayer. Roberts entered a preparatory school for the ministry at Newcastle

Emlyn when he was about 26, just before revival broke out. He never completed his studies.

Roberts's praying more than his preaching sparked the revival which spread throughout Wales. People became convicted and converted with no visible leaders present. It was said that most of the population of Wales turned to Christ in repentance and faith. Roberts ministered with a team of Spirit-filled young people including his brother and sisters. His name became known throughout the world as revival spread to other countries.

Broken in health from the short but intense period of prayer, ministry, and what he regarded as conflict with Satanic forces, he retired from public view for the remaining 50 years of his life.

Roberts was convinced that he must go into exile to give himself to a ministry of prayer for worldwide revival. Years later he said, "By preaching I would reach the limited few, but by and through prayer I can reach the whole of mankind for God." Those in high positions and also the common people continued to seek him out for counsel. He was respected by all for being the channel God used so briefly to bring revival fires.

* * *

APPROXIMATE DATE: 1904

The proposed interview with Evan Roberts in Wales took an unexpected turn. Evan, the world-famous young revivalist, the most publicized preacher of his day, would not grant an interview. Instead of being able to question him directly about the Holy Spirit's work, we are going to see the Spirit in action in one of his meetings.

I was able to "interview" Evan's brother, Dan, with

whom I "attended" the meeting, asking Dan to explain what was going on. Evan was willing to make a few comments to me after the meeting concluded at three a.m. The year was 1904.

QUESTION: *Dan, I understand your brother, Evan, won't consent to an interview.*
DAN ROBERTS: Newspaper men from all over the world are after him. Many publishers are asking whether they might write about him, but he refused them all.

Q: *Why? I would think free publicity would increase attendance at his meetings.*
DAN: Evan believes that this awakening is of God and not from himself. If people idolize him, the Shekinah Glory would be withdrawn. He feels that the Holy Spirit would have none of it because it would rob God of the glory due to His holy name alone.

Q: *Is it true that sometimes Evan doesn't even announce when and where he will preach?*
DAN: That goes for all of our team. Evan simply states a day or two ahead, if at all, that he hopes to be in a certain place at a given time. Even then it is not sure when, where or *if* he is going to preach. He moves only with the Spirit. He feels it should be for God that people come to meetings. Sometimes he even leaves during a meeting if he senses that people came only to see and hear him. I have heard him plead with agonized spirit for the people to look away from him as the center of attraction and to Christ alone, or else the Holy Spirit would withdraw Himself from the movement. At other times he purposely refrained from speaking for this same reason. "I have nothing to offer

you. It is Jesus Christ who has the blessing for you," he tells them.

Q: Are there other preachers in this revival?
DAN: Oh yes. Now, at the height of the moving of God, there are at least a hundred pastors, evangelists and so-called lay people as God's instruments.

Q: Does Evan travel widely for preaching?
DAN: Actually, he doesn't. His ministry is confined to only one of the counties of Wales. The fire of God burned in towns and villages which he did not even visit. And in many places he did visit, he found the fire was already there. His visit only fanned the flame.

Q: Your team members seem unusually young.
DAN: Well, I'm 20, so is Sydney Evans, our teammate and my brother's closest friend. Evan is 26 and our sister Mary, actively witnessing with us, is 16. Our music group, "The Singing Sisters," ranges in age from 18 to 22.

Q: Incredible! I do see mostly young people going into the chapel.
DAN: I believe God is using youth in a unique way. Thousands of them, since they have become converted, are going everywhere testifying. Even little children have their own prayer and praise meetings.

Q: What education or training does Evan have for evangelism?
DAN: He worked in the coal mines from a very early age, then did blacksmithing. God's hand has been upon him for many years, and he felt called to preach, but he had no education. Actually, he had prayed for 15 years for a mighty visitation of the Holy Spirit. Just recently

he has become a student to prepare himself to serve God.

Q: Did something special happen in Evan's life to thrust him into the mainstream of such a revival?
DAN: Even before he went away to school, in our home in the countryside, God was revealing Himself to Evan in an amazing, overwhelming manner, which filled his soul with divine awe. He could not even explain it to us, but we all sensed it. About that time Evan went with his youth group to a Christian convention where, through an evangelist, God spoke to him and burned into his heart the prayer, "Bend me, O Lord!" The Holy Spirit came and melted his whole being by the revelation of Calvary love to his heart. From that point Evan had such a great burden for souls that he intercedes for the people of Wales with sweat, tears and agonized prayers.

Q: I heard that he had a vision that this revival would happen.
DAN: While at school and communing with God one midnight, he shared with Sydney that he had a vision of the mightiest revival Wales had ever known—that the Holy Spirit was coming and we must get ready, and that we must prepare a little team and go all over the country preaching. God gave him the faith to ask for 100,000 souls to be saved.

Q: Has that figure been reached?
DAN: Even more. It began with Evan being faithful to follow God's specific leading to go back to our home church and preach to our youth group for a week. A spontaneous revival broke out among them. A sense of the Lord's presence was everywhere—in the homes, on

the streets, in the mines, factories, schools and even in the drinking saloons and amusement places.

Q: Would you explain how you got the revival started—money, organization, advertising, personnel?

DAN: What has happened in Wales is a spontaneous spiritual awakening generated only by prayer, *not* a planned and organized evangelistic campaign. The astounding feature of this awakening is the lack of commercialism. There are no hymn books, no song leaders, no committees, no choirs, no great preachers, no offerings, no organization. As Lord Pontypridd remarked, "The revival finances and advertises itself. Therefore there are no bills, no hired halls, no salaries."

Q: Let's put it another way then—how did the Holy Spirit prepare Wales for this revival?

DAN: Some of our young Welsh pastors, after being fruitless and discouraged in their ministries, found the experience of the fullness of the Holy Spirit, and their preaching was absolutely transformed. Thousands started accepting Christ. This commenced about seven years ago when Evan was only 19. Through some of the Keswick Deeper Christian Life Conferences, the Spirit broke forth among many in glorious power. Here and there all over the country, pastors and their churches and thousands of people were broken before the Lord. They began without any compulsion from the outside to remove the hindrances from their lives, to surrender fully to Christ and to receive the Spirit in His fullness. Young people between 16 and 18 were especially touched and traveled with their pastors to preach in other towns with outstanding results. Churches were crowded out nightly.

Q: Who led the meetings?

DAN: It may seem strange to you, but they were carried on largely by the people themselves, although pastors were present. All day and all night the meetings would go on. In the evening after the services there were great processions marching through the towns singing hymns. This gave rise to much prayer all over the land. As many as 40,000 desperate and seeking believers, unknown to each other in most cases, in various parts of the land, had been waiting on the Lord for an even greater demonstration of the mighty power of God.

Q: There certainly must have been a holy atmosphere everywhere.

DAN: Just the opposite! It was a dark day in Wales. Religiously, higher criticism had upset the churches and caused many to be indifferent or doubters. Everywhere bars were crowded. Wales was in the grip of football fever when tens of thousands of working-class men thought and talked only of football. They gambled on the results of the games. Cock fighting, prize fighting, pigeon flying and betting and gambling on anything and everything were big in our country.

Q: It seems the meeting is beginning. Are we late? Maybe I misunderstood what time it was to start.

DAN: Time limits are of no consequence in these meetings. People gather an hour or two before the announced time, and meetings close whenever they end— maybe three a.m., if they began at seven the previous evening.

Q: When do people work? Surely life has not completely stopped in this country.

DAN: In many places all work does cease during Evan's

visits. Factories and shops sometimes close for one to three days so people can attend meetings. Miners often come directly from the pits in their coal-stained clothes.

Q: *The singing is tremendous! But I can't figure out who is leading the music, or who is leading the meeting, for that matter. There's no one on the platform.*
DAN: Evan always tells us, "We must obey the Spirit. He must control the meeting." The last person to lead the meeting in any way would be Evan. You can watch what we call "the influence of the power of the Spirit" playing over the congregation like wind rippling over the surface of a pond. There is no instrumental music and the pipe organs go unused. The Welsh are famous for their native gift of congregational singing—but this is more than that. Every person singing is like part of a huge musical instrument with every string swept by the breath of the Spirit of God.

Q: *I feel it! And the hymns never seem out of harmony with the theme of what the Spirit is doing among the people. The mood and purpose seem to bear testimony to a unity created only by the Spirit of God. Are there special singers though?*
DAN: There are soloists, some duets and singing groups, but they are never announced to sing. When they do sing, it is under the compulsion of the Spirit. They are never called upon by the evangelist. When they are present, sometimes they sing, sometimes they don't, according to the prompting of the Spirit. The young ladies in the groups, sometimes instead of singing, break out in fervent prayer and exultation. And sometimes when they do rise to sing they aren't able to finish

the song because they are so overcome by the power of God.

Q: The format of the meeting seems to be—well, there doesn't seem to be any. Prayer by just anybody and everybody all at one time, praise and exclamations of adoration, just anytime, no matter what else is going on—testimonies, little sermons by anyone who wants to speak. . . .

DAN: That's it. The people themselves carry on the meeting under the influence of the Spirit, leader or no leader. That simultaneous prayer is something new that just happened in this revival. We were not accustomed to everyone praying aloud at once, sometimes for hours, standing, sitting, kneeling. Young people and even children pray boldly and freely.

Q: Why is that small boy coming to the platform?

DAN: He is waiting for a break in the meeting—now he reads a portion in Welsh from his Bible and goes back to his seat. He has obeyed the Spirit.

Q: Who is that person who stood to sing one verse of a hymn and then broke into sobbing?

DAN: He is a newly converted young miner. Now the congregation takes up the hymn and sings it over and over, deeply moved.

Q: I counted—they sang the chorus, "O, for thee He is waiting," almost 40 times! The building seems filled with the glory of the Lord! But it is not disorderly. Everyone is very sober and serious. One can't deny that there is a lot of emotion though.

DAN: When thousands of people are convicted of their sins by the Spirit and are gloriously saved by the grace of God, even right in the meeting, how can they contain their joy? Why should they quench it? And when believers are filled with the Spirit and mountains of hindrances are melted from their lives, they are drunk with the new wine of the Spirit. They are oblivious to everything other than their blessed Lord Jesus.

The same people who criticize emotionalism in our response to Christ believe in full expression of it in the football stadium. Tens of thousands in our stadiums are hypnotized and drunk with the sport. They pack the stadiums in all kinds of weather.

Q: *That fellow giving a testimony looks like an athlete.*
DAN: He is W. Rogers, one of Wales's most famous football players. Many of them are now converted and join open-air street meetings to testify what glorious things the Lord has done for them. Many of the teams have been disbanded because the players are now involved in full-time witness and the stadiums are empty anyway. Some of the players hold underground prayer meetings in the coal pits.

Q: *Is there preaching from the pulpit against football?*
DAN: Not at all, nor against any of the other social evils. *Only Christ is preached*, and when people experience a new life in Him they have new interests and desires.

Q: *There must be about 1,500 people crowded into this church. Are they all local people?*
DAN: The majority are, but there are a lot of strangers. Outstanding Christian leaders from all over the world have come to Wales especially to see what the Holy Spirit is doing. F.B. Meyer, Gypsy Smith, G. Campbell Morgan, General Booth—all have been here.

Q: Are such noted leaders asked to speak when they come?

DAN: No. At most they may pray or join with others in praise while they remain seated with the congregation — never on the platform. Generally they sit quietly recognizing that here is a revival that has not come through great preachers or great preaching, but a supernatural work altogether apart from either. They feel that their very personalities would hinder the meetings. And why should great Christian leaders preach sermons when here before them they see their sermons fulfilled? It really doesn't matter whether they have seen or heard Evan at all. They have said that it was worth coming even from Australia, New Zealand or America just to hear the dynamic testimonies of the spiritual experiences of the Christians in Wales.

Q: Is your brother going to preach tonight?

DAN: I really don't know. Sometimes he comes and just sits among the people for three hours praying quietly. Then he might stand up, pray or preach for 10 or 15 minutes and then sit down. The people then carry on in the Spirit. Oh, there he comes now, trying to make his way through the crowd jamming the aisles.

Q: He is speaking in Welsh. Would you interpret for me please?

DAN: Evan is praying, committing the service to Jesus through the Holy Spirit, asking to put us all under His blood. In the name of Jesus he is binding the devil this moment and asking us to open our hearts to Calvary love. Claiming victory. Claiming the Holy Spirit's work on us all. Asking God to speak in power to us. Now people all over the audience are praying, standing up in the balcony, all over, some shouting, "Lord, save me!"

231

Shouts of praise. Now singing again. Evan begins his message now. He is not long speaking when he, himself, is broken down. He is trying again to picture the depths of the suffering Savior for us. Now he is interrupted by people standing up and testifying of being saved right this moment. Now a hymn. The whole crowd is on its feet, swayed by intense spiritual enthusiasm and pouring out feelings in praise, more hymns of worship, and messages from the Bible from unknown persons. . . .

Q: Why doesn't the crowd let Evan speak? He did not get to finish his message.
DAN: He is very sensitive to the Spirit. Doesn't want to hinder what God is doing by putting himself forward. Now he starts again. No, he is interrupted again. A little girl in the balcony with a thin, piping voice is beginning to unburden her soul in prayer. Evan waits.

Q: The congregation is crying "Hush! Sh!" to her. They want to hear Evan.
DAN: Evan is motioning to stop the rebuking voices and is waiting until the little girl is finished. I think he will not go on preaching. Almost a hundred persons are on their feet engaged in prayer at one time. Do you notice, though, how everything seems to be in perfect harmony? All are gloriously conscious of the wonderful presence of God in our midst by the Holy Spirit. See how radiantly happy Evan is? He knows the Holy Spirit is in control, not he.

Q: Now it is nearly three in the morning. People are leaving. Shall we go? I have a few more questions if you aren't too tired.
DAN: Go right ahead. Let's wait outside. Perhaps you can meet Evan for a few minutes before he leaves.

Q: Good. I still wonder about the concrete results of this kind of moving of the Spirit. Do people spend all their time in meetings and neglect Bible study?

DAN: On the contrary, many of the recent prayer meetings have resolved themselves into serious Bible classes. A great interest in the Holy Scriptures has resulted from this revival. And the Bible Society's records show that over three times as many Bibles were being sold after the revival broke out as before. The new converts are immediately being instructed in the Word and the believers who are now filled with the Spirit are eagerly absorbing the Bible.

Q: How about changes in society? That's where the real test comes.

DAN: In some towns a drunken man is a thing of the past and police are having an easy time of it. Street disturbances have become conspicuous by their absence. Longstanding debts are paid, stolen goods returned, taverns forsaken, language is cleaned up. Political meetings have had to be postponed during the revival because members of the Houses of Parliament were taking part in the revival meetings. Theatrical companies are making sure they don't come to Wales because they know they would go bankrupt. Prisons are empty. Even in universities, revival scenes are commonplace during these past few months.

Q: Oh, here comes Evan! He must be exhausted, but I can't believe how his serious, handsome face doesn't show any stress from such an experience. May I ask you only one question, Mr. Roberts? How would you explain the Holy Spirit's part in all that is going on in this movement?

EVAN: First, we need to define the Holy Spirit as personally as the Bible does. That prepares us for what He wants to do. Do you know what people called Him in the past? They called Him "something." If we speak of Him thus, we shall remain without the Spirit.

We should not pray, "Send power down!" There is no need. The Holy Spirit is with us already. I realize that He is here. We need not pray that He should come. In the second chapter of Acts you will find that He has already been sent. We have an accurate account that He came. Have you any account that He went back?

Our prayer should be, "Open our hearts to receive Him!" The Spirit is calling us continually, but the danger is that we don't heed His voice. *Obedience, obedience, obedience*—that is the great thing! It is no good getting thousands of people to churches unless we learn the lesson of obedience to the Spirit. If we speak of the Spirit, we must obey the Spirit. And from doing that, great results are sure to follow. If I had not given up everything to the Spirit, I should not be here today. I am obliged to say things that make some people regard me almost as insane. But though the whole world sneers at me, I know that I must obey the Spirit!

* * *

Writings by and about Roberts and *books used in research (not intended to be exhaustive):

*The Great Revivalists
*Invasion of Wales by the Spirit: Through Evan Roberts
  (Also titled When the Spirit Came)
*Pioneers of Revival

Albert Benjamin Simpson

[1843–1919]

THE ULTIMATE
TRANSFORMER

ORN AT BAY VIEW, Prince Edward Island, Canada, Simpson was of Scottish ancestry. Known as a mischievous lad, he liked to sneak off to go hunting. At age 14, he felt God's call to the ministry.

Because he lacked financial help from his family, Simpson struggled to study on his own, and became overworked and ill. His conversion took place during that difficult period. He successfully worked his way through Knox College at the University of Toronto, winning several awards and scholarships.

After graduation he was ordained, accepted his first

pastorate in Hamilton, Ontario, and was married the next day. Later pastorates took him to Louisville, Kentucky, and to New York City where he founded the Gospel Tabernacle in 1882.

Simpson published the *Alliance Life* magazine (then titled, *The Word, Work and World,* and later, *The Alliance Weekly*) and authored close to 100 books on Christian doctrine and living. His extensive ministry involved conventions, camp meetings, evangelistic campaigns and missionary convocations. Out of his missionary labors came the Evangelical Missionary Alliance, which later became The Christian and Missionary Alliance.

* * *

APPROXIMATE DATE: 1915

QUESTION: *Dr. Simpson, what were you missing even in the midst of your outstanding success in public ministry?*
A.B. SIMPSON: I had always felt a great lack of spiritual power for life and service. My personal life was the conflict of Romans chapter seven. It was by reading W.E. Boardman's book, *The Higher Christian Life,* that I was awakened to the truth of the filling of the Holy Spirit and led to seek it.

Looking back, I would say there were three experiences which mark great epochs in my life. The first, when I accepted Jesus as my Savior. Fifteen years later I believed in Jesus as my Sanctifier. Seven years after that Christ showed me it was His blessed will to be my complete Savior for my body as well as my soul.

Q: *Isn't the filling of the Holy Spirit a part of the conversion experience?*
SIMPSON: No, the coming of the Holy Spirit to a human

heart is the second great epoch of our spiritual life. It marks a crisis just as distinct as conversion itself.

Q: What is implied in the word "fill"?

SIMPSON: The emphatic word "filled" in both Ephesians 5:18, "be *filled* with the Spirit," and Colossians 2:10, "ye are *complete* in Him," is the Greek *pleroo*. It means to fill full, so full that there will be no room left empty.

It does not mean to have only a measure of the Holy Spirit, but to be wholly filled with and possessed by the Holy Ghost—to be utterly lost in the life and fullness of Jesus. It is the completeness of the filling which constitutes the essence of the sanctified life.

All is connected with a living Person. We are not filled with an influence; we are not filled with a sensation; we are not filled with a set of ideas and truths; we are not filled with a blessing—we are filled with a Person. Christianity centers in a living Person and its very essence is the indwelling life of Christ Himself. This Person is the true fullness of *every part* of our life.

Q: Is there a difference between having the Spirit and being filled with the Spirit?

SIMPSON: Yes, there is a difference. It is true that there is a measure of the Holy Spirit's life in every regenerate soul, that He is given to all who accept the Lord Jesus. But the Holy Spirit is given to believers in very diverse measures. He is the agent in conversion and regeneration. But it is a very different thing when the converted soul voluntarily yields itself in surrender and dedication and invites the Holy Spirit to fill and control its life. Then the Holy Spirit becomes not only the builder of the house but the ever-present occupant. The abiding of John 15 has become a reality; we abide in Christ and He abides in us. He does not become the Abiding Guest of the heart until there is full surrender.

It is when every part of our being is filled with His love and possessed for His glory that we are wholly sanctified and we bring forth all the fruit of the Spirit and manifest His gifts.

Q: *Could you illustrate the difference?*
SIMPSON: We all easily understand the difference between the shallow stream and the overflowing river. In both cases there is water; in one case it is a weak current, while in the other it is an overflowing stream that drives the innumerable wheels of the factories along the shores. The power all comes from the fullness which causes the overflow.

Again, we can understand the difference between a boiler full of water and a boiler full of boiling water. In one case it is only water which fills, but has no power; in the other it is the water converted into steam, driving the wheels of a mighty engine and carrying cars across the continent along the railroad track. That single degree of temperature makes all the difference in the world between power and impotence.

Paul explains it in Second Timothy 1:6 when he speaks of "stirring up the gift of God which is in thee." The gift was already bestowed and fully recognized, but it was like an expiring flame – the embers of the fire were falling into ashes, and the flame was almost dead. The word used is *rekindle* the fire – be filled with the Spirit.

Q: *Doesn't First Corinthians 12:13 indicate only the one experience of being baptized into one body at conversion?*
SIMPSON: You are referring to "For by one Spirit are we

all baptized into one body, whether we be Jews or Gentiles, whether we be bond or free; and have been all made to drink into one Spirit." Well, it is one thing to be baptized into the one body by the Spirit; it is another thing to drink of that one Spirit. The first is an act; the second is a habit. The first brings us into a relationship; the drinking of His fullness until we become filled is the habit of abiding in His fullness so that we are always filled.

Q: Why did Jesus say "from within you" shall flow rivers of living water? Isn't the filling of the Spirit an action upon us?
SIMPSON: The secret of this is that the direction has been changed. We do not have to bring the Spirit down now because He is here. There is no need for excitement, noisy demonstration and incantations. Faith can calmly take what the Spirit is lovingly waiting to give. The rivers – note that it is not only one river but many outflowing streams – are flowing out, not in. The Spirit is already indwelling; the waters are there.

Numbers 21:16–18 illustrates this. The people were thirsty and there was no water in sight. They gathered in a circle on the sand and dug a well, accompanying the digging with a song of faith and invocation, "Spring up, O well, sing ye unto it." The waters began to gush up from subterranean fountains and they drank in abundance. The waters were running as a river beneath their feet all the time; all they had to do was dip in the river and drink to satisfy their thirst.

We may not always see the river of God's fullness flowing in our lives, nor be distinctly conscious of the Spirit's gracious presence. Often we shall be entirely without religious feeling or emotion. But the Holy Spirit is still there in the depths of our subconscious being. In the moment of need we can, like them, dig a well by faith and prayer, best of all by song and praise, and lo, the fountains will gush forth. The living waters will flow and our happy hearts will sing, "There is a river whose streams make glad the city of our God."

Q: *Would you share more specifically what happened to you in your second crisis experience?*
SIMPSON: One day my heart's full consecration was made with unreserved surrender. I entered upon a consecrated, crucified and Christ-devoted life. I used to think that we were sanctified at the last moment before entering heaven. But the Lord Jesus Christ tells us that we are sanctified in order to serve Him here. Separation must come first, then consecration and the filling of the Spirit – the first two are our work, the third is His.

Q: *Do you teach that we become perfected and sinless at the moment we are filled with the Holy Spirit?*
SIMPSON: First, may I say emphatically that I believe this experience of Christ our Sanctifier marks a definite and distinct crisis in the history of a soul. We do not grow into it but we cross a definite line of demarcation as clear as when the hosts of Joshua crossed the Jordan over into the promised land. They set up a great heap of stones so that they would never forget that crisis hour.

That being clear, I do not preach *perfection* but a *perfect Christ* abiding in the sanctified believer. Sanctification is *divine holiness*, not human self-improvement nor perfection. It is the inflow into man's being of the life and purity of God's own perfection and the working out of His own will. We remain as insignificant and insufficient as ever. It is the Person who dwells within us who possesses and exercises all the gifts and powers of our ministry. Only as we abide in Him and He works in us are we able to exercise this power.

Q: It is still somewhat of a gradual process, is it not?
SIMPSON: It is *complete* but not *completed*; it is *perfect* but not *perfected*. The true attitude of the consecrated heart is that of constant yielding and constant receiving. This view of sanctification gives boundless scope to our spiritual progress.

It is here that the *gradual* phase of sanctification begins. Commencing with a complete separation from evil and dedication to God, it now advances into all the fullness of Christ and grows up to the measure of the stature of perfect manhood in Him. Then every part of our being and every part of our life is filled with God and becomes a channel to receive and a medium to reflect His grace and glory.

Q: When the Holy Spirit brings some new grace or gift into prominence in our life and work, is that another baptism?
SIMPSON: The possibilities of the indwelling Spirit are limitless and infinitely varied. He works in us at different times as may seem best to His sovereign will. But we are not, therefore, to say that our old experience is void and that we have received a new baptism of the Spirit. It is the same blessed wellspring flowing in new streams and springing up in new fullness.

Q: Is the baptism with fire different from the baptism with the Holy Spirit?
SIMPSON: It is not different but simply an expletive phrase qualifying and completing the thought expressed in the first phrase. The Holy Ghost is Himself a divine fire, and when He takes possession of a soul, His opera-

tions are similar to the effect of fire in the natural world.

The baptism with fire, however, suggests a stronger and more searching operation of the Spirit. He has a purifying, refining and consuming effect within us as does a fire. There are things in all of us that we are not able to eliminate ourselves and would give any price to have consumed. God's fire burns out our inmost being. The Holy Ghost kindles the flame that melts our selfishness and pours out our being in tenderness, sacrifice and service.

The same fire of love is the fusing, uniting flame, which makes Christians one, even as the volcanic tide that rolls down the mountain fuses into one current everything in its course. Above all things, fire is the mightiest of forces. It drives our engines and propels our commerce. It is the only thing that can move the heart of man and the church of God. Oh, for the fire of the Holy Ghost!

Q: What are some of the evidences of the filling of the Holy Spirit?

SIMPSON: In the first place, to be filled with the Spirit will bring us the fullness of Jesus. The person and work of the Holy Ghost must never be recognized apart from the person of Christ—to do this is sure to lead us into spiritualism. The Holy Ghost never comes to us apart from Jesus because the blessed Spirit witnesses not of Himself but of the Lord Jesus Christ. Let us be very careful of this. The more we are filled with the Holy Ghost, the more we recognize Christ, depend upon Christ, live upon Christ alone.

Therefore, this very word "filled" is used in connection with Christ in Colossians 2:9-10, "In him dwelleth all the fulness of the Godhead bodily. And ye are complete in him." Literally translated, it is ". . . and ye are filled with Him." God fills Jesus; Jesus fills us. To be filled with the Spirit is to be filled with Christ and to so live that our constant experience and testimony will be, "I live; yet not I, but Christ liveth in me."

Q: *What is the nature of the power we receive from the Holy Spirit?*
SIMPSON: The right translation of Acts 1:8 is ". . . ye shall receive the power of the Holy Ghost coming upon you. . ." It is not your power, but His power. It is not abstract power under your control, but it is a Person whose presence with you is necessary to your possessing and retaining the power. He has the power and you have Him. So the power of the Holy Ghost is power from above, received from Him moment by moment.

Q: *Is this power mainly for serving the Lord?*
SIMPSON: It is *not* primarily power for service, but it is also power to receive the life of Christ; power *to be*, rather than *to say* and *to do*. Our service and testimony will be the outcome of a life filled with the Holy Spirit.

Q: *Are there more evidences of this filling?*
SIMPSON: The fruit of the Holy Spirit listed in Galatians chapter five spring spontaneously from the fullness; a life of holiness, righteousness and obedience develops. Our mind and understanding is filled with knowledge and light. He controls our thoughts with harmony, sweetness, strength and peace.

Q: *Will our physical bodies be affected or are the evidences purely spiritual?*
SIMPSON: Yes, our very bodies will feel the fullness. The Holy Ghost is a true tonic for physical energy and good

health. The fullness of the Spirit is the elixir for body and brain and being. To be filled with His blessed life will make our feet spring, our nerves steady, our brain strong, our circulation regular and our whole being at its best for God and holy service.

Beside that, our very circumstances will keep time to the blessed fullness of the heart within. As the presence of God touches everything that comes into our life, we will find that all things work together for good to us if we love God and fulfill His purpose. Our circumstances will become adjusted to us, or we become adjusted to our circumstances. The whole of our life, "fitly framed together," will become full of vigor, full of power and blessing.

Q: Does the quickening power of the Spirit on our bodies referred to in Romans 8:11 happen at the resurrection?

SIMPSON: I believe that verse is usually given the wrong exegesis. It is not the Spirit but Jesus' voice that shall raise the dead; the Spirit does not dwell in dead bodies; the bodies spoken of are "mortal." I believe it refers to our bodies *here and now*. It means the invigorating, vitalizing, stimulating of a body weak and failing. It precisely applies to the healing of disease by the touch of the Holy Spirit.

If He dwells in the house, He will repair it and take good care of it. We are thus introduced to God's great secret of true physical life. It is not nerve force, muscular force, the effect of food and air and constitution—although these have their place and none of them must be neglected or despised. But it is a direct infusion into our mortal frame and our vital centers of a supernatural and divine vitality through the Holy Ghost.

This is something not communicated by drugs or

electrical applications, or even air and food; it is life from the primal source of life, the Creator Himself. It is another kind of life, a higher kind of life, an added life. That is the very life of which Paul writes in Second Corinthians 4:11, "The life also of Jesus might be made manifest in our mortal flesh."

Q: Does the filling of the Spirit also affect our minds?
SIMPSON: Christ will fill all the needs of our intellectual life. Our mental capacities will never know their full wealth of power and spiritual effectiveness until they become simply the vessels of His quickening life. These brains of ours are to be laid at His feet simply as the censers which are to hold His holy fire. The fullness of the Holy Spirit will be within us a perpetual source of physical and mental energy, sufficient for every function and test of human life.

Q: Are the supernatural manifestations and gifts of the Spirit still for us today?
SIMPSON: They were never intended to be interrupted. But let us never make the mistake of regarding them as a goal, or allowing them to take the place of the higher truths that relate to our spiritual life. At the same time, let us not ignore them. The church is one through all the ages: "Jesus Christ, the same yesterday, and today, and forever." The Holy Spirit is unchanged, and the design of the church today is identical with First Corinthians 12 and the plan which God gave at Pentecost.

Q: Some teach that we should minimize the supernatural aspects of the Holy Spirit's power and emphasize the greatest miracle of all—salvation through the gospel.
SIMPSON: We cannot leave out any part of the gospel

without weakening the rest. If there ever was an age when the world needed the witness of God's supernatural working, it is in this day of unbelief and Satanic power.

Q: Do you think the supernatural aspects might even be accelerated today?

SIMPSON: We ought to expect yet more wonderful manifestations in these last days before the coming of the Lord Jesus Christ. As the end approaches the Holy Ghost will work in the healing of sickness, in the casting out of demons, in remarkable answers to prayer, in special and wonderful providences and in such ways as may please His sovereign will.

Q: What will be the effect on the world?

SIMPSON: It will prove to an unbelieving world that the power of Jesus' name is still unchanged and "all the promises of God in Him are yea, and in Him, Amen, forever." Let us not fear to claim His power for our physical as well as our spiritual needs.

Q: What is your view on the gifts of the Spirit?

SIMPSON: Much attention is being given at this time to the supernatural gifts of the Spirit. No Bible Christian can for a moment question the value and permanency of these gifts which the apostle describes so fully in the 12th chapter of First Corinthians. There is every reason to believe that all these gifts were meant to be in operation in the church of Christ until the end of the age. There is an apparent revival of them at the present time.

Q: To which gifts are you referring?

SIMPSON: The one most especially in evidence of late is the gift of tongues. Along with this we sometimes hear the teaching of the extreme view that this gift is *essential evidence* of the baptism of the Holy Spirit. That is most unscriptural.

Q: In what respect?
SIMPSON: In the first place, the erroneous teaching referred to is sure to lead people to seek for manifestations and peculiar experiences rather than for God Himself. That will decentralize and distract the heart from its supreme goal.

In the next place, such teaching is directly contrary to the emphatic statement of the apostle that the Holy Spirit exercises His sovereignty in bestowing these gifts on whomsoever He will. He knows the particular forms of divine enduement that are best suited for our different ministries and qualifications.

More important still, such a view would place undue emphasis on spectacular gifts rather than the spirit of love, and turn us aside from the practical and useful to the sensational.

Q: What is the scriptural balance of the gifts of the Spirit?
SIMPSON: The true scriptural balance is to make the Lord Jesus Himself the central object of our thought and affection, to seek to be filled with His Spirit for His service and glory. We are to cultivate the disposition of love and the graces that tend to make us a blessing to others. Then we can trust Him to give to us and to others whatever special gifts He sees best suited to each of us.

Q: What safeguards does the Bible give for the use of the Spirit's gifts?
SIMPSON: Their exercise in Christian work and worship

is carefully regulated by the apostle in the 14th chapter of First Corinthians. Certain principles are clearly laid down which should control the worship of the assembly. The first is edification. Nothing should be encouraged that does not tend to promote the spiritual good of the largest number. The second is order. All confusion, extravagance and exaggerated emotion should be avoided. The third is self control. "The spirits of the prophets are subject to the prophets." Even the Holy Spirit does not take away our mental poise or expect us to surrender our common sense and will or yield ourselves to any hypnotic influence.

But above all else we are exhorted to seek for the grace of love. Not only is it the highest end to be pursued, but it is the surest means of accomplishing the very goal that many are pursuing—a deeper filling of the Spirit. The apostle says, "I show unto you a more excellent way," and that is a better way for obtaining the blessing you seek. That way is to forget yourself in a spirit of love and aim to be a blessing to others.

Q: *Many Bible teachers differ with you on the necessity of waiting to receive the filling of the Holy Spirit.*
SIMPSON: The promises of God are for those who wait for Him. The spiritual life, in some respects instantaneous in its operations, is progressive in others. There is a moment when we definitely receive the Holy Ghost. But there is a preparation for His coming, and a waiting for His fullness in us.

Q: *How can we wait for the Spirit's coming since He has already come at Pentecost and is now dwelling in the believer?*
SIMPSON: Doubtless there is a sense of waiting which people in the Old Testament and the disciples before

Pentecost experienced, which cannot be true of us. For them the Holy Ghost was not yet sent from heaven. After Pentecost, in that same sense, we cannot wait for the coming of the Comforter, for indeed He has come and He is here. But there is a preparation *on our part* just as necessary in these days.

Q: *Please define the nature of our waiting.*
SIMPSON: It is not waiting *for* the Lord, but it is waiting *on* the Lord. It is not looking forward to a distant blessing, but it is continuing in the attitude of receiving and claiming the blessing, giving time for the Holy Spirit to fill the waiting heart with all His fullness. It is more than expectation of a future blessing. It is rather accepting a present blessing, and yet a blessing so large and full that it cannot be taken by us in all its completeness in a moment of time. It requires the opening of every vessel of our being and the continuance of our heart in the attitude of receiving.

Q: *Does waiting benefit us personally?*
SIMPSON: God uses seasons of waiting to mark great transitions in our lives, epochs of spiritual new departure, when we are led to new planes and new advances. Sometimes it is very desirable that there should be a complete break, to get us out of the old ruts, that we may become free to take a higher place and make a bolder advance.

Another reason is the necessity to cease from ourselves. As with the disciples who had to wait before Pentecost, the greatest danger for them was not in what they might *fail* to do, but in what they might *try* to do. The greatest harm that we can do is the attempt to do anything at all when we are not prepared and when we do not understand our Master's will. They waited for days and learned to be silent. They formed the habit of suspension of their own activity and the dependence of their own will entirely upon the direction of the Holy Ghost.

There are times when the most masterly thing we can exercise is inactivity; there are times when the most mischievous thing we can do is to do anything at all.

Q: Does waiting contribute to the emptying of ourselves which you said was essential before filling?

SIMPSON: There is no wiser nor better thing to do on the eve of a season of blessing than to make an inventory—not of our riches, but of our poverty. We need a time to count up all the voids and vacuums and places of insufficiency. We need to make the valley full of ditches and then to bring to God the depths of our need for Him to fill them. For that reason, too, God wants us to go apart and quietly wait upon Him, until He searches into the depths of our being and shows us our folly, our failures and our need.

There are some spiritual conditions that cannot be accomplished in a moment. The breaking up of the fallow ground takes time; the frosts of winter are as necessary as the rains of spring to prepare the soil for fertility. God has to break our hearts to pieces by the slow processes of His discipline and grind every particle to powder. Then He can mellow us and saturate us with His blessed Spirit until we are open for the blessing He has to give us.

Q: What makes waiting so essential?

SIMPSON: There is a cumulative power in waiting prayer to bring the answer and the blessing, breath by breath, and moment by moment. We must drink, and drink, and drink again, and yet again if we would know all the fullness of the river of His grace.

Sometimes our hearts are so dry that we need to wait upon the Lord for days and days before there is any impression. But all the while the dry ground is filling, and the thirsty soil is absorbing. After the waiting is completed, we shall know that it was not in vain.

We do not wait enough upon the Lord. We do not spend sufficient time at the Mercy Seat. We allow the rush and hurry of life to drive us off, and we lose time by our reckless haste instead of gain it.

Q: How did you personally come into the third crisis of your life concerning healing?
SIMPSON: I saw cases where God did definitely heal and I never doubted or questioned them. For myself, however, the truth had no really practical or effectual power, for I never could feel that I had any clear authority in a given case of need to trust myself to Him.

Q: Was your own physical condition so robust that healing was not a significant need?
SIMPSON: On the contrary, for more than 20 years I suffered from many physical infirmities and disabilities. When I was only 14 and preparing for college, I developed a nervous prostration from overwork in studying. The doctor did not even permit me to look at a book for months.

As an ambitious pastor at 21, I plunged headlong into my work and again broke down with heart trouble, necessitating months of rest.

Several times in my life it seemed as if I would die. I recovered only in part with the aid of constant remedies and preventatives. I never went anywhere without ammonia in my pocket to revive me from my suffocating agonies. Two other collapses of long duration over-took me. Only a few months before I took Christ as my Healer, a prominent physician in New York told me that I did not have constitutional strength enough to last more than a few months.

Q: How did you begin to move toward faith in God's healing?
SIMPSON: Through the simple words of a song I hap-pened to overhear while at a campground: "My Jesus is the Lord of lords; No man can work like Him." Such an ordinary thought—but it fascinated me, possessed my whole being and seemed like a voice from heaven. So I took Him also to be *my* Lord of lords, and to work *for me.*

Soon after, while resting at the seashore at Old Or-chard, Maine, I heard a great number of people testify that they had been healed by simply trusting the Word of Christ, just as they would for salvation. It drove me to my Bible. I determined that I must settle this matter one way or the other. I am so glad I did not go to other people.

At His feet, alone, with my Bible open, and with no one to help or guide me, I became convinced that this was part of Christ's glorious gospel for a sinful and suffering world, for all who would believe and receive His Word. That was enough. I could not believe this and then refuse to take it *for myself.* I felt that I dare not hold any truth in God's Word as a mere theory or teach to others what I had not personally proved.

Q: What did you do about it?
SIMPSON: That Friday afternoon at three o'clock I went out into the silent pine woods—I remember the very spot—and there I raised my right hand to heaven and

made three great and eternal pledges, as if I had seen God before me face-to-face: I believed healing to be part of God's Word; I would henceforth take Jesus as Lord for all my physical life; and I solemnly promised *to use this blessing* for the glory of God and the good of others in speaking and ministry in the future.

Q: *Did you immediately enjoy the restoration of perfect health?*
SIMPSON: Physically I do not think I am even now any more robust than before. But I am intensely conscious with every breath that I am drawing my vitality from a directly supernatural source, and that it keeps pace with the calls and necessities of my work. I believe and am sure that it is nothing else than the life Christ manifested in my mortal flesh.

A few months after my healing God called me into a special pastoral, literary and missionary work which has since engaged my time and energy. It has involved much more labor than any previous period of my life.

I desire to record my testimony to the honor and glory of Christ that it has been a continual delight and much easier in every way than the far lighter tasks of former years. I am conscious, however, all the time, that I am not using my own natural strength but His.

Q: *Once healed by the Lord, is a person thereafter immune from sickness?*
SIMPSON: Not at all. I have felt myself to be wholly dependent upon a vital and continuous connection with the Lord for His life. There was a time when my physical strength, like a heap of ashes, was burned out. But lo! I found a vessel of oil, the blessed Holy Ghost. As God poured His fullness on my exhausted frame, a divine strength came, full of sweet exhilaration and

unwearied buoyancy and energy. In that light and life of God I am working without exhaustion and trust still to work in His glorious all-sufficiency until my work is done.

Q: Faith healing became part of your ministry after that?

SIMPSON: I, and my friends associated with me in this ministry, do not use that term "faith healing" nor "faith cure." We always say "divine healing" because we believe that *faith* has no power intrinsically to cure anybody. The real power in every case of true healing must be a personal God and not a mere subjective state of mind in the person concerned or anybody else.

Q: Do you sponsor meetings where people might be healed?

SIMPSON: Friday afternoon meetings for healing began in my own home in 1883 and have been carried on uninterruptedly since then in various meeting places. Teaching on healing, testimonies of those healed, requests for prayer from those present and from all over the world are shared. The meeting always closes with an anointing service according to the instruction in the epistle of James.

Other "Homes for Physical Healing" have been carried on for many years in other places in New York and cities of the East and Midwest. People may come and stay or attend meetings for biblical instruction on healing and for healing itself.

Q: Under what circumstances do you believe in anointing with oil for healing?

SIMPSON: I believe the Bible teaches it and we practice it—but not indiscriminately. I am careful to instruct those receiving it to look to the Lord and not to the anointing or the anointer. It is very solemn ground and can never be made a professional business or a public parade. Its mightiest victories will always be silent and out of sight, and its power will keep pace with our humility and holiness.

We solemnly warn the people of God against caricatures and counterfeits of this solemn truth which they may expect on every side. We greatly deprecate the indiscriminate anointing of all who come forward, of which we hear in various quarters.

Q: Is it necessary to be anointed with oil in order to be healed?
SIMPSON: Every believer has the right to claim healing directly for himself. The Lord Jesus has purchased and provided for His believing children physical strength, life and healing as freely as the spiritual blessings of the gospel. We do not need the intervention of any man or woman as our priest. He alone is our Great High Priest, able to be touched with the feeling of our infirmities. It is still as true as ever, "As many as touched him were made perfectly whole." Thousands who have no circle of believing prayer surrounding them can be encouraged to trust the Great Physician.

Q: Please summarize your biblical basis and philosophy of healing.
SIMPSON: I believe there are three epochs in the revelation of Jesus Christ about divine healing: The first is when we see it in the Bible and believe it as a scriptural doctrine; the second is when we see it in His blood and receive it as part of our redemption rights; the third is when we see it in the risen life of Jesus Christ and take Him into vital union with all our being as the life of our

life and the strength of our mortal frame. This then is the nature of divine healing. It is not the mere restoration of ordinary health, but it is the impartation of the strength of Christ through the Holy Ghost. It is often most marked alongside of the greatest physical weakness.

Q: What are the conditions necessary in the believer in order to be healed?

SIMPSON: There are three conditions of this great blessing. First, that we are wholly yielded to Him to use the life He gives for His glory and service. Second, that we believe without doubt the promise of His Word for our physical healing. Third, that we abide in Him for our physical life and draw our strength moment by moment through personal dependence upon Him.

The secret is that we do not possess this strength in ourselves; it is the strength of Another. We just appropriate it because Christ is our life. It is not self-contained strength, but strength derived each moment from the One above us, beyond us, and yet within us.

Q: Dr. Simpson, why are some not healed despite much prayer and faith of all concerned?

SIMPSON: First, I would say that I do not know. And probably you do not know. And we will not know absolutely until we know even as we are known (1 Corinthians 13:12). One of the first lessons God wants us to learn is to *be still and know that He is God.*

Then I would say that undoubtedly some persons have not been healed because their life work was completed and their Lord was calling them to Himself. There comes such an hour in every accomplished life. Sometimes, however, this is not fully understood by the suffering one or the surrounding friends, and there is the natural struggle and the earnest prayer—and then deep disappointment when it seems unanswered.

But I believe that if we wait upon the Lord in a life of faith, obedience and communion, the heart will usually be able, with quietness, to understand enough of His will to triumph even in death itself.

Sometimes, I believe, life is shortened by disobedience to God. For if we would judge ourselves, we should not be judged. Then sometimes there is a lack of real faith on the part of the sick even when the external conditions of faith have apparently been fulfilled and others may suppose there has been real faith in God for healing.

Q: What is the nature of this "real faith for healing"?
SIMPSON: Faith for divine healing is not mere abstinence from remedies, or an act of intellect or will, or a submission to the ordinance of anointing. It is the real, spiritual touch of Christ. It is much more rare than many suppose.

There is plenty of faith in the doctrine, plenty of readiness to give up remedies, plenty of faith in the prayers of others—especially if they are eminent saints—plenty of faith for healing in the future. But personal, real faith takes Christ *now*, and pressing through the crowd, touches His garment. This faith is not much oftener found now than in the days when only *one person*, struggling through the crowd that surrounded Jesus, *really touched Him.*

Q: What is the biblical perspective on spiritual awakenings in the church through the ages—their meaning and function?
SIMPSON: I believe the key is in Isaiah 44:3, "I will pour water on him that is thirsty, and floods upon the dry

ground." Two forms of the Spirit's operations are here set forth—the ordinary and the extraordinary. Even the ordinary work of the Spirit is expressed by the strongest figure, "I will *pour water.*" But His extraordinary ministry is described by a more emphatic figure, I will "*pour floods* upon the dry ground." These floods represent the occasional outpouring of the Spirit of God in seasons of great revival which the church is witnessing now in many places and which earnest Christian hearts are longing to see everywhere.

Q: What do such revivals demonstrate?

SIMPSON: Such seasons of mighty blessing are powerful witnesses for God, awakening the attention of a careless world and compelling even the most skeptical and indifferent to recognize the reality and power of the gospel of Jesus Christ. Such seasons, for a time at least, lift up a standard against the enemy and check the prevalence and power of evil as no mere human words or authorities ever can. God becomes His own witness and the scoffer and the sinner are awed and humbled before the majesty of the Lord.

Q: What happens in the lives of individuals during revivals?

SIMPSON: Personal conversions take place spontaneously, sometimes irrespective of preaching, confession of identification of individuals with the Lord's people, consecration and higher spiritual blessings. In awakenings we should not be satisfied until people have been led to *all* the fullness of Christ. Every convert should know that it is his *privilege* to be baptized with the Holy Ghost, to be delivered from the power of self and sin and to enter into a life of abiding victory, rest and power.

Q: Should we be praying and expecting an awakening today?

SIMPSON: Let us pray for such a mighty outpouring of the Holy Ghost in our day. We are warranted to expect such manifestations of divine power especially as the coming of our Lord draws nigh. These are to be the very signs that will herald His return: "I will pour out My Spirit upon all flesh," He says, "and I will show signs and wonders before the coming of that great and notable day of the Lord."

Q: Do revivals have a direct connection with the return of our Lord?

SIMPSON: The Holy Ghost is preparing for Christ's return by the spiritual enrobing of His children. There is a marked movement in all sections of the Christian church toward separation from the world and entire consecration to Christ, that we may receive the filling of the Holy Ghost and be transformed and conformed to Christ. This is the very sign that the Bridegroom is near at hand. When the Bride is found robed and ready, her Lord's coming will not be long.

Q: Is witness to others a biblical manifestation of this wonderful filling?

SIMPSON: Because the blessing is enough and to spare, it will overflow and bless the world. God cannot use us until we are running over. If we would be filled, we must learn to give out as well as to receive. We must empty our hearts that we may be refilled.

God is a great economist and loves to bless those who make the best use of their blessings and become in turn a source of blessing to others. The Holy Ghost is given for service; God cannot bless a selfish soul. In this blessed work of winning the lost and giving the gospel

to the world, we shall find our own rich reward and
"the fullness of the blessing of Christ."

Q: Does this filling of the Holy Spirit have anything to do with world missions?

SIMPSON: Most definitely! And this is also a sign of His
near coming. It is the Holy Ghost who is sending us
forth to evangelize the world according to Acts 1:8. We
are witnessing the mighty working of the Holy Ghost
among the nations.

If we are truly filled with the Holy Ghost and longing
for the coming of Christ, we shall be active witnesses
and workers in preparing for Him. We will be soul
winners at home, and if we cannot go abroad, we will
help others go and give the gospel quickly to all the
world. The Holy Ghost always puts the *go* in us and
turns our blessing into the multiplied blessing of our
fellowmen.

* * *

Writings by and about Simpson and *books used in research
(not intended to be exhaustive):

*All For Jesus
The Best of A.B. Simpson
Christ in the Tabernacle
The Christ Life
Days of Heaven on Earth
The Fourfold Gospel
The Gentle Love of the Holy Spirit
*The Gospel of Healing
*The Holy Spirit (Power from on High) 2 Vol.
A Larger Christian Life
*The Life of A.B. Simpson
*The Lord for the Body

Missionary Messages
The Self-Life and The Christ-Life
Songs of the Spirit
*When the Comforter Came
Wholly Sanctified
Wingspread

Hannah Whitall Smith

[1832–1911]

THE HAPPY SECRET

HANNAH, THE DAUGHTER of a Philadelphia Quaker and wealthy glass manufacturer, spent a happy childhood in a loving family atmosphere. Well-educated and physically beautiful, she married Robert Pearsall Smith, a young businessman, when she was 19.

The Smiths were not satisfied with the spiritual deadness of 19th-century Quaker doctrine and became caught up in revivalist activities. Both preached, wrote tracts and engaged in evangelism among all classes of people. They were especially successful among high society and professional circles both in America and England. The Smiths eventually settled in England.

Hannah was the mother of five children, two of whom died in their youth. The rest became prominent in society and professions. Her husband became conceited and unstable with his apparent spiritual effectiveness and popularity among famous people, and became a religious fanatic. He died a bitter, disappointed, unhappy man.

Hannah, however difficult her life, maintained an optimistic, spiritually buoyant attitude throughout her life. She spent her final years confined to a wheelchair, living with her son in Sussex, England.

Hannah wrote several books, but the most celebrated was the religious classic, *The Christian's Secret of a Happy Life*. Published in 1875, it is still in print.

* * *

APPROXIMATE DATE: 1885

QUESTION: *Mrs. Smith, you wrote an entire book on Christians being happy. Do you think most Christians are not?*

HANNAH WHITALL SMITH: That is my observation. This lack of joy does not attract people to our Lord. A friend once said to me, "You Christians have a religion that seems to make you miserable. You are like a man with a headache—he does not want to get rid of his head, but it hurts him to keep it. You cannot expect outsiders to seek very earnestly for anything so obviously uncomfortable."

Q: Is Christian happiness a secret?

SMITH: Not in the sense of a secret deliberately hidden from us but as a very precious thing which is delightful to find. Believers often begin their Christian lives with victory and the optimism that they will never be defeated. But before long the victories become few and fleeting, the defeats many and disastrous.

Q: *What causes that?*

SMITH: Partly, a wrong conception of God. A great many Christians seem to think that their Father in heaven wants to make them miserable and take away all their blessings. I am ashamed to write the words, but this idea is making hundreds of lives wretched. We must correctly realize that better and sweeter than health, or friends, or money, or fame, or ease, or prosperity, is the adorable will of our God. He wants nothing but our good.

Q: *Are there other factors contributing to unhappy and powerless Christian lives?*

SMITH: The new Christian perhaps has had a clear understanding of doctrinal truths but not the possession of their life and power. He has rejoiced in the knowledge of things revealed in the Scriptures but not a living realization of the things themselves. Christ is believed in, talked about and served. But He is not known as the soul's actual and very life, abiding there forever and revealing Himself continually in His beauty. The Christian has found Jesus as Savior from the penalty of sin but not from its power.

Q: *That could describe most Christians. Surely that can't be the normal scriptural experience?*

SMITH: Certainly God has not planned for us to live at such a low level. But many people settle for it and are convinced that the best you can expect from your Christian life is alternate failure and victory—one hour sinning, the next repenting, then beginning again, only to fail again, and again to repent. Is this what Jesus had in mind when He laid down His precious life to deliver us from our sore and cruel bondage to sin? Did He provide only this partial deliverance? Are we left to struggle under the weary consciousness of defeat and discouragement? Surely not!

Q: I guess many Christians think we have to wait for heaven to experience ultimate victory.
SMITH: Now we are coming to the basis of the problem. We must accept one scriptural premise—that Jesus came to save us now, in this life, from the power and dominion of sin and to make us more than conquerors through His power.

Q: Does God accomplish all our victories for us and we need do nothing?
SMITH: That is not the complete picture of God's truth. There are two distinct sides to it, contrasting but not contradictory—God's side and man's side. Without this understanding, wrong impressions will be created.

Q: Who then is responsible for what?
SMITH: To state it briefly, I would say that man's part is to trust, and God's part is to work. It can be seen at a glance how these two parts balance. I mean, there is a certain work to be accomplished. We are to be delivered from the power of sin and to be made perfect in every good work to do the will of God. We are to be transformed by the renewing of our minds. Besetting sins are to be conquered, evil habits to be overcome, wrong attitudes and feelings are to be rooted out.

Q: Shouldn't we take care of all that ourselves?
SMITH: That is the mistake! Of course somebody must do this—either we must do it for ourselves, or another must do it for us. Most of us have tried to do it for ourselves at first and have grievously failed. Then we discover from the Scriptures and from our own experi-

ence that it is something we are unable to do, but that the Lord Jesus Christ has come on purpose to do it. He will do it for all who put themselves wholly into His hands and trust Him without reserve.

Q: *Wouldn't that make the Christian life passive?*
SMITH: No, we do not sit down from that point in a sort of religious easy chair. When we trust, the Lord works; a great deal is done – not by us, but by Him. Having put ourselves wholly and absolutely into His hands, we must now expect Him to begin work. God's work in and through us, however, does take time. Maturity of Christian experience cannot be reached in a moment. It is the result of the work of God's Holy Spirit who, by His energizing and transforming power, causes us to grow up into Christ in all things. We will find ourselves doing impossible things.

Q: *You said we should do nothing but trust, but at the same time that we will do impossible things. Isn't that contradictory?*
SMITH: The two can be reconciled, just as we reconcile statements concerning a saw in a carpenter's shop. We may say at one moment that the saw has sawn asunder a log. The next moment we declare that the carpenter has done it. The saw is the instrument used, the power that uses it is the carpenter's. And so we, yielding ourselves unto God and our members as instruments of righteousness unto Him, find that He works in us to will and to do of His good pleasure. Then we can say with Paul, "I laboured . . . : yet not I, but the grace of God which was with me" (1 Corinthians 15:10b).

Q: *You have termed such an experience as "the higher life." Who is eligible for that?*

SMITH: Actually, it is the only true and normal Christian life. I like to call it "the life hid with Christ in God." It is the life the Lord wants *all* Christians to live, but it differs from much that we see in ordinary Christian experience.

Q: *How can one attain to this higher life?*
SMITH: First, do not look upon it as an *attainment* but an *obtainment*. We cannot earn it; we cannot climb up to it; we cannot win it; we can do nothing but ask for it and receive it. It is the gift of God in Christ Jesus. When something is a gift, the only course left for the receiver is to take it and thank the giver. We never say of a gift, "See to what I have attained." We boast of the love, wealth and generosity of the giver.

Q: *Upon whom then does God bestow the gift and how are they to receive it?*
SMITH: He can bestow it only upon the fully consecrated person – the first condition; second, it is to be received by faith.

Q: *What is involved in consecration?*
SMITH: Let's examine our motivation. Consecration is not in order to *deserve the blessing* but to *remove the difficulties* and make it possible for God to bestow it. Some people like to use the word *abandonment*. Whatever word we use, we mean an entire surrender of the whole being to God – spirit, soul and body – placed under His absolute control so that He may do with us just what He pleases. The language of our hearts, under all circumstances and in view of every act, is to be "Thy will be done." We give up all liberty of choice. We live a life of complete obedience.

But I beg of you, don't look at it as a hard and stern

demand. You must do it gladly, thankfully, enthusiastically. You must go in on what I call the privileged side of consecration. I can assure you, from the universal testimony of all who have tried it, that you will find it the happiest place you have ever entered yet!

Q: How does faith operate in this experience?
SMITH: It must follow surrender as the absolutely necessary element to receive any gift.

Q: But did we not exercise faith at conversion? Is not everything covered by that initial belief?
SMITH: This is all meant, of course, experimentally and practically. Theologically and judicially every believer certainly has everything as soon as he is converted; but experimentally *nothing* is his until he claims it by faith. This faith of which I am speaking must be a *present* faith. No faith that is exercised in the future tense amounts to anything.

Q: If one takes those two steps—consecration and faith—are they certain to lead to the higher life?
SMITH: You may be perfectly sure of this: No matter what may be the complications of your peculiar experience, no matter what your difficulties, or your surroundings, or your "peculiar temperament," these two steps, definitely taken and unwaveringly persevered in, will certainly bring you out sooner or later into the green pastures and still waters of this life hid with Christ in God. And if you will let every other consideration go, and simply devote your attention to these two points, and be very clear and definite about them, your progress will be rapid, and your soul will reach its desired haven far sooner than you can now think possible.

* * *

Writings by and about Smith and *books used in research (not intended to be exhaustive):

*The Christian's Secret of a Happy Life
God is Enough
The God of All Comfort
*The Great Revivalists
*The Transatlantic Smiths

Charles Haddon Spurgeon

[1834–1892]

THE IMPERATIVE OF POWER

BORN AT KELVEDON, ESSEX, ENGLAND, the son of an independent minister, Spurgeon has been called the greatest preacher since the apostle Paul. He attended Colchester School, a school in Newmarket, and joined the Baptist church in 1850.

Spurgeon began preaching soon after his conversion at age 16, and served his first pastorate when he was 18. By the time he was 20, people thronged to hear him in what had been a small deteriorating church in South London. Eventually his congregation built him the great Metropolitan Tabernacle, seating 6,000. He preached there for the rest of his life.

In his lifetime he published more than 2,000 sermons and 49 volumes of commentaries, anecdotes and illustrations, besides editing the monthly *Sword and Trowel*.

His diligent study and exposition of the Bible, his simple but eloquent presentation, his powerful voice and his use of stories in his sermons were great assets to his preaching. This man called "the prince of preachers" attributed the secret of his power to the Spirit of God and to the hundreds of thousands who prayed for him around the world.

* * *

APPROXIMATE DATE: 1870

QUESTION: Mr. Spurgeon, how vital do you think the power of the Holy Spirit is to the churches and the leadership of God's work?
CHARLES HADDON SPURGEON: If we do not have the Spirit of God, it is better to shut the churches, to nail up the doors, to put a black cross on them and say, "God have mercy on us!" If ministers do not have the Spirit of God, they had better not preach, and the people would do better to stay home. I think I do not speak too strongly when I say that any church without the Spirit of God is a curse rather than a blessing.

If a Christian worker does not have the Spirit of God, he is standing in somebody else's way; he is a tree bearing no fruit but standing where another fruitful tree might grow. This is a solemn work. It must be the Holy Spirit or nothing.

Death and condemnation is preferable to a church that is not yearning after the Spirit, crying and groaning until the Spirit has worked mightily in her midst. The Holy Spirit is here. He has never gone back since He descended at Pentecost. He is often grieved and vexed for He is peculiarly jealous and sensitive. The one sin God cannot forgive has to do with His blessed person.

Therefore let us be very tender toward Him, walk humbly before Him, wait on Him very earnestly. Let us resolve to knowingly continue nothing which would prevent His dwelling in us and being with us now and forever.

Q: Does the Holy Spirit have any work related to the church which He still needs to accomplish?
SPURGEON: Yes, I believe one work is to bring on the latter-day glory.

Q: What is that, and when do you think it will happen?
SPURGEON: In a few more years—I don't know when or how—God will pour out the Holy Spirit in a far different style from the present. We may expect diversities of His operations but during the past few years very little of His Spirit has been poured out.

Q: Please explain.
SPURGEON: Ministers have gone on in dull routine, continually preaching, preaching, preaching, and it does very little good. The hour is coming, and it may be even now, when God will pour out the Holy Spirit again in a wonderful manner.

Q: What evidence would we see?
SPURGEON: It will be according to Scripture: many shall run to and fro and knowledge shall be increased, the knowledge of the Lord shall cover the earth as the waters cover the surface of the great deep. His kingdom shall come and His will shall be done on earth as it is in

heaven. We are not going to drag on forever like Pharaoh with the wheels off his chariot.

Q: Do you think those days are relatively imminent?
SPURGEON: My heart exults, and my eyes flash with the thought that very likely I may live to see the outpouring of the Spirit when the sons and daughters of God again shall prophesy, and the young men shall see visions, and the old men shall dream dreams (Acts 2:17).

Q: Will miracles accompany such an outpouring?
SPURGEON: Perhaps there shall be no miraculous gifts for they will not be required. Yet there shall be such a miraculous amount of holiness, such an extraordinary fervor of prayer, such a real communion with God, and so much vital religion, and such a spread of the doctrines of the cross, that everyone will see that truly God is pouring out the Spirit like water and the rains are descending from above.

Q: What should Christians do in anticipation?
SPURGEON: Let us pray for that outpouring; let us continually labor for it and seek it from God.

* * *

Writings by and about Spurgeon and *books used in research (not intended to be exhaustive):

The Comforter
Evening by Evening
Gleanings Among the Sheaves
Lectures to My Students
Life of Charles Haddon Spurgeon
Metropolitan Tabernacle Pulpit
Morning by Morning

Necessity of the Spirit's Work
The Power of the Holy Ghost
The Soul Winner
Spiritual Revival: The Want of the Church
The Treasury of David: A Commentary on the Psalms, 3 Vol.
Treasury of the Bible, 4 Vol.

James Hudson Taylor

[1832–1905]

IT IS NO SECRET

T HE SON OF A METHODIST MINISTER who had desired to become a missionary to China, Taylor was born at Barnsley, England. A weak and frail child, he received his early education from his godly parents. Taylor did not became a Christian, however, until the age of 17.

After medical training at the London Ophthalmic Hospital, and brief theological training, the China Evangelization Society asked him to begin work in China immediately. Taylor set sail for China when he was only 21. In 1857 he married Maria Dyer, a teacher in China at the time. Taylor became exhausted after seven years of strenuous work at a small hospital and in intensive evangelistic work. Only a period of convalescence in England saved his life. He finished his medical studies during that time and translated the New Testament into the Ningpo dialect.

Burdened for the millions of Chinese who never had an opportunity to hear the gospel, Taylor established the China Inland Mission in 1866. Before his death it had expanded to 205 mission stations with 849 missionaries from England and 125,000 witnessing Chinese Christians.

Taylor was gifted in sharing his missionary vision and spent much of his life recruiting missionaries from around the world. His philosophy of Christian service was to look to God in faith for funds without direct solicitation.

He returned to China once more at the age of 73 and was buried in the land for which he had prayed and labored so faithfully.

* * *

APPROXIMATE DATE: 1895

QUESTION: *Many books have been written about you and your pioneer mission work in inland China. Each points to a certain experience called your "spiritual secret" as being critical to your spiritual success. Is your secret exclusive?*
JAMES HUDSON TAYLOR: It is not a secret that should be hidden, although it took me many years to discover it. I was already 37 and had labored for the Lord in China more than 15 years.

Q: *What was your spiritual condition before that experience?*
TAYLOR: I was constantly under pressure of strain and stress. My spiritual life hardly kept pace with demands upon it. Outwardly it may not have seemed so, but I knew my own heart before the Lord.

Q: What were your spiritual frustrations?

TAYLOR: Not the work, in spite of all its difficulty and trial. When consciously in communion with the Lord, work seemed light. Not the shortness of funds, nor anxiety about those dearest to me. It was just myself— the unsatisfied longing of my heart, my inward struggle to abide in Christ, my frequent failure and disappointment. I was face-to-face with heathenism and all the claims that pressed around me. But—alas—too often out of touch with Christ.

Q: Did your heavy responsibilities as founder and director of the Mission contribute to your feelings of inadequacy?

TAYLOR: Had I been responsible only for myself, this would have been bad enough, but with all the demands upon me for others, it was unbearable. Prior to my experience, my mind had been greatly exercised for six or eight months. I felt not only my personal need, but also the need of our missionaries, for more holiness, life and power in our souls.

Personal need stood first and was the greatest. I prayed, agonized, fasted, strove, made resolutions, read the Word more diligently, sought more time for quiet and meditation—all without success. Every day, almost every hour, the consciousness of sin oppressed me. I knew that if I could only abide in Christ, all would be well—but I could not.

Q: Did you continue to seek God daily for strength and wisdom?

TAYLOR: Indeed, I began the day with prayer and determined not to take my eye from Him for a moment. But pressure of duties, sometimes very trying, constant interruptions apt to be so wearing, often caused me to forget Him. Then one's nerves get so fretted in that climate that temptations to irritability, hard thoughts and sometimes unkind words are all the more difficult to control. Each day brought its register of sin and failure, of lack of power. The will was certainly present with me, but how to perform, I could not determine.

Q: *What accelerated your search for a more victorious experience?*
TAYLOR: At that very time, the pages of *REVIVAL* magazine, published in England, were largely occupied with a genuine holiness movement. This was destined, in the providence of God, to lead to the Keswick Convention with its worldwide influences for good. Copies found their way to all the stations of our Mission and brought the subject of a deeper spiritual life prominently before all of us. Many besides myself were hungering for a fuller experience because we saw that it was in accord with the Word of God. I read in the magazine, "The Holy Spirit never creates hungering and thirsting after righteousness except for the purpose that Christ may fill the longing soul."

Q: *How did the prospect of a deeper spiritual life affect you?*
TAYLOR: It became my deepest longing, but oh, how different were the actual experiences of my soul! With the growth of the Mission, sometimes I was buoyed up by hope, sometimes almost in despair with my own inward need. I wrote to my parents asking their prayers because I continually mourned my following the Lord at such a distance, and learning so slowly to imitate my precious Master. I told them I never knew how bad a heart I had, though I did love God and His work. Often I was tempted to think that one so full of sin could not

even be a child of God at all, but then I dismissed that and tried to rejoice all the more in the preciousness of Jesus.

Q: *Your crisis was near, was it not?*

TAYLOR: I can remember clearly that it was Saturday, September 4, 1869, when a letter arrived from my close friend and fellow missionary, Mr. McCarthy. He had come into this full experience recently and shared it with me because he knew of my longing for it. He had experienced the same failures and unrest, the same ups and downs. He wrote of such things as "abiding, not striving nor struggling, trusting Christ for present power, resting in the Savior, complete salvation."

When I read his letter, I suddenly saw it all: Not striving to have faith, or to increase our faith, but looking to the Faithful One seems to be all we need. It was resting in the Loved One entirely, for time and for eternity. Then I looked to Jesus, and when I saw, oh, how joy flowed!

Q: *These truths were surely not new to you?*

TAYLOR: I echoed my friend, Mr. McCarthy, that this was not new, and yet new to me, and formerly misapprehended. But now I grasped the reality for *myself.* Yes, I had long and truly known the Lord and served Him by faith. Because I had known the nearness of Christ as so precious, I could not bear such ups and downs and habitual failures.

Q: *Did you immediately share your new experience with others?*

TAYLOR: After praying and thanking and praising God with the tide of joy and life more abundant sweeping through my soul, I wanted everyone to know how to enter this fullness of life. I gathered the household in the sitting room upstairs, told out what my whole experience was, and other hearts were moved and blessed too. The streams began to flow. I arranged for our many missionary house guests that weekend to stay over Sunday so we might have special prayer concerning it.

Others in our Mission had already experienced this blessing before I did. In fact, my wife viewed all of this with a joy mixed with wonder because the experiences we all were finding as something new and further had long been her secret of victory and peace. Now we were more united than ever, and helpers of each others' faith.

Q: *What differences did you begin to notice in yourself?*

TAYLOR: Pressed though I was with business and Mission matters, I now had a leisure in my spirit by resting completely in Jesus. No longer was I striving to have faith. How shall I explain it? Not asking God to help me get the sap or power *out* of the Vine and *into* myself, but realizing that Jesus *is* the Vine and I am *in* Him, one with Him, and He in me, and consequently *I have all His fullness in me!* And I may take all I need of His fullness! It is not trying to be holy, but rejoicing that Christ *is* perfect holiness, and He is *in me* to be holy. I am inseparably one with Him—that is the secret!

Oh, God made me a new man! I had known these things theoretically, certainly, without really apprehending them. I had seen it long enough in the Bible, but now I believed it as a living reality for myself.

Q: *Many said that your new experience completely changed your disposition. What was so noticeable?*

TAYLOR: Simple as was my change in point of view, it

changed everything. My coworkers said I was now a joyous, bright, happy Christian. I had been a toiling, burdened one before without much rest of soul. I was resting in Jesus now, and letting Him do the work – that makes all the difference!

Whenever I spoke in meetings, I was told that a new power seemed to possess me and flow through me. Troubles did not worry me as before, and in the practical things of life I had new peace. I cast everything on God in a new way, and I gave more time to prayer.

Instead of working late at night, I began to go to bed earlier, rising at five to give two hours before the work of the day to Bible study and prayer. Thus my own soul was fed, and the living waters of God's power could flow through me to others. It was an abiding fullness of Jesus that did not cease.

Q: Were you able to explain your experience to your family in England?
TAYLOR: My sister had been my lifelong intimate friend and correspondent. She and my mother had wrestled in prayer for my conversion when I was 17. I naturally had a great longing to help her into the same experience. She was sorely pressed with her growing family, outward responsibilities and inward conflicts. I witnessed to her that my work was never so plentiful, so responsible or so difficult, but that the weight and strain were all gone. I said that the last month or more of my life had been perhaps the happiest of my life. I was not sure I could make myself clear, for there was nothing new or strange about it – and yet, all was new! In a word, I told her that once I was blind, now I see.

Q: Looking back on your past, what mistaken ideas did you have about the Christian life?

TAYLOR: I unconsciously had the idea that victory may not be for this life, which God may have meant to be one of continual conflict. Maybe God didn't want to give complete deliverance to us now so that heaven would be sweeter. Perhaps practical holiness was to be gradually attained by a diligent use of the means of grace.

I was not really striving to attain it in my own strength because I knew very well that I was powerless. I told God so repeatedly. I reminded Him that I knew all the power was in Christ, but I just didn't know how to get it *out of Him and into me.* Looking at His wonderful fullness, I felt all the more helpless and guilty for not having the faith to make it my own.

Q: Faith seemed to be your strongest point! You continually trusted God for the supply of finances and missionaries in your work in China.
TAYLOR: It was in my *personal life* before the Lord that I harbored the sin of unbelief. I had prayed for faith but it did not come.

Q: Do you feel that you are a better Christian since this deeper experience?
TAYLOR: I am no better than before, nor do I want to say any longer that I'm striving to be better. No, that is not the point. But I am dead and buried with Christ, yes, and risen too and ascended. Now Christ lives in me and "the life which I now live in the flesh I live by the faith of the Son of God, who loved me, and gave himself for me" (Galatians 2:20b).

I know I am as capable of sinning as ever, but I realize Christ's presence as never before. He cannot sin, and He can keep me from sinning. I cannot say that since I have seen this light I have not sinned. I do feel there was no need to have done so. Walking more in the light, my conscience has been more tender, sin has been instantly seen, confessed, pardoned, and peace and joy, with humility, instantly restored.

Q: After what you call "the exchanged life," you went through most excruciating trials, sorrows, pressures and problems, didn't you?

TAYLOR: Difficulties greater and more serious than I had ever experienced crowded around me with unparalleled pressures and constant movement. Riots, massacres of our missionaries, wars and almost overwhelming adversities took place. And much sickness. Several of my own precious children died. My darling wife, Maria, died from an illness at the age of 33.

Q: What crushing blows to come so soon after your deeper experience!

TAYLOR: My heart was overwhelmed with pain, but at the same time with gratitude and praise. My eyes flowed with tears of mingled joy and sorrow. My fifth son, only one week old, was buried just before his mother. But I still rejoiced in God through our Lord Jesus Christ—in His works, His ways, His providence, *in Himself.*

I had to return to England repeatedly due to my own ill health. For a time I was paralyzed from a fall and advised by physicians that I would probably never walk again nor return to China. The whole burden of the Mission was upon me and I could not even move.

Q: How did you recover?

TAYLOR: Praise God, in answer to the prayers of friends I was healed and raised up. Then 58 of our missionaries perished in the persecution of the Boxer Rebellion in China, along with 21 of their children. From the time

Maria died, I had to be separated from my other dear children for years on end.

But I want to say that though I was deeply moved and burdened with trials almost to my own death, *nothing* has hindered my joy in Jesus Himself dwelling in me since God revealed this full truth to me.

Q: *Do you think God prepared you through that experience for the trials to come?*
TAYLOR: I do. Business and ministry are always pressing, but now He makes my work light and gives me joy in seeing Him blessing others. I have no fear of our work being too heavy *for Him*, either in China or in the home department. We are not our own, nor is the work ours. He whose we are and whom we serve will prove equal to any emergency.

Q: *Mr. Taylor, your "secret" experience—this reality of oneness and fullness of Jesus in you—seems to be such a deep truth that only mature Christians might grasp it. Is it meant only for Christian workers?*
TAYLOR: Oh, no! We should not look upon this truth as for the few, but as the birthright of every child of God. No one can dispense with it without dishonor to our Lord. This experience is the only power for deliverance from sin and for true service for Christ.

Q: *Isn't it more difficult to understand than salvation?*
TAYLOR: When I wrote to my own motherless children, the oldest only nine, I explained this truth to them on their level. In fact, on the same childlike level is the only way we should understand it. I longed for them to learn early, and once for all, the precious truths which

came so late to me concerning oneness with and the indwelling of Christ.

These do not seem more difficult to apprehend than the truths about redemption. Both need the teaching of the Holy Spirit, nothing more. It is heaven begun below, is it not? May we ever enjoy it! This truth makes one feel so utterly childlike. It is like playing in the shallows of a boundless ocean. Oh, the unsearchable riches of His fullness! And all is ours—for He is ours and we are His!

* * *

Writings by and about Taylor and *books used in research (not intended to be exhaustive):

Hudson Taylor
Hudson Taylor and the China Inland Mission
Hudson Taylor and Maria
Hudson Taylor in Early Years: The Growth of a Soul
Hudson Taylor's Spiritual Secret
Pioneers of Revival
They Found the Secret
Union and Communion

William Henry Griffith Thomas

[1861–1924]

THE GLORY SIDE OF POWER

THOMAS WAS BORN in Oswestry, Shropshire, England and dated his conversion from his 17th year. He studied three years at King's College in London and was ordained by the Bishop of London in 1885.

He served as curate at St. Peter's, Clerkenwell, for nearly four years. He continued his ecclesiastical training at Oxford while senior curate at St. Aldate's, completing it in 1895.

Thomas continued his ministry for nine years in London at St. Paul's, Portman Square. He became principal of Wycliffe Hall, Oxford, from 1905 to 1910. During that period he completed work on his doctor of divinity degree. Thomas was involved in conference ministry at Keswick, England, from 1906 to 1908.

Moving to Canada, he became professor of Old Testament Literature and Exegesis at Wycliffe College, Toronto, for nine years. He returned to England at intervals for numerous conference engagements at Keswick.

Thomas lived his last five years in Philadelphia engaging in Bible conference ministry and literary work. He was associated with the early stages of the Philadelphia College of the Bible and a recognized leader in fundamentalist circles.

Closely associated with Lewis Sperry Chafer and A.B. Winchester, Thomas was instrumental in the establishment of the Evangelical Theological College, later renamed Dallas Theological Seminary. He died at age 63 a few months prior to the opening of the seminary, which he was to have served as head of the theology department.

* * *

APPROXIMATE DATE: 1906

QUESTION: *Would you explain the three aspects of salvation to which you refer in your writings?*
W.H. GRIFFITH THOMAS: Concerning the past, a Christian can say, "I was saved"—from the penalty of sin. Concerning the present, a Christian can say, "I am being saved"—from the power of sin. Concerning the future, he can say, "I shall be saved"—from the presence of sin.

Q: *Some people say that we must do our best as Christians, hope for the best, but that we obviously cannot expect complete and constant victory. What do you teach?*

287

THOMAS: I believe the Bible absolutely opposes that view. What I think is not important—God's ideas are. The Bible teaches a possible life of victory and power in our *now* experience.

Many verses declare that God gives us the victory, we shall reign in life, and God always causes us to triumph. If we cannot experience this victory, the only alternative is that sin is inevitable and the verses to which I have referred are invalid. God promised victory and made provision for it in the person of His Son.

Q: Then why do so many Christians live without power and victory?
THOMAS: It may be partly because they still live on the other side of Pentecost. They live as if they were in Old Testament times when the Spirit came upon just a few on special occasions. In this dispensation of the Holy Spirit, however, God's purpose is for all to have this fullness of the Spirit. This luxury is not for a favored few. It is for all Christians, for all times and all circumstances.

Q: How about terminology? Does the Holy Spirit baptize us or fill us?
THOMAS: I realize not everyone will endorse some of my expressions but I can only pass on what I think. Phraseology may differ, but I suggest that you should be particularly careful when you talk about the "baptism" of the Holy Ghost. Scripture does not use that phrase. You read that Christians received the baptism of the Holy Ghost, but while we have a right experience, we may have a wrong description.

I believe baptism in the Holy Ghost is exactly on the same plane as baptism in water—we never need to repeat it. We never baptize people in water twice, at least we should not. The baptism of the Spirit is an elementary and initial act that we never need to repeat.

Q: *May we not experience great power from God in our lives more than once?*
THOMAS: I believe with all my heart in the statement "One baptism, many fillings." The New Testament always associates the word "baptism" in connection with the Holy Ghost with the *beginning* of an experience. "Ye shall be baptized with the Holy Ghost" referred to the day of Pentecost. First Corinthians 12:13 is worthy of careful consideration. "For by one Spirit are we all baptized into one body." When we first accept Jesus Christ as our Savior, the Holy Ghost baptizes us. That is not by water, but by the Holy Ghost. The Holy Ghost baptized us and put us into the Body of Christ, that is, the Church.

Q: *What place do feelings or emotions have in our experience with the Holy Spirit?*
THOMAS: We obtain this power by *faith*, not feelings. Many invariably associate the Holy Ghost with great tides of emotion. Not necessarily. Emotions largely depend on our temperaments. Some people are stolid English people who do not express much emotion. Wonderfully enthusiastic Welsh people, on the other hand, are simply always in emotion. You cannot expect the Holy Ghost to work in the same way among entirely different people—the warm-hearted enthusiastic Celts and the phlegmatic Saxons. The Holy Ghost must deal with them differently. But the Celt and the Saxon must obtain this victory and power by the same means—faith.

Q: *How can we remain permanently full?*
THOMAS: They key is in the meaning of the Greek words

huparchou pleres in Acts 7:55. Faith obtains, and faithfulness maintains. By continually yielding ourselves to God, we develop an attitude. The Holy Ghost, without any necessary tides of emotion, is simply and solely lived day by day.

We must also keep close to the Word of God. God speaks through the Word; God's Spirit uses the Word. Then we experience the reality of the Spirit of God as our power.

* * *

Writings by Thomas and *books used in research (not intended to be exhaustive):

The Apostle John: Studies in His Life and Writings
The Apostle Peter: Outline Studies in His Life, Character and Writings
Christianity is Christ
A Devotional Commentary on Genesis
Hebrews: A Devotional Commentary
*The Holy Spirit of God
Outline Studies in the Acts of the Apostles
Outline Studies in the Gospel of Luke
Outline Studies in the Gospel of Matthew
St. Paul's Epistle to the Romans
Studies in Colossians and Philemon
Through the Pentateuch
*The Victorious Life

Reuben Archer Torrey

[1856–1928]

EXPLORING
POWER

 A. TORREY WAS BORN in Hoboken, New Jersey. A graduate of both Yale University and Seminary, he continued his studies abroad at Leipzig and Erlangen Universities in Germany. As an ordained Congregational minister, Torrey served as superintendent of the Minneapolis City Mission Society. He accepted the invitation to supervise the Moody Bible Institute in Chicago and serve as pastor of Moody Memorial Church.

A noted educator, a man of prayer and an evangelist with a world vision, Torrey's evangelistic tours abroad resulted in 100,000 professions of faith.

Also known as a Bible expositor, he wrote 40 books on salvation, soul-winning and theology. Bible students still regard his books as classics.

Later Torrey served as dean of the Bible Institute of Los Angeles (Biola) and served as pastor of The Church of the Open Door in the same city.

* * *

APPROXIMATE DATE: 1898

QUESTION: Dr. Torrey, is it true that Mr. D.L. Moody was the only person who could tell you what to preach?
R.A. TORREY: Yes, no one else dared. But I recognized his wisdom from God. "Be sure to preach on the baptism with the Holy Spirit," he used to tell me.

Q: As one of the most popular lecturers at Moody's Northfield Conference Grounds in Massachusetts, on what topics did you speak?
TORREY: The Word of God, the second coming of Christ, praying and the work of the Holy Spirit. I guess my stress on the importance and necessity of the baptism with the Holy Spirit became a hallmark of my preaching.

Q: Do different terms for that experience describe different experiences?
TORREY: Baptism with the Holy Spirit, filled with the Spirit, gift of the Spirit, poured out, receiving the Holy Spirit, the promise of the Father—I believe describe one and the same experience in the New Testament.

Q: Do you teach that the baptism with the Spirit happens at the time of conversion?
TORREY: No, and I also believe that baptism with the Holy Spirit is a definite experience of which one may and ought to know whether he has received it or not. In

the account in Acts regenerated people received it at Pentecost. It is an operation of the Spirit distinct from, subsequent to, and additional to His regenerating work. A man may be regenerated by the Holy Spirit and still not be baptized with the Spirit. In regeneration there is an impartation of *life*, and the one who receives it is saved. In the baptism with the Holy Spirit there is an impartation of *power* and the one who receives it is fitted for service.

Q: When do we actually receive the Holy Spirit?
TORREY: Every true believer has the Holy Spirit (Romans 8:9, I Corinthians 6:19). But not every believer has the baptism with the Holy Spirit, although every believer may have it.

Q: When can the baptism with the Spirit be received?
TORREY: Immediately after the new birth, as in the household of Cornelius. In a normal state of the church, every believer would have the baptism with the Spirit, as in the church at Corinth. The Spirit would be received immediately upon repentance and baptism into the name of Jesus Christ for the remission of sins (Acts 2:38).

Q: What prevents this from happening more often to people who are newly born again?
TORREY: The doctrine of the baptism with the Spirit has been so little taught that it has almost dropped out of sight. The church has so little expectancy along this line that much of the church is in the position of the churches in Samaria and Ephesus. Someone has to come and call the attention of the mass of believers to their privilege in the risen Christ which they may claim.

Q: *Is the purpose of the baptism to make us holier and more victorious in life?*

TORREY: No, the baptism is an experience connected with and primarily for the purpose of service. It is not basically intended to make believers happy nor holy but to make them useful. In every Bible passage in which the results of the baptism with the Holy Spirit are mentioned they are related to testimony and service. No direct references are to cleansing from sin.

It has to do with gifts for service rather than for character. The steps by which one naturally receives the baptism with the Spirit are such that it is ordinarily accompanied by a great moral uplift, even a radical transformation. But the baptism is not in itself either an eradication of the carnal nature or cleansing from the impure heart. It is the impartation of supernatural power or gifts in service. Sometimes one may have rare gifts by the Spirit's power and unfortunately few graces.

Q: *But isn't the Spirit's ministry in the Christian to cleanse from sin and empower one to lead a life of victory over the world, the flesh and the devil?*

TORREY: These are indeed some of the Spirit's great works in us. But this is not the baptism with the Holy Spirit.

Q: *Did Jesus promise two separate baptisms—one with the Holy Ghost and one with fire?*

TORREY: Jesus' statement cannot be interpreted as two contrasting baptisms, one of blessing and the other of judgment. The Greek terms do not permit this interpretation. It is one twofold baptism. Many seem to get only part of it, "the Holy Wind," but the "fire" is for us too, if we claim it. And the fire searches, refines, consumes, illuminates, makes to glow, energizes and spreads.

"Fire" is what many need today and it is available to us.

Q: Are the manifestations of baptism with the Spirit the same in all persons?
TORREY: They are not. "There are diversities of gifts, but the same Spirit" (1 Corinthians 12:4). The gifts vary with the different lines of service to which God has called each person. The church is a body and different parts of the body have different functions. The Spirit imparts to one who is baptized with the Spirit those gifts which fit him for the work to which the Spirit has called him.

For example, many in the early church who were baptized with the Holy Spirit spoke with tongues (Acts 10:46, 19:6), but not all (1 Corinthians 12:27–30). Likewise today the Holy Spirit imparts to some gifts as an evangelist's, to others as pastors and teachers, to others as helps, governments, etc.

Q: Does everyone baptized with the Spirit receive some gift, and can we ask for or choose what we would like?
TORREY: Without question there will be some gift to everyone baptized with the Spirit. But the Holy Spirit divides to each one severally as He will (1 Corinthians 12:11). He is absolutely sovereign in deciding how—in what special gift, operation or power—the baptism shall manifest itself. It is not for us to pick out some place of service and then ask the Holy Spirit to qualify us for that service. It is not for us to select some gift and then ask the Holy Spirit to impart that gift. We must simply put ourselves entirely at the disposal of the Holy Spirit to send us where He will, to select for us what kind of service He will and to impart what gift He will. Our position is to unconditionally surrender to Him. Some are trying to select the gift and so get none. Of course,

it is scriptural, while recognizing and rejoicing in the sovereignty of the Holy Spirit, to "covet earnestly the best gifts" (1 Corinthians 12:31).

Q: What kind of power do we receive after being baptized with the Spirit?
TORREY: He always imparts power in service. The power may be of one kind in one person and a different kind in another, but there will always be power – and the very power of God, at that. If anyone is reading these pages and has not yet received the baptism with the Holy Spirit, he will receive it if he seeks it in God's way. Then there will come into his service a power that was never there before – power for the very work God has for him to do. The results of that power may not be manifest at once in conversions (Acts 7:55–60). But the Spirit will impart boldness in testimony and service. The baptism changes cowards into heroes.

Q: Are there other evidences of this baptism?
TORREY: The baptism causes one to be occupied with God and Christ and spiritual things. The Spirit of God comes upon the believer and fills his mind with a real apprehension of truth. The Spirit takes possession of his faculties, imparting to him gifts not otherwise his but which qualify him for the service to which God has called him.

Q: Since the baptism is so distinctly for the service of God, is it primarily for clergy or so-called full-time Christian workers?
TORREY: There is no limitation on who should have this experience. The baptism was not merely for the apostles, not merely for those of the apostolic age, but for "all that are afar off, even as many as the Lord our God

shall call" (Acts 2:39). It is for every believer in every age of the church's history. If any believer in any age does not have this baptism, it is solely because he does not claim his privilege in Christ.

Q: Is it a one-time experience?

TORREY: No, it is not enough for one to be filled with the Holy Spirit once. We need a new filling of the Spirit for each new emergency of Christian service. Peter is said to have been "filled with the Holy Spirit" on three different occasions.

Q: What conditions must we meet to receive the baptism?

TORREY: I want to say first that I aim to be just as dogmatic as the Bible. I do not think I have attained to that yet. But if the Bible says in the most positive and dogmatic terms that *if* you do certain things, you *shall* be baptized with the Holy Spirit, I do not hesitate to affirm that. I do not have the slightest fear that my affirmation will prove untrue. Anyone who does these certain things, who takes these certain steps, will be immediately baptized with the Holy Spirit.

Q: What are those steps?

TORREY: They are seven: acceptance of Christ as personal Savior, repentance of sin, open confession of faith in Christ, full surrender to Christ, an earnest desire for the baptism, prayer for it and acceptance of it by faith. I base these squarely on Acts 2:38; Acts 5:32; John 7:37–39; Luke 11:13; and Mark 11:24.

Q: How noticeable have been the changes in the lives of those who have taken these steps?

TORREY: I know for a fact that as a result of my preach-

ing and counselling on this subject, the lives and ministries of multitudes of ministers, students and laymen
have been completely transformed. I must say that the
experimental reception of the baptism with the Holy
Spirit is sometimes conditioned on the believer's knowing that there is such a blessing available and that it is
actually for him now.

Q: What part does obedience play in the baptism with the Holy Spirit?

TORREY: Obedience means absolute surrender. This
really involves true repentance and faith in Jesus Christ.
It is one of the most fundamental conditions of entering into this blessing. It is the point at which thousands
fail today.

Q: What part does prayer have?

TORREY: There may be much earnest praying and still
the Holy Spirit does not come because the prayer is not
in faith (James 1:6–7). The faith that receives this baptism, as every other blessing, is the faith that counts it as
its own (Mark 11:24, 1 John 5:14–15).

Q: Do all Bible teachers agree with your approach to this subject of the Spirit's baptism?

TORREY: I know that many wince at my terminology,
believing that the baptism with the Spirit was either
confined to the apostolic age or that it referred to an
incorporation of the believer into the body of Christ.
Even a number of Moody's close associates and teachers
at Northfield hold to this latter position.

Q: Did they confront you about it?

TORREY: Mr. Moody called them together at his home
after one of the conference sessions one night and

asked me "to talk this thing out with them." The talk lasted for hours and the discussion was friendly—but there was no appreciable change of viewpoint on either my side or theirs.

Q: What did Mr. Moody say to that?
TORREY: He requested me to linger for awhile, and after some serious reflection said, "Oh, why will they split hairs? They are good teachers, they are wonderful teachers, and I am so glad to have them here. But why will they not see that the baptism with the Holy Spirit is just the one touch *that they themselves need?*"

Q: Were your differences with these Bible teachers simply a matter of terminology?
TORREY: No, it involved the important question as to whether a believer has the right to pray for and expect a special enduement of power from the Holy Spirit. I am still firm in my conviction about proper Bible terminology, but I say that I do not care how you phrase it. You may call it "the filling with the Spirit," "the baptism with the Spirit," "the enduement of power," or whatever you please. I would rather have the right thing with the wrong name any day than to have the wrong thing with the right name. I am adamant about a personal appropriation of the Holy Spirit for power.

* * *

Writings by and about Torrey and *books used in research (not intended to be exhaustive):

Baptism with the Holy Spirit
The Power of Prayer
*R.A. Torrey: Apostle of Certainty
*What the Bible Teaches

Charles Gallaudet Trumbull

[1872–1941]

DON'T PADDLE YOUR OWN CANOE

TRUMBULL WAS BORN in Hartford, Connecticut where he spent his early years. He graduated from Hamilton School in Philadelphia, later earning a B.A. degree from Yale University in 1893. Trumbull was awarded his Litt.D. from Wheaton College, Wheaton, Illinois in 1928.

He worked with the *Sunday School Times* publication from 1893 and became editor in 1903. He was vice president, secretary and director of the Sunday School Times Company for many years.

Trumbull became staff writer for *The Toronto Globe* newspaper and wrote weekly for the *Philadelphia Evening Public Ledger.* Other publications for which he wrote were: *Morning Sun,* Bradenton, Florida; a newspaper in Sioux Falls, South Dakota; *The Daily Argus-Leader,* Long Beach, California; *The Herald,* Augusta, Georgia; *The Chronicle* and *The Times,* in Johnson City, Tennessee.

He was a Companion of First Class Military Order Loyal Legion and a member of the Victory Institute in England. Trumbull was associated with the Palestine Exploration Fund in England and the Archeological Institute of America.

His denominational persuasion was Presbyterian. He served for a number of years as treasurer of the Belgian Gospel Mission and director of Pioneer Mission Agency, Keswick Colony of Mercy. He played a key part in the establishment of the Victorious Life Testimony, American Keswick in New Jersey.

Trumbull was vice president of World's Christian Fundamentals Association, and associated with the American Tract Society. He made his home in the Philadelphia area most of his life.

* * *

APPROXIMATE DATE: 1902

QUESTION: Dr. Trumbull, why do you say that your spiritual experience was like Jesus healing the man who was sick 38 years?
CHARLES G. TRUMBULL: For 38 years I had an infirmity of spiritual paralysis through my bondage to sin—always longing to be made whole. One day the Lord also said to me, "Arise and walk." I was a boy of 13 when I first made public confession of Jesus Christ as my Savior,

301

but not until 25 years later did I even know Christ offered life and power for victory over sin.

Q: Weren't you already a busy, dedicated, successful Christian worker for many years?
TRUMBULL: I certainly was. But there were great fluctuations in my spiritual life, alternating heights and depths, failure before besetting sins, no habitual deliverance. I lacked dynamic, convincing, spiritual power in my ministry. I was going through the motions, even doing personal work, the hardest kind of all, talking with people one by one about giving themselves to my Savior. But I wasn't seeing results. I was sometimes heartsick over the spiritual barrenness of my Christian service.

Q: What is the big mistake you refer to that keeps Christians powerless?
TRUMBULL: They are paralyzed, as I was, by thinking that we must share in doing that which only God can do. Jesus, you know, makes two offers to everyone. He offers to set us free from the *penalty* of our sin, and to set us free from the *power* of our sin. Both of these offers are on exactly the same terms. We can accept them only by letting Him do it all.

Every Christian has accepted the first offer; many Christians have not accepted the second. They think they must have some part in overcoming the power of their sin, that their efforts, their will, their determination, strengthened and helped by the power of Christ, is the way to victory. As long as they mistakenly believe this, they are doomed to defeat. We don't have to "paddle our own canoe" to walk in newness of life. Christian experience is wholly the result of the Producer of Christian experience – the Holy Spirit. We must let the Holy Spirit do it all.

Q: How do you get into this victorious life?

TRUMBULL: Only two very simple conditions—surrender and faith. "Let go and let God." We must turn over to Him, for time and eternity, all we have and all we are, for His complete mastery and use and disposal—every habit of our life, every ambition, every hope, every loved one, every possession, all of ourselves. Christ must be made *our life*.

Q: Aren't some people entirely surrendered but still not experiencing the victorious life?

TRUMBULL: Oh yes, because surrender is only the first step but not the whole. The surrendered life is not necessarily the victorious life. There is no victory without surrender, but there may be surrender without victory. We may have "let go" but if we have not yet "let God" we are sure to be defeated. We may not have realized that the work of victory is wholly and exclusively God's.

Q: After surrender, should we keep praying for victory?

TRUMBULL: No. That may even postpone and prevent victory. Jesus is waiting for us to praise Him for it as *already* done. As one has said, we are not to ask Him to *make* His grace sufficient for us. He tells us that it *is* already so. It is our part simply to take Him at His word and say, "I thank Thee, Lord." We should then let Him do His work and know that Jesus is meeting all our needs now. This is a different kind of victory than trying in vain to be Christlike or asking for Christ's help.

Q: How did you personally come into the experience of Christ's power?

TRUMBULL: I was confronted with the concept of Christ

as one's whole life by the lives and preaching of some others. I knew I did not experience Him the way they did. I came to a crisis at a youth missionary conference one August. I was ministering there for a week feeling miserable, hopelessly unfit and incompetent. I was in the midst of a recurring time of failure and defeat. A missionary bishop was one of the first speakers, and he told us it was Christ's desire and purpose for every follower of His to be a wellspring of living, gushing water of life to others *all the time*. Not intermittently, but with continuous and irresistible flow.

I knew that was not my Christian experience. The next morning, Sunday, alone in my room, I prayed it out with God, and I asked Him to show me the way out of my misery and defeat. He gave me what I asked. He gave me a new view of Christ—a wholly new conception and consciousness of Christ.

Q: *What is the difference between your concept of Christ now and your former one?*
TRUMBULL: It is hard to put into words, and yet it is, oh, so new, and real, and wonderful, and miracle-working in both my own life and the lives of others. I realized that Christ in you, and you in Christ, Christ our life, and abiding in Christ, are literal, actual, blessed facts, and not figures of speech.

I had always known Christ was my Savior, but I had looked upon Him as an *external* Savior, one who did a saving work for me from outside, as it were. I believed He was ready to come close alongside and stay by me, *helping* me in all I needed. But now I knew something better! At last I realized Jesus Christ was actually and literally *within* me. And even more: that He had constituted Himself as my very life, taking me—my body, mind and spirit—into union with Himself. But I still had my own identity, and free will, and full moral responsibility.

Was this not better than having Him as a helper? It meant I never again needed to ask Him for help as though He were one and I another; instead He would simply do His work, His will, in me and with me and through me. My body was His, my mind was His, my will was His, my spirit was His—and not merely His, but literally a part of Him!

Q: *Did this concept change your life?*

TRUMBULL: It has meant a revolutionized, fundamental change in my thinking and my life, within and without. The three great lacks or needs of which I spoke have been miraculously met. It transformed my ministry to realize that Jesus Christ does not want me to work for Him. He wants me to let Him do His work through me, using me. Christ creates spiritual power in me, yes, but Christ Himself is better than power. I may have Christ Himself!

But we must be careful of any counterfeit victory. Victory over the power of any sin in your life, which you must achieve by *working* for it, is counterfeit. Victory, which you must obtain by *trying* for it, is counterfeit. It is not the real thing, the thing God offers you.

Q: *Do we gradually gain victory over sin in our lives?*

TRUMBULL: No, God's Word does not teach that. Victory gained by a gradual conquest over evil, getting one sin after another out of our life, like pulling weeds out of our garden, is likewise counterfeit victory. No, the Lord Jesus does not offer to give us any such thing as a gradual gift. It is not growth. "Thanks be unto God which giveth us the victory through our Lord Jesus Christ" (1 Corinthians 15:57).

But please do not misunderstand that in the victorious life there is no growth. That would be absolutely false to the Word of God. We only begin to grow normally, grow as God wants us to grow, *after* we have entered into victory. No, victory is not fighting your wrong desires or concealing your wrong feelings; that would mean a struggle. In real victory, He does it all. We do not dare to help. When the Lord Jesus Christ by the Holy Spirit works in our life to give us this victory, it is a miracle every time. If it is not a miracle, it is not victory.

Q: Does the Christian church today teach about victory in the sense that you have explained it?
TRUMBULL: Unfortunately, we often start new converts off on the wrong track. We advise them as soon as they are born again to get busy for God. Works certainly have a place in the Christian's life, but they follow the grace of God, never precede it, and they are never the conditions of God's grace. I was on that wrong path for 25 years. Grace is not a joint effort. Grace is not cooperation. Grace is absolutely exclusive. Grace means God does it all.

The same is true of God's work in the church and in the world. It is God's work and not our work for God. I cannot repeat that often enough. He insists on doing it through us. This is the most important concept to transform our witness and our work.

Q: Did you say that some serious perils face Christians who have entered this life of victory? Shouldn't it be easier?
TRUMBULL: To be sure, no life in the world is so perilous as the victorious life. Does that surprise you? Yet there is no life so safe. Where the onslaughts of the adversary

are the most fierce, the grace of the Captain of our salvation is the most effectively demonstrated. Some of the perils are so subtle, so unexpected, they may not be recognized unless we frankly face them in advance as terribly real possibilities—no, not possibilities, but certainties. We need a supernaturally sensitized consciousness of these perils to be safeguarded.

Q: Would you share with us what some of these perils are so we may be forewarned?
TRUMBULL: I will mention a number of them briefly. I am sure you can ask the Lord what to do about them. This life of victory is not an untempted one; in fact, it is the most tempted life anyone can live. No one knows the full meaning of temptation until he has dared to trust Christ for full victory. Then come temptations as never before: desperate, diabolical, hellish, subtle, refined, gross, spiritual, fleshly—the whole gamut of all the deception and the down pull the world, the flesh and the devil can bring to you. But God sees them all, and He is standing on sentry-guard in our lives against them. The Word of God has disclosed them all to us, and the "sword of the Spirit" (Ephesians 6:17) is our sure weapon.

Q: Suppose we do fail under some of these temptations or perils?
TRUMBULL: If we fail or sin through not trusting God completely for victory, and this is not a life of sinless perfection, the peril is to think we never had the blessing, or that it will now take us some time to get back into the blessing. But our Lord wants us to believe Him for *instant* cleansing and restoration.

Q: Aren't we stronger and safer from sin or temptation the longer we have lived in victory?

TRUMBULL: Absolutely not. Nor are we weaker, on the other hand, because we have sinned or broken our victory. Our continued record in victory adds nothing to our assurance of victory because it adds nothing to Christ. He alone is our assurance of victory. In ourselves we are just as weak and helpless, just as sinful, just as impotent, after 10 years of unbroken victory as we were the first moment of our new birth. The veteran warrior in this deeper life is equally capable of unbelief and of disastrous defeat in sin. He needs the moment by moment looking away unto Jesus as His only Savior as much as the young Christian who has just entered upon that life. We should not get over-confident through continued victory, or become weakened with fear through failure. We will always have our sinful nature, which can sin and will sin any moment that we fail to trust Christ for His victory in us. But as we trust Him, His victory in us is absolute.

Q: As time goes on, don't we become more sensitive to the leading of the Holy Spirit in this deeper spiritual life?
TRUMBULL: We do, but we must be careful of following excessive impulses or "leadings" to do specific things. They may be of God; on the other hand, they may be of Satan or of self. We can go into the fog by following them. We need to ask God for the gift of discernment to test them.

Q: Are there other extremes about which we should be careful?
TRUMBULL: We need to maintain a balance between asceticism and luxury. We are to take care of our personal appearance, our cleanliness, our clothing, to be attractive to our fellow men. It is a positive duty to be attrac-

tive Christians in dress and appearance so others may be won to us in order that we may win them to our Lord.

We are to do *all* things to the glory of God (1 Corinthians 10:31). This includes our pleasures. We are not to believe the lie of Satan that everything pleasurable or attractive is sinful. We are to enjoy our meals, for instance, not reduce them to the minimum of mere physical sustenance. Likewise other temporal details of life.

We may also have the mistaken idea that when we have a choice between something hard and something easy, the hard thing is always God's will. His will may be just the opposite. There is not necessarily any virtue in difficulty, and there is not necessarily any sin in ease. The only question is, what is God's will for us in each matter? We are never to abandon our God-given common sense in the victorious life.

Q: The victorious life must be very exciting—a supernatural life, a living miracle, a thrilling adventure demonstrating God's power. . . .

TRUMBULL: Right there lies another peril—to mistakenly expect thrilling, unexpected, supernatural evidences of God's power. And if these phenomena do not occur, we are tempted to think something is wrong. God wants us to trust, not in supernatural experiences, but in Himself. He will decide when the unusual shall come into our life, and when our life shall be commonplace and humdrum, so far as things of sight and sense are concerned. It is safe to say that God's purpose for the supernatural, so far as circumstances and experience are concerned, is the unusual rather than the usual for His wholly trusting children. Don't test God or your victory by circumstances or manifestations. Trust only Jesus Himself.

Q: We hear some Spirit-filled Christians state, "God said this to me," or "God led me to do that." It's hard to argue with such statements.

TRUMBULL: That's another peril—to unconsciously assume an infallible knowledge of God's will. If we are not on our guard, we thoughtlessly slip into such habitual expressions about God leading us. Some true and yielded Christians almost never speak of any action or decision without prefacing it with words that God told them to do this or that. Quite often, later circumstances show plainly that God did not tell them to do it; they had misunderstood His leading. That is possible at any time for any believer, even one wholly yielded.

Q: How should we speak of what we think is God's guidance for us?

TRUMBULL: Instead of saying, "God told me to do this," let us say, "I believe God would have me do this." Let us recognize that we *may* be mistaken. Even if we are quite certain in our own hearts and minds of God's leading, let us avoid claiming infallible knowledge, without qualification, in our conversation with others.

Q: Do you have any more of these very practical cautions?

TRUMBULL: The blessings of God in this life in the Spirit are so wonderful that we are in danger of thinking more about the blessings than of the Blesser. God does not want us to worship the fruit or gifts of the Spirit, but the Spirit. A helpful saying is attributed to Spurgeon: "I looked at Jesus and the dove of peace flew into my heart; I looked at the dove of peace and she flew away."

Q: Why do some Spirit-filled Christians have an air of

elite exclusiveness that offends other Christians who have not yet gone deeper with God?
TRUMBULL: A very important point. We must be careful of pride and regarding fellow Christians who are "not in on the secret" with a condescending attitude of "holier than thou." The only good thing about the victorious Christian is Christ; we deserve no credit for Christ—the glory and honor and victory are all His. True victory should keep us humble, and it will. This is related to the peril of being unteachable.

Q: How does that show up?
TRUMBULL: We get so excited because the Holy Spirit has given us new illumination on God's Word, new knowledge of things never before known, new wisdom, unmistakable and directly from God. We enjoy a flood of light on duties. We are able to counsel others as never before. All this is not imaginary; it is genuine and vital. And we praise God with gratitude unspeakable.

Suppose such a Spirit-filled Christian gets criticized by a fellow Christian who may not know Christ as his victory. This victorious Christian may say to himself about the other, "Who is he to tell me anything about this? He does not know the secret of victory. The Bible has not been opened to him by the Holy Spirit as it has been to me. He does not have the light I have." And we become unteachable.

Perhaps the criticism received is actually sound and true, and God sent it for his guidance and correction. A victorious Christian can certainly learn even from the criticism of unsaved, unregenerate people! Often he ought to. The victorious life is no guarantee of omniscience, of infallibility in knowledge.

Q: Why do some Spirit-filled Christians get off on spiritual tangents?

TRUMBULL: We must be careful not to think we can get along with less of the written Word of God just because we have the Holy Spirit within us. Time after time in history, those with so-called "higher life" experiences, either individuals or groups of Christians, have gone onto the rocks and been wrecked. The reason? They supposed that because Christ and the Holy Spirit dwelled within them, they could safely pay little attention to the Bible. Our new experience of Christ should result in *more* time with His Word and in prayer, not *less*.

Q: It seems so incongruous that sometimes Spirit-filled Christians fall into the most serious sins.

TRUMBULL: We should never take sin lightly just because we have recourse to instant forgiveness by confessing to the Lord. Danger lies ahead when we begin to tolerate breaks and failures as the expected rather than the unexpected, the usual instead of the unusual, and it becomes habitual. Hard to explain, but when the life of spiritual power and victory is broken into in the slightest way by unbelief, we are exposed most vulnerably to sins of gross immorality and degradation. Those who have gone highest with the Lord can go lowest.

Let us recognize this peril; let us confess this possibility of our utterly sinful nature. Then let us yield ourselves afresh to the mastery of our holy Lord, and trust Him afresh for His sufficiency to safeguard us from this awful denial of His name and betrayal of our stewardship.

If we *should* slip in any slightest way, let us instantly stop anything we are doing, take the time necessary to confess to Him, claim His forgiveness and entire cleansing, and trust Him at once for His complete restoration and victory. Satan would like us to delay doing so. That is deadly peril!

Q: What safeguards can the Christian take against the danger of immoral relationships?
TRUMBULL: It is common sense and wise spiritual judgment to share deeper spiritual relationships between men and men, and between women and women, rather than between two persons of the opposite sex–unless God is bringing the two together in marriage. There should not be any unnaturalness, or any unhealthy self-consciousness when men and women, older or younger, properly talk or pray together about their Lord and their possessions in Christ. But Satan, as an angel of light, may lead two such persons into a spiritual intimacy and dependence upon each other which is not of God, and which can lead to unhappiness in more than one life–or real disaster. Because it is the Holy Spirit who gives us the victorious life, we must live holy lives.

Q: I suppose that can be carried to the extreme as well?
TRUMBULL: It certainly can. A final peril is the danger of not being human enough. Because of the depth and intensity of our spiritual life, we can forget we have responsible, temporal interests as well as eternal ones. Let's not be criticized for only having a concern for people's souls and none at all for their bodies. Let us be human.

We should deliberately cultivate certain secular, human interests to have points of contact with the many around us who know nothing of the spiritual interests so precious to us. We should develop hobbies, music, amusements, sports and other healthy interests which will keep us from the peril of narrowness in the victorious life.

There is still plenty in this world that is not of the devil; God wants us to keep close to our fellows in a joyous healthy way. Let us also be careful about common social courtesies and thoughtfulness toward others. Especially let us maintain balance with our married partners and children, and in our family and home circle relationships. We should not neglect them while we are concerned for the spiritual needs of the world. The victorious life is really the only well-balanced life on earth.

Q: God is not the one who puts all these dangers in the path of Spirit-filled Christians, is He?
TRUMBULL: It is the enemy, Satan, who tries a thousand and one ways to find a crack in our armor. But here is an extra peril to avoid—we are not to think more about Satan than of Christ. We are to recognize the terrible reality of Satan. We are to study the Word of God to learn about our adversary, but then we are to *look away* from Satan unto Jesus. To look unto Jesus is our life and our victory!

* * *

Writings by and about Trumbull and *books used in research (not intended to be exhaustive):

Charles Gallaudet Trumbull: Apostle of the Victorious Life
C.I. Scofield, A Biography by Trumbull
Genesis and Yourself
**The Life that Wins*
Men Who Dared
**Perils of the Victorious Life*
A Pilgrimage to Jerusalem

Prophecy's Light on Today
Taking Men Alive: Studies in Soul-winning
*They Found the Secret
*The Victorious Life: Messages from Summer Conferences
*Victory in Christ

BIBLIOGRAPHY

America's Great Revivals. Booklet: Compiled reprints from *Christian Life* magazine. Chicago: Moody Press, n.d.

Barabas, Steven. *So Great Salvation*. London: Marshall, Morgan & Scott, 1952.

Boardman, W.E. *The Higher Christian Life*. Boston: Henry Hoyt, 1858.

Bounds, E.M. *Power Through Prayer*. Springdale, PA: Whitaker House, 1982.

————. *Prayer and Praying Men*. Grand Rapids, MI: Baker Book House, 1977.

————. *Purpose in Prayer*. New York: Fleming H. Revell, 1920.

Brengle, S.L. *When the Holy Ghost is Come*. New York: Salvation Army Book Dept., 1909.

Brookman, David W. *Basic Books For The Minister's Library*. Shippensburg, PA: Destiny Image, 1986.

Chadwick, Samuel. *The Way to Pentecost*. Ft. Washington, PA: Christian Literature Crusade, 1973.

Chafer, Lewis Sperry. *He That is Spiritual*. Chicago: Moody Press, 1943.

Chambers, Oswald. *God's Workmanship*. Ft. Washington, PA: Christian Literature Crusade, 1953.

————. *He Shall Glorify Me*. Ft. Washington, PA: Christian Literature Crusade, 1975.

————. *Talks on the Soul of a Christian*. London: Simpkin Marshall, 1941.

Choy, Leona Frances. *Andrew Murray: Apostle of Abiding Love*. Ft. Washington, PA: Christian Literature Crusade, 1978.

Clarke, Charles. *Pioneers of Revival*. Plainfield, IL: Logos International, 1971.

Conwell, Russell H. *Life of Charles Haddon Spurgeon*. (no location): Edgewood Publishing, 1892.

Cumming, James Elder. *Through the Eternal Spirit*. New York: Revell, 1896.

Dallas Theological Seminary: 1924–1974. Dallas: Office of Publications, Dallas Theological Seminary, n.d.

Douglas, W.M. *Andrew Murray and His Message*. London: Oliphants, 1957.

Du Plessis, J. *The Life of Andrew Murray of South Africa*. London: Marshall Brothers, 1919.

Edman, V. Raymond. *Finney Lives On*. Wheaton, IL: Scripture Press, 1951.

————. *They Found the Secret*. Grand Rapids, MI: Zondervan, 1960.

Finney, Charles G. *Memoirs of Charles G. Finney: Written by Himself*. New York: A.S. Barnes, 1876.

————. *Power From On High*. Ft. Washington, PA: Christian Literature Crusade, 1975.

Fullerton, W.Y. *F.B. Meyer: A Biography*. London, Edinburgh: Marshall, Morgan & Scott, n.d.

Godwin, George. *The Great Revivalists*. Boston: The Beacon Press, 1950.

Goforth, Jonathan. *By My Spirit*. Minneapolis: Bethany Fellowship, 1942.

Goforth, Rosalind. *Goforth of China*. Minneapolis: Bethany House Publishers, 1937.

Gordon, Ernest. *Adonirum Judson Gordon*. New York: Fleming H. Revell, 1896.

Gordon, A.J. *The Ministry of Healing.* Harrisburg, PA: Christian Publications, 1961.

—————. *The Ministry of the Spirit.* Grand Rapids, MI: Baker Book House, 1964.

Gordon, S.D. *Quiet Talks on Prayer.* New York: Fleming H. Revell, 1941.

—————. *Quiet Talks on Power.* New York: Fleming H. Revell, 1903.

Hall, Clarence W. *Samuel Logan Brengle: Portrait of a Prophet.* New York: Salvation Army, 1933.

Hannah, John D. *The Early Years of Lewis Sperry Chafer.* Dallas: Office of Publications, Dallas Theological Seminary, n.d.

Harrison, E. Myers. *Heroes of Faith on Pioneer Trails.* Chicago: Moody Press, 1945.

Hefley, James C. *How Great Christians Met Christ.* Chicago: Moody Press, 1973.

Hopkins, Evan Henry. *The Law of Liberty in the Spiritual Life.* Philadelphia: Sunday School Times, 1954.

Howard, Philip Eugene. *Charles Gallaudet Trumbull: Apostle of the Victorious Life.* Philadelphia: Sunday School Times, 1944.

Martin, Roger. *R.A. Torrey: Apostle of Certainty.* Murfreesboro, TN: Sword of the Lord, 1976.

McConkey, James H. *Give God a Chance.* Chicago: Moody Press, 1975.

—————. *The Three-Fold Secret of the Holy Spirit.* Chicago: Moody Press, 1897.

McCraw, Louise Harrison. *James H. McConkey: Man of God.* Scottsdale, PA: Herald Press, n.d.

Meyer, F.B. *Five Musts of the Christian Life.* Chicago: Moody Press, 1927.

—————. *Meet for the Master's Use.* Chicago: Bible Institute Colportage, 1898.

————. *The Secret of Guidance.* Chicago: Moody Press, n.d.

Miller, Park Hays. *Heroes of the Church.* Philadelphia: Westminster Press, 1922.

Moody, Dwight L. *Moody's Latest Sermons.* Grand Rapids, MI: Baker Book House, 1965.

————. *Secret Power: The Secret of Success in Christian Life & Work.* Chicago: Bible Institute Colportage, 1908.

Moody, William R. *The Life of Dwight L. Moody.* New York: Fleming H. Revell, 1900.

Morgan, George Campbell. *The Acts of the Apostles.* New York: Fleming H. Revell, 1924.

————. *The Spirit of God.* New York: Fleming H. Revell, 1900.

Moule, Handley C.G. *Veni Creator: Thoughts on the Person and Work of the Holy Spirit of Promise.* New York: Thomas Whittaker, 1890.

Murray, Andrew. *Divine Healing.* London: Victory Press, 1934.

————. *The Full Blessing of Pentecost.* London: Oliphants, 1954.

————. *Key to the Missionary Problem.* Ft. Washington, PA: Christian Literature Crusade, 1979.

————. *The Spirit of Christ.* Ft. Washington, PA: Christian Literature Crusade, 1978.

————. *The State of the Church.* Ft. Washington, PA: Christian Literature Crusade, 1983.

Niklaus, Robert L., John S. Sawin and Samuel J. Stoesz. *All For Jesus.* Camp Hill, PA: Christian Publications, 1986.

Parker, Robert Allerton. *The Transatlantic Smiths.* New York: Random House, 1959.

Paxson, Ruth. *Life on the Highest Plane.* Chicago: Moody Press, 1928.

————. *Rivers of Living Water.* Chicago: Moody Press, n.d.

————. *The Wealth, Walk and Warfare of the Christian.* New York: Fleming H. Revell, 1939.

Roberts, Philip Ilott. *Frederick Brotherton Meyer.* New York: Fleming H. Revell, 1929.

Simpson, A.B. *The Gospel of Healing.* Camp Hill, PA: Christian Publications, 1986.

————. *The Holy Spirit (Power from on High),* Vol. 1. Harrisburg: Christian Publications, n.d.

————. *The Lord for the Body.* Harrisburg: Christian Publications, 1959.

————. *When the Comforter Came.* Harrisburg: Christian Publications, n.d.

Smith, Hannah Whitall. *The Christian's Secret of a Happy Life.* New York: Fleming H. Revell, 1952.

Spurgeon, Charles H. *The Comforter.* Wilmington: Cross Publishing, n.d.

————. *Necessity of the Spirit's Work.* Wilmington: Cross Publishing, n.d.

————. *The Power of the Holy Ghost.* Wilmington: Cross Publishing, n.d.

————. *Spiritual Revival: The Want of the Church.* Wilmington: Cross Publishing, n.d.

Stewart, James A. *Invasion of Wales by the Spirit: Through Evan Roberts.* Ft. Washington, PA: Christian Literature Crusade, 1963.

Sweet, William Warren. *Makers of Christianity.* New York: Henry Holt, 1937.

Taylor, Dr. and Mrs. Howard. *Hudson Taylor and the China Inland Mission.* London: China Inland Mission, 1918.

————. *Hudson Taylor in Early Years.* London: China Inland Mission, 1912.

————. *Hudson Taylor's Spiritual Secret.* Philadelphia:

China Inland Mission/Overseas Missionary Fellowship, 1958.

Taylor, J. Hudson. *Union and Communion*. Chicago: Moody Press, n.d.

Thomas, W.H. Griffith. *The Holy Spirit of God*. Grand Rapids, MI: Wm. B. Eerdman, 1950.

Thompson, A.E. *The Life of A.B. Simpson*. New York: Christian Alliance Publishing Co., 1920.

Thornbury, John F. *God Sent Revival*. Grand Rapids, MI: Evangelical Press, 1977.

Torrey, R.A. *What the Bible Teaches*. New York: Fleming H. Revell, 1898.

Trumbull, Charles G. *The Life That Wins*. Philadelphia: Sunday School Times, n.d.

————. *Perils of the Victorious Life*. Ft. Washington, PA: Christian Literature Crusade, 1959.

————. *Victory in Christ*. Ft. Washington, PA: Christian Literature Crusade, 1976.

The Victorious Life. (Messages from the Summer Conference at Whittier, CA, June, and Princeton, NJ, July, and Cedar Lake, IN, August, 1918.) Philadelphia: Board of Managers, Victorious Life Conference, 1918.